The Privatization of Health Care Reform

The

Privatization

of

Health Care
Reform

Legal and

Regulatory Perspectives

Edited by

M. GREGG BLOCHE

OXFORD
UNIVERSITY PRESS
2003

OXFORD
UNIVERSITY PRESS

Oxford   New York
Auckland   Bangkok   Buenos Aires   Cape Town   Chennai
Dar es Salaam   Delhi   Hong Kong   Istanbul   Karachi   Kolkata
Kuala Lumpur   Madrid   Melbourne   Mexico City   Mumbai
Nairobi   São Paulo   Shanghai   Taipei   Tokyo   Toronto

Copyright © 2003 by Oxford University Press, Inc.

Published by Oxford University Press, Inc.
198 Madison Avenue, New York, New York 10016
http://www.oup-usa.org

Oxford is a registered trademark of Oxford University Press

Library of Congress Cataloging-in-Publication Data
The privitization of health care reform : legal and regulatory perspectives /
edited by M. Gregg Bloche
p. cm.
Includes bibliographical references and index.
ISBN 0-19-510868-X
1. Medical care—Law and legislation—United States.
2. Privatization—Law and legislation—United States.
3. Health care reform—United States.
I. Bloche, Maxwell Gregg.

KF3825 .P75 2002   344.73'0321—dc21   2002022447

9 8 7 6 5 4 3 2 1

Printed in the United States of America
on acid-free paper

To the memory of
R. J. B.
and
R.E.B.

Acknowledgments

I am deeply grateful to those who made this book possible. Preparation of four of the chapters was supported in part by Robert Wood Johnson Foundation Investigator Awards in Health Policy Research. Three chapters originated as presentations to a conference on the privatization of health care reform, sponsored by the Georgetown University Law Center. Alvin Tarlov, Barbara Krimgold, David Mechanic, and Lynn Rogut of the Robert Wood Johnson Foundation Investigator Awards created ongoing opportunities for exchange among most of the contributors through the Foundation's "cluster group" program. Dean Judith Areen of the Georgetown University Law Center encouraged and funded the conference that led to this volume. At Oxford University Press, Jeff House saw the importance of this project early on, after the collapse of the Clinton health plan; he played a large role in shaping the book's coverage, and supported me through to its completion. Lynda Crawford and her copyediting staff gently nudged the manuscript toward greater readability and endured, with grace, our tender egos.

The extraordinary efforts of Elizabeth Jungman, my gifted research assistant, played a critical role in bringing this project to completion. Ms. Jungman managed the editing process, prevailed over computer glitches, and herded cats to keep production on track. Genevieve Grabman, Michael Sapoznikow, and William Tarantino also provided invaluable research assistance. Sylvia Johnson,

Pauline Latty, Anna Selden, and John Showalter provided vital photocopying and word processing support and rescued me from my ineptitude at all things Microsoft. My daughter Cecilia, seven years old as this book goes to press, reassured me, "Daddy, you know it doesn't have to be perfect," and told me, "you talk too much about medical necessity."

M.G.B.

Washington, D.C.

Contents

Contributors

GERARD F. ANDERSON
Johns Hopkins University
Bloomberg School of Public Health
Baltimore, Maryland

M. GREGG BLOCHE
Georgetown University Law Center
Washington, DC

RICHARD A. BRIFFAULT
Columbia Law School
New York, New York

LARRY S. GAGE
Powell, Goldstein, Frazer & Murphy
Washington, DC

SHERRY GLIED
Columbia University
Mailman School of Public Health
New York, New York

MARK A. HALL
Wake Forest University School of Law
Winston-Salem, North Carolina

PETER J. HAMMER
Unversity of Michigan Law School
Ann Arbor, Michigan

CLARK C. HAVIGHURST
Duke University School of Law
Durham, North Carolina

THOMAS RICE
UCLA School of Public Health
Los Angeles, California

Introduction

Is medicine a market commodity, like cosmetics? Or is it "different"—in ways that make commerce in health care crass, even indecent? Americans, it would seem, want it both ways. Since colonial times, Americans have both embraced and rebelled against commercialism in the health sphere. Market-driven change in the United States health system has varied in pace but never ceased. In the 1990s, it accelerated dramatically.

The failure of President Clinton's health reform plan in 1994 set off a surge of entrepreneurship. With the prospect of comprehensive legislation gone, insurers, doctors and hospitals, and health care purchasers were free to act without high political and regulatory risk. Motivated by soaring medical costs, they did so aggressively. Health care payers and providers forged novel business arrangements and organizational forms, aimed at controlling costs while meeting consumers' expectations. Employers shopped the medical marketplace energetically, searching for coverage that could enable them to compete for labor at manageable cost. Taking reform into their own hands, these actors remade the business of medicine. The health care system that emerged at the end of the 1990s bore little resemblance to what either market proponents or market skeptics had predicted a decade before.

This book considers the transformation the market has wrought. Its authors, for the most part, take American reliance upon the medical marketplace as a given:

this is not a book about whether or to what degree health care should be provided or paid for by government versus the private sector. Rather, the essays in this volume address challenges that rapid change in the medical marketplace present for the law and for regulatory policymakers. The authors start from the premise that systemic, state-sponsored overhaul of the American way of paying for and providing health care is unlikely in the foreseeable future. Courts and regulators, the authors therefore presume, must make do with the current patchwork of legal regimes that cover health care.

The legislators and judges who crafted these legal regimes did so without medical care specifically in mind. Indeed, the drafters of the statutory schemes that have most shaped the medical marketplace had no inkling that their handiwork would apply to the health sphere. American health law is thus a story of unintended consequences. The confusion, incoherence, and serendipity that have ensued is a central theme of the essays in this book. Another, related theme is the mismatch between law's pursuit of consistency within doctrinal spheres—for example tort and contract, antitrust, and the statutory scheme governing employees' fringe benefits—and the singular complexities of health care markets and institutions. The resulting fragmentation of health care lawmaking has foreclosed coordinated, system-wide policy responses. Beyond this, lack of national consensus on many of the central questions in health care policy has translated into legal contradiction and bitter controversy. These questions include the extent to which access to medical care should track (or depart from) prevailing distributions of wealth; how doctors, hospitals, and health care payers should limit clinical spending; how regulatory powers ought to be spread among federal, state, and local government; and when autonomy, privacy, and other ethical concerns should constrain public and private decision makers.

The speed of entrepreneurial development poses further challenges for health care lawmaking, challenges that several of the chapters in this volume consider. Courts, legislatures, and regulatory agencies are slow, unwieldy decision makers, rarely able to keep pace with private innovation. The very constraints that render judicial and regulatory authority legitimate in a democratic society—norms of due process, reasoned decision making, citizen participation, and political accountability—limit government's ability to gather information and to act quickly and efficiently.[1]

Some might object to this book's treatment of the medical marketplace as a given—and to the authors' inattention to the possibility of state action to supplant the role of market forces. In the eyes of many market skeptics, government's failure to so act has little to do with popular preferences and much to do with corporate political influence. Seen from this vantage point, analysis aimed at making markets work better errs by accepting a way of doing things that serves the wealthy and the powerful at the public's expense. To be sure, corporate money and webs of influence helped to quash the Clinton Administration's health reform program,[2] and the political power of health care providers has periodically stymied reform efforts since the Roosevelt Administration. But missing from this critical view is any allowance for health care commercialism's popular appeal. This appeal is powerful, and it is too often underestimated. It is tied to something classically American—the felt need for tools to check established authority. Repeatedly in United States history, skepticism about the competence and benevolence of professional and government authority has fueled interest in market competition as a way to empower lay people in medical matters. In the 1830s, as Enlightenment-era reverence for science and medicine devolved into fashionable doubt about what doctors knew, Jacksonian America embraced consumer choice, unmediated by physician judgment. Raucous competition between clinical nostrums and between physicians and other kinds of practitioners continued through the nineteenth century, largely unconstrained by prescription, licensing, or other regulatory limits.[3]

Physician resistance to the competition paradigm stiffened toward the end of the century. Popular distrust and disdain for no–holds-barred commercialism overtook doubts about professional judgment, and medical societies campaigned successfully for state licensing schemes that excluded non-physician practitioners. In the early decades of the twentieth century, the profession took unprecedented control of its own market, closing down large numbers of medical schools and imposing tough accreditation standards on the survivors. This strategy reduced physician supply, raised quality, and built public confidence in professional judgment.[4] Stunning advances in the technology of medicine—surgical anesthesia and antisepsis, the x-ray and the EKG, and the antibiotic revolution—fed this confidence. By the 1950s, regard for doctors' competence and ethical commitment had reached a historic high.[5]

Americans' confidence in physicians and health care institutions has been in decline ever since. The flood tide of skepticism toward authority that swept the nation in the 1960s and 1970s brought with it renewed doubts about medical authority. Critics targeted professional paternalism and questioned physician benevolence.[6] Revelations that clinical researchers had exposed patients to radiation, mind-altering drugs, and other unconscionable risks without their knowledge for national security and other non-therapeutic purposes reinforced these doubts. As in the 1830s, the ideal of personal choice in medical matters gained strength as a substitute for faith in professional authority. The bioethics movement that emerged in the 1960s and 1970s made patient autonomy its central precept, and courts and regulators crafted informed consent requirements for treatment and research.

The bioethics movement's pioneers paid little heed to health care financing or organization; their focus was on empowering patients in their relations with doctors. But proponents of a larger role for markets in the health sphere built on bioethics thinking about patient empowerment. Personal choice, they said, should extend beyond the decision to reject or consent to a doctor's advice. Price-conscious selection of physicians, hospitals, and levels of care empowers patients as consumers,[7] they contended, and courts and regulators should reshape the law to expand opportunities for consumer choice.[8] More controversially, they have argued since the 1980s that the law should more tightly bind consumers to their health plans' cost containment policies, on the ground that subscription to a plan constitutes consent to its controls on spending.[9]

Neither the law nor the American consumer fully embraced the ideal of personal empowerment through the market for medical coverage. Yet this ideal has gained traction, in the courts and among consumers, through its fit with widespread thinking about patient autonomy. The growing realization that much of medicine is a matter of discretion, ill-constrained by hard science,[10] has added to the appeal of the market as a check on professional and elite authority. The health insurance industry's infamous *Harry and Louise* TV spots, which targeted President Clinton's health reform plan with such deadly effect,[11] traded on voters" fears of loss of control in medical matters. To be sure, voters are far from ready to embrace health insurers as benign alternatives to professional or government authority. Political candidates' focus group-tested promises to take health care decisions out of the hands of HMO bureaucrats and return them to doctors and patients underscore citizens' worries about the power of insurers. But market choice has a large place in the American toolkit for controlling the power of elites in the medical sphere, and a distinguishing feature of the U.S. health system is its proliferation of checks on centers of authority.

The metamorphosis of the medical marketplace since the collapse of the Clinton plan reflects both the appeal of consumer choice and our national insistence that institutional authority be contained. This metamorphosis has surprised both market skeptics and the free-market faithful. Conventional wisdom in the early 1990s held that competition between health plans would eventually result in rival, nationwide managed care organizations, each with its own regional networks of doctors, hospitals, and other facilities. Forecasters predicted that these competing networks would consolidate insurance coverage, hospital care, and outpatient services under the same management. These rival, "vertically" integrated enterprises would develop distinctive brand names, management strategies, and medical practice styles. They would run their own hospitals and employ or contract exclusively with their own doctors. They would thereby develop separate clinical cultures and intra-firm referral networks among plan doctors, hospitals, and other facilities. "Feeder" patient flows from doctors to community hospitals to elite tertiary care centers within each health plan would ensure efficient use of personnel and facilities. Participation of doctors in just one or a few health plans would engender organizational loyalty and compliance with plan-wide clinical practice and cost control policies. Consumers would choose from among these plans based on price, practice style, amenities, and objective measures of quality.

Things have not played out this way. Nationwide health plans have emerged, but they have not consolidated insurance, hospital, and outpatient services under the same corporate roof. Nor have they forged enduring, exclusive relationships with doctors, hospitals, and other providers. Instead, health plans have mostly stayed in the businesses of insurance and benefit administration, using their buying power to obtain discounted prices from doctors and hospitals. Medical practices, community hospitals, and elite tertiary care centers have remained free-standing institutions. They have consolidated "horizontally" to some degree: group medical practices are larger and many hospitals have joined regional or national non-profit and investor-owned systems. But providers typically affiliate with multiple health plans, adding and dropping these affiliations from year to year in response to changing market conditions. Plans adapt to rapidly changing markets by eschewing long-term commitments, like owning hospitals and employing doctors, in favor of shifting affiliations with providers. Intermediary organizations offer plans additional flexibility by organizing myriad, custom-tailored provider networks and by managing such specialized services as mental health and physical rehabilitation.

The upshot is that health plans have gained marketing flexibility at the price of the institutional authority necessary to develop distinctive, plan-wide clinical practice styles and management strategies. The story of managed-care entrepreneurship over the past ten years has been, in large measure, a story of successive efforts to control costs without this institutional authority. Health plans have tried preauthorization review of proposed treatments, selective affiliation with frugal providers, hard bargaining for discounted payment rates, and financial incentives to physicians to limit spending. Consumer and provider resistance to these methods has led plans to pull back from each, in turn. At no point did the medical marketplace reach equilibrium in regard to cost containment methods. As this book goes to press, no equilibrium is in sight. To the contrary, costs began to rise again at double digit rates in this decade's early years, and health plans seemed at sea in their efforts to limit spending without fierce resistance from patients and providers.

Challenges to the managed care industry's cost control efforts have been a central theme in the law of health care provision. The law's treatment of these challenges is this book's main focus. The authors consider some of the principal legal and regulatory regimes that govern the industry's cost containment efforts and constrain consumer and provider resistance to these efforts. They do so from diverse analytic and ideological perspectives, and they do not reach a unified set of conclusions. Indeed, they often disagree outright.

The contributions to this book, however, have several things in common. First, they seek the big picture. The arcane complexity of health care law is a barrier to understanding its treatment of the health sphere's core social policy questions. This book's authors pay heed to relevant legal detail, but their broader focus is the law's response to the social and moral dilemmas posed by the managed care revolution. The authors neither review legal doctrine in comprehensive fashion nor track health care trends in detail. Rather, they take the long view of the relation between legal and regulatory developments and health care industry change. Second, the authors draw upon insights from economic, ethical, and political theory to an extent unusual in commentary on health law and policy. This commentary tends to overlook parallels between market failure in the health sphere and in other industries with analogous characteristics. Insights from theory can help legal decision makers to spot such parallels and to take advantage of lessons they may offer. Third, these authors are not hostages to theory. They take the technical, institutional, and psychological complexities of health care seriously, and they eschew abstract propositions that do not fit with real world experience. To be sure, each author eyes these complexities through a lens shaped by his or her theoretical commitments. But they share a concern for facts, even inconvenient ones, and their contributions to this book sacrifice elegance when necessary to account for awkward realities.

This small volume is not an exhaustive review of developments in the medical marketplace and the law of health care provision. Its authors do, however, offer in-depth understandings of some of the managed care revolution's widely-perceived failings and the law's relationship to these failings. Some of the contributors treat law as a cause of these failings; others emphasize the law's potential and limits as a corrective tool when the market disappoints. The first two chapters present contrasting overviews of how the disparate doctrines and decision makers that constitute health law work together, for better or worse, to constrain the medical marketplace. The next six chapters address particular market developments and the regulatory dilemmas they present. Problems considered include the power of state versus federal government in the health sphere, conflict between insurers and patients and providers over medical need, financial rewards to physicians for frugal practice, the role of antitrust law in the organization of health care provision and financing, the future of public hospitals, and the place of investor-owned versus non-profit firms.

The first chapter, "American Health Care and the Law," by Clark C. Havighurst, contends that health law's disparate doctrines, diverse sources, and lack of a unifying paradigm render it ill-prepared to bring reason and order to the governance of the medical marketplace. Havighurst, a former health policy advisor to President Reagan and a pioneering advocate of competition and consumer choice as organizing precepts for American medicine, urges that health care law be reconceived to promote well-functioning medical markets. To this end, he proposes a dialogue between stakeholders in the health sphere and those who make, interpret, and apply health law. In the second chapter, "One Step Ahead of the Law: Market Pressures and the Evolution of Managed Care," I consider the interplay between health care law and markets from a different angle. I argue that medical markets have proven more responsive to consumer concerns than market skeptics expected, but the resulting institutional change has disappointed market proponents, and that market actors' anticipation of legal developments has done more to change the way health plans do business than have courts or regulators themselves.

Chapter 3, "Federalism and the Future of Health Care Reform," by Richard A. Briffault and Sherry Glied, tackles a problem that has come close to paralyzing government's efforts to make rules for the medical marketplace—the relationship between federal and state regulatory authority. The federal statute that governs employment-based medical coverage, and thus functions as a virtual constitution for private health plans, imposes few substantive duties on plans and employers and has been read to broadly preempt the states' regulatory power. Briffault, an authority on federalism issues, and Glied, a health economist and advisor to the Clinton administration on health care reform, review the constraints that federalism imposes on government's ability to respond to market failures in the health sphere.

The next two chapters address clinical cost management methods. In Chapter 4, "The Management of Conflict Over Health Insurance Coverage," Gerard F. Anderson and Mark A. Hall consider the courts' role in resolving contentious disputes over preauthorization and payment for medical treatment. Drawing upon their own empirical research, Anderson and Hall (another pairing between a health economist and a legal scholar) review the factors that have influenced judges' decisions in these cases, then offer proposals that could reduce litigation (and bitterness) over medical coverage issues. Chapter 5, "Financial Incentives as a Cost Control Mechanism," by Thomas Rice, reviews theory and evidence on financial incentives meant to influence physicians' practice behavior. Rice, a health economist more skeptical about markets than are most in his discipline, considers how financial incentives might affect physicians, then assesses evidence on the degree to which different incentive systems are used in the United States. He notes that doctors and patients are troubled by such incentives, then closes with a discussion of two regulatory options: requiring the disclosure of financial incentives and limiting the extent to which payers can put physicians at financial risk for the cost of care.

The last three chapters consider institutional form in the health care industry. Chapter 6, "Medical Antitrust and the Changing Structure of the Firm," by Peter J. Hammer, assesses the case for applying traditional, procompetitive antitrust principles to health care markets. In response to the rise of managed care, doctors and hospitals have sought legislative exemptions from antitrust law's prohibitions on collective action. "These proposals," Hammer writes, "raise questions about when markets should be trusted and when they should be displaced by various nonmarket institutions." Hammer, a health law scholar and economist whose work boldly challenges conventional antitrust thinking, examines the logic of medical antitrust law from a perspective informed by Ronald Coase's writings on industrial organization and Kenneth Arrow's ideas about the regulatory role of non-market norms. In Chapter 7, "Why Do Public Teaching Hospitals Privatize," Larry S. Gage employs case studies to consider the trend toward privatization of public hospitals that serve the poor, as providers of last resort. Gage, president of the National Association of Public Hospitals and a partner at the law firm of Powell, Goldstein, Frazer & Murphy, defends privatization as a pragmatic solution, in some cases, to bureaucratic and legal rigidities that limit public hospitals' ability to adjust to changing market conditions. In the final chapter, "Should the Law Prefer Nonprofits?," I evaluate, and find wanting, the case for tax and regulatory preferences for the nonprofit form over investor ownership in the hospital and health insurance sectors.

The picture of health policy and law that emerges from this book will unsettle scholars and policy makers who strive for simplicity and clarity in their explanations and prescriptions. Trends in the health sector are difficult to track, and legal and regulatory governance is the product of myriad, mostly uncoordinated power centers. These power centers often act with little understanding of health care. Statutes, common law doctrines, and norms restraining the exercise of judicial and regulatory agency discretion limit their power to produce coherent, rational health care policy. Well-financed interest groups impose tight political constraints. Yet a measure of rationality is possible within these limits. Scholarship that concedes the health sphere's complexities and seeks remedies that fit this country's legal, political, and cultural constraints can contribute to reasoned regulatory governance. The essays collected here aspire to this end.

M. Gregg Bloche

Notes

1. James Q. Wilson, *Bureaucracy: What Government Agencies Do and Why They Do It* (1989).
2. David S. Broder & Haynes B. Johnson, *The System: The American Way of Politics at the Breaking Point* (1996).
3. Rosemary Stevens, *In Sickness and in Wealth* (1989).
4. Paul Starr, *The Social Transformation of American Medicine* (1982) 198–232.
5. Id. at 338–47.
6. E.g. David Rothman, *Strangers at the Bedside: A History of How Law and Bioethics Transformed Medical Decision Making* (1991).
7. Alain C. Enthoven, *Health Plan: The Only Practical Solution to the Soaring Cost of Medical Care* (1980).
8. E. Haavi Morreim, Cost Containment and the Standard of Medical Care, 75 *Cal. L. Rev.* 1719, 1757–64 (1987).
9. E.g. Clark Havighurst, *Health Care Choices: Private Contracts as Instruments of Health Care Reform* (1995); Mark A. Hall, *Making Medical Spending Decisions: The Law, Ethics, and Economics of Rationing Mechanisms* (1997).

10. See, e.g., David M. Eddy, The Use of Evidence and Cost Effectiveness By the Courts: How Can It Help Improve Health Care, 26 *J. Health Polit., Policy, & L.* 387, 396 (2001).
11. See Johnson & Broder, supra note 2, at 205–13. This series of TV ads featured an anxious, middle class couple at home, talking unreassuringly about the prospect of government control over their health care decisions.

The Privatization of Health Care Reform

1

AMERICAN HEALTH CARE AND THE LAW

Clark C. Havighurst

Once upon a time, the U.S. health care industry was not beset on all sides by law and lawyers. Indeed, when I first surveyed the field of health law in the late 1960s, the list of emergent legal issues in health care was quite short. In addition, the salient issues arose within relatively few fields of law, principally medical malpractice (including the area of informed consent), occupational licensure, the tort liability of hospitals, abortion, prescription drug development, human experimentation, and several other aspects of what we now call bioethics. Although the federal Medicare and Medicaid legislation had recently been enacted, those programs did not yet present major legal problems, largely because they were still operating under widely accepted principles borrowed almost intact from private, nonprofit health insurance—which itself had not yet become controversial or raised high-profile legal questions. Scholars and practitioners in the field did not anticipate an explosion of new laws and of legal attacks on time-honored institutions and industry practices. Health care was generally viewed as a charitable or public service and not as a business requiring a sophisticated legal regime to ensure that it performed responsibly. In short, the health care industry was largely left alone by the law and lawyers, and nearly everyone expected that it would always be so.

This chapter offers some observations concerning the disorderly state of health care law today, suggesting in the process some possible answers to such questions

1

as the following: What has happened since the 1960s to create today's legal jungle? Are there explanations, logical or otherwise, for the proliferation of legal rules and the associated legal risks that have only lately engulfed health care providers, financing institutions, and others? Where did all this law come from? Did an imperialistic legal system unfairly single out the health care industry as a fruitful new field in which to extend its dominance? Were the new legal rules and enforcement mechanisms put in place by rational planners carrying out a coherent national policy toward the health care industry? Is the law, as it has evolved to this point, internally consistent and clear about the objectives it seeks to achieve? If not, what can be done about it?

After briefly reviewing five areas of law where the public was blindsided by unheralded but crucially-important changes in public policies toward the health care industry, I observe a number of anomalies and fundamental contradictions in health care law, which also reflect a high degree of cognitive dissonance—the simultaneous holding of incongruous attitudes or beliefs—both in public attitudes toward health care and in health policy itself. I conclude by suggesting that the apparent legal confusion, attributable in part to the absence of a single source of law governing health care in the United States, reveals a need for a private synthesizing effort to bridge gaps between different policy-making authorities and between conflicting paradigms, legal doctrines, and public policies that coexist only because they have never had to be reconciled.

Watershed events in American health care: the law and unintended consequences

The United States legal system has been a major factor, for better or worse, in creating the conditions that determined how American health care would evolve in the past half-century. In several watershed events, important implications of the legal changes were not recognized at the time by the public, industry insiders, or even the decision makers themselves. Yet each of these events set in motion powerful economic and political forces that dramatically altered the face of the industry. Although it is too much to expect that law will always evolve according to pure logic, lawmaking for the health care industry has been driven by chance to a particularly surprising degree.

The history of American health care in the past two generations has featured, first, the growth of provider-sponsored, employer-financed private health insurance, followed by the extension of similar public coverage to the over-65 population, the disabled, and certain categories of poor families. These expressions of third-party financing carried with them new degrees of moral hazard—economists' term for the tendency of decision makers to incur higher costs when someone else stands to bear them. Uncontrolled, this moral hazard eventually gave rise to unprecedented cost escalation, as benefit–cost ratios were almost totally neglected in physicians' clinical choices and, consequently, also in decision making on capital spending and technological development. The cost explosion initially triggered a struggle for control of the system between the medical profession, which had taken responsibility for decision making in most elements of medical care, and government, which sought to impose regulatory controls as a forerunner to adopting universal health coverage. In the late 1970s, however, a third way appeared in national health-policy debates, as advocates of greater reliance on market forces and competition began to win converts by pointing to the potential of health maintenance organizations (HMOs) and other innovations—for example, selective contracting, incentive arrangements, and predetermination of coverage limits—to control moral hazard by consensual means, all in a context of accountability to purchasers.

With the defeat in 1979 of the Carter administration's proposal for universal hospital revenue controls, and the election in 1980 of a conservative president, national health policy toward the private sector suddenly became one of benign neglect, as private purchasers and competitive markets were given a chance to show what they could do to control costs. Since that time there have been revolutionary changes in the way health services are bought and paid for in the private sector, and some movement in public programs to build on these developments. These changes have succeeded in slowing the rate of cost increases but have also occasioned unhappiness about the entities that took responsibility for controlling costs, about their motives and methods, and about their accountability for any questionable practices or erroneous decisions.

The law was present at the creation of each of the major problems that has surfaced in the health care industry at various points in its recent history. It also was responsible for imposing or lifting, as the case may be, many of the constraints operating on industry actors as they addressed these problems. The following paragraphs show how the path taken by the health care industry was influenced by conditions that the legal system largely created with little awareness of what it was doing.

Subsidizing Employer-Based Health Coverage

During World War II wage controls prevented private employers from raising their workers' take-home pay. A loophole, however, allowed them to offer generous health benefits—which the tight labor market prompted them to do. After the war, employers and workers lobbied successfully to have these benefits—to which they had become accustomed—made tax-free. Subsidizing the purchase of health coverage and other fringe benefits seemed like a good, progressive idea at the time. But, having aided middle-class employees in this way, government has since found it difficult to muster voter support for a more extensive program to ensure coverage for those whose jobs do not carry health benefits. By building this modest concession into the tax system, government laid the groundwork for the system of employer-based health coverage that we still have today.

The exclusion of employer-paid health premiums from taxable income has given the great majority of consumers a strong inducement to pay as many of their health bills as possible through an employer-sponsored health plan rather than out-of-pocket. In taking optimal advantage of this tax loophole, consumers have over-insured themselves, eschewing coverage with demand-suppressing deductibles and coinsurance (which would have to be paid from after-tax rather than untaxed income) and seeking coverage that is more comprehensive than would be optimal if they were merely seeking protection against unpredictable costs. These choices by consumers, although rational, widened the impact of the moral hazard associated with health insurance, inviting more spending on health care than consumers would have normally elected. The tax subsidy also gave consumers an incentive to purchase their coverage through the workplace, where the true cost of coverage was effectively hidden from them. This encouraged labor unions and many employers to use overly-generous health benefits strategically, to demonstrate their concern for workers' welfare. Employment-based health coverage—in which benefits are highly visible and costs are not—helped to breed the pervasive entitlement mentality that still distorts political discussions about health care. Today's backlash against managed health care owes a lot to working Americans' ability to see only the possible drawbacks of their new coverage and not the substantial savings that managed care has added to their paychecks.

In many ways, therefore, the tax policy adopted naïvely in the postwar period continues to color the political, institutional, and legal climate in which health care is financed and provided. Policy wonks have long advocated capping the tax subsidy at an appropriate level, but proposals to do so have not fared well over the years; opportunistic politicians can easily persuade voters to oppose the "taxing" of health benefits. A tax subsidy of this kind is insidious precisely because—in addition to being an off-budget public expenditure (amounting to about $125 billion in 1998)—it can misallocate huge amounts of society's resources, yet be almost entirely invisible and painless at the level of individual producers, consumers, and taxpayers.[1] Since the affected interests simply adjust their behavior to the incentives created, they have no occasion to complain or to call for political attention to the fact that United States spending on personal health care exceeds that of any other nation by several whole percentage points of gross domestic product (GDP).[2] This extravagance suggests the magnitude of the problem that we inadvertently created for ourselves when government elected to use the tax code to encourage employed persons—those who could best afford its true cost—to purchase health coverage.

Infusion of New Money through Medicare and Medicaid

The launching of the Medicare and Medicaid programs in the mid-1960s was a well-recognized watershed in health policy. Although many physicians opposed Medicare in the belief that federal involvement would be detrimental to their calling (although not to their incomes), these warnings were discounted as reactionary. Moreover, Congress could not have foreseen how the infusion of so much new public money into the health care industry, coupled with the moral hazard that accompanies any form of third-party payment, would forever alter not just the economics but also the culture of medical care. Perhaps Medicare's most significant side effect was to make the health care sector, more than ever before, an arena for profit-seeking activity. For the first time, hospitals and physicians could expect to be paid well for much of the care they had previously provided for less. They also saw a huge increase in demand for even the costliest of their services. Entrepreneurs suddenly saw new opportunities in health care, and physicians saw opportunities to become entrepreneurs themselves. With so much money on the table, law and lawyers could not be far behind— not so much because they were lured by the money at stake as because their services would be needed (and worth paying for) as entrepreneurs rushed in and as the legal system was called upon to referee the inevitable disputes.

To be sure, the United States government's plunge into the financing of health care for the elderly and the poor probably could not have occurred without dramatic expansion in the role of law and lawyers. But the potential for legal problems was exacerbated by the way the programs were designed. In a political compromise, Medicare was fashioned to resemble the Blue Cross and Blue Shield plans. Hospitals and physicians had devised these plans to enable consumers to purchase financial protection against unpredictable health care costs without intruding on providers' freedom or introducing price competition. Although the program thus avoided immediate confrontation with providers, its inflationary potential was clear, since it contained few tools for combating moral hazard. The rising costs of the public programs led eventually to regulation-like reforms, all of which increased the need for lawyers on all sides of every issue.

After Medicare shifted in 1983 from retrospective cost reimbursement to prospectively determined payments based on patient diagnosis, there were fewer occasions to litigate reimbursement issues. Nevertheless, the program's regulatory and entitlement features continue to generate legal disputes. An arguable virtue of proposals to shift away from a system of financing defined benefits (that is, entitlements) to one based on defined contributions (subsidizing beneficiaries' enrollment in private health plans) might be a decrease in legal problems—at least between government and providers. Legal disputes would then be largely confined to the familiar private-law areas of torts and contracts and to application of state and federal regulatory schemes, such as those governing managed care.

The recent spectacular boom in law business associated with the government's campaign against so-called fraud and abuse reveals another legal time bomb in the original design of Medicare. As part of the political deal, Medicare gave beneficiaries a free choice of providers and permitted any provider to participate unless the government could show cause for disqualification. The government thus deprived itself of powers such as those that private payers use to protect themselves against exploitation through inappropriate kickbacks and self-referrals (for example, the power to select and deselect providers without due process). Although it took time for the problem to materialize, Medicare eventually became highly vulnerable to sophisticated schemes to induce lucrative referrals of beneficiaries. To be sure, the harm to either beneficiaries or the government was not always apparent as entrepreneurs scrambled for the available business. But the government was unable to assure itself that utilization abuses were not occurring and was offended by apparent profiteering at its expense. It therefore moved to address the problem by enacting increasingly stringent antifraud legislation on at least seven occasions between 1972 and 1996.

Under these laws, the federal government now uses the threat of criminal prosecution and heavy civil penalties against providers and entrepreneurs who may be guilty of nothing more reprehensible than adapting to the more entrepreneurial, incentive-driven health care marketplace and of taking advantage of weaknesses in Medicare's design and administration. Although some providers are unduly opportunistic, much of the conduct subject to penalty under the anti-kickback and Stark legislation (aimed to curb referral abuses) appears fairly well accepted and manageable in the private sector. Nevertheless, government has found it convenient to characterize provider conduct that exploits the program's shortcomings as "fraud and abuse," and to criminalize it. The moral spin was necessary to overcome the presumption that all providers are entitled to participate in Medicare, and to shift responsibility for the program's deficiencies away from its designers. What is notable for present purposes is how decisions on the details of Medicare, which were made to satisfy providers' interests as well as certain ideological predilections of its sponsors, led the health care industry in unanticipated directions, and into activities that have necessitated the enlistment of many, many lawyers.

Applying Antitrust Law to Physicians

Crucial changes have occurred in medical care as a result of the enforcement of the antitrust laws in the health care sector since the mid-1970s. The watershed event was the Supreme Court's 1975 decision in *Goldfarb v. Virginia State Bar,* which provided the warrant for this enforcement campaign.[3] In *Goldfarb* (which involved price fixing by real estate lawyers), the court held that the so-called learned professions are engaged in "trade or commerce," and therefore do not enjoy an implied exemption from the Sherman Act. It is ironic that the case that opened up antitrust law as a new field of legal activity in the health care industry itself dealt with a restraint of trade in the legal profession.

The significance of the *Goldfarb* decision for national health policy can hardly be overstated. Previously, both government and the private sector had largely acquiesced in the medical profession's view of itself as a self-regulating body, and accepted the profession's hegemony over major portions of the health care system. Thus, nearly everyone discounted any substantial role for competition in the health care industry and tolerated infringements on the operation of market forces. *Goldfarb,* however, effectively overturned a policy based on the view that professionals could be trusted to determine the basic rules under which health care was provided. Its effect was suddenly to make health care competition mandatory, in the sense that competitors could not lawfully agree to restrain it. Not only did this fundamental policy shift occur without any public debate or legislative action, it is doubtful that a legislative campaign to change the old, tolerant policy would have commanded much support. Nevertheless, one stroke of the Supreme Court's pen changed the basic legal regime governing professional services, and opened the door to procompetitive private innovations that the medical profession had previously been able to suppress.

An equally significant consequence of *Goldfarb* was to increase the relevance of the previously embryonic debate over whether competition could be a desirable force in health care. Indeed, *Goldfarb,* or something like it, was necessary to make a market-oriented health policy plausible, since so long as the medical profession could exercise effective control over the economic environment of physicians, it could prevent the emergence of corporate middlemen able and willing to act as purchasing agents for consumers in procuring physician services on competitive terms. After *Goldfarb,* significant reform could be realistically expected in the private sector, without direct government intervention. Partly on this basis, Congress defeated the Carter administration's hospital cost-containment bill in 1979 and, with the support of the Reagan administration, began to rely explicitly on competition and consumer choice to shape the health care industry's future. The antitrust battles that ensued thus paved the way for the revolution that occurred in the health care industry in the 1980s and 1990s. It is at least arguable, on this basis, that *Goldfarb* was the most important event ever in the evolution of American health policy.

In any event, without the antitrust enforcement effort against physicians that began in earnest after *Goldfarb,* the nation would have had to wait much longer for private innovations that made providers accountable to consumers for the cost as well as the quality of medical care. More likely, without antitrust enforcement clearing the way for private innovation, government would have assumed a dominant role in American health care, as it has in other countries.[4] Thus, a seemingly technical clarification of the law, adopted without policy debate, had a truly fateful effect on the course of history.

Preemption of State Laws

Another largely serendipitous event that has had profound effects on the course of American health care was the enactment in 1974 of the Employee Retirement Income Security Act (ERISA). ERISA's principal effect in the health care field has been to preempt state laws "insofar as they may now or hereafter relate to any employee [health] benefit plan." Despite recent interpretations granting the states somewhat more regulatory freedom with respect to health care than they were previously thought to have, ERISA remains a serious impediment to many state regulatory and other initiatives and to many lawsuits against employers or organized health plans. Because ERISA itself provides very little regulatory control over employee health plans and offers only minor remedies for aggrieved enrollees in such plans, it represents a sizable loophole in the law. This loophole is troublesome in some respects, but ERISA preemption has made possible a great deal of generally desirable innovation by employers and health plans that might otherwise have been precluded or discouraged by state regulation or by the threat of litigation under state law.

ERISA's effect in limiting the ability of state law to deal with health plans was as unintended on the part of Congress as it was significant in shaping the industry's course. ERISA was enacted in response to some highly-publicized instances of pension-fund fraud and mismanagement and was not perceived by Congress as a health care measure at all. Indeed, it was specifically designed not to interfere with the business of insurance or with state regulation thereof. To this end, it included an exception—the so-called saving clause—from the preemption provision for state laws regulating the business of insurance. Because Congress assumed that health coverage would continue to be governed by state law, it did not devise ERISA's regulatory scheme with health benefits in mind.

However, ERISA eventually proved to have important unintended consequences for health care. One of its main effects was, over time, to induce nearly all employers large enough to do so to self-insure their health benefits, usually with the help of a third-party administrator—an insurance company providing "administrative services only," or a managed-care plan assuming some of the employer's risk. The inducement to self-insure was inherent in ERISA's preemptive provisions, which permit self-insured plans alone to escape both the burdens of state insurance regulation and the impact of other state laws applicable to health insurers. Once again, the law inadvertently reinforced the role of employers in procuring health coverage. Unfortunately, the need for an employer to self-insure to qualify for ERISA preemption limited ERISA's value to small employers, which must purchase coverage for their employees from health insurers or HMOs that are subject to state regulatory requirements. These requirements raise the cost of coverage, making it prohibitive for some employers.

It is reasonable to argue that ERISA leaves a vital part of American health care underregulated or inadequately policed by the courts. Yet the revolution that began in American health care in the late 1970s would have been much less dramatic if ERISA-protected health plans had not been free from regulatory restraints and thus able to adopt innovative approaches to the design and administration of health benefits. Most of these innovations have benefitted consumers. In any event, ERISA is still another legal guest at the party whom no policymaker ever intended to invite. For some it added to the fun; for others it has been a wet blanket.

Recognizing Corporate Responsibility for Medical Care

In the 1965 Illinois case *Darling v. Charleston Memorial Hospital*,[5] the law took another important policy leap largely out of public view—recognizing for the first time that health care institutions have direct legal responsibilities to patients for the quality of medical care provided by physician-independent contractors. In *Darling*, a hospital was held legally responsible for injuries caused in the first instance by a physician in the emergency room. Although *Darling* was recognized as a landmark decision at the time, it is not obvious, looking at it today, why it was so notable. After all, the court merely held a hospital liable for injuries received by a patient as a result of negligent treatment by a staff physician taking a turn on call in the emergency room, and there had been many earlier cases in which hospitals had been held liable for the torts of their physician agents. Indeed, if the *Darling* court had simply applied the doctrine of apparent agency and held the hospital vicariously liable because the patient believed that the doctor was its agent, the decision would have attracted little attention. But the court went further, holding that the jury could find the hospital itself negligent, either in its nurses' inattention to the poor care provided by the doctor or in its own failure to monitor that care. Given then-prevalent notions of professionalism and the law's general hostility to "the corporate practice of medicine," the court's recognition of a hospital's duty to supervise a physician's treatment was indeed surprising.

Because it recognized that corporations, as well as individual professionals, may have direct obligations to patients and thus the right to oversee the work of affiliated physicians, the *Darling* case was a watershed in health care law. Just as the paradigm undermined in *Darling* had been enshrined in previous public policy without much conscious thought or explicit consideration of alternatives, the *Darling* court gave little indication that it appreciated it was embracing a new policy with important implications for power relationships throughout the industry. Nevertheless, *Darling* attracted attention at the time because it recognized a controversial role for hospitals vis-à-vis physicians, one that, although it may have been gradually emerging in practice, had not previously been explicitly recognized in law. Certainly it was this aspect of *Darling* that elicited applause among hospital administrators, who had long sensed a need to exercise some control over physicians and who were probably glad—even at the cost of new liability fears— to have a convincing, legitimizing excuse for moving in that direction. In health care today, corporate or institutional responsibility is widely recognized, even if the old paradigm also continues to color much legal, policy, and professional thinking.

Contradictions in U.S. health policy: the law and cognitive dissonance

Because health care law comprises many different fields of law and springs from many different sources rather than from a single policymaking body, it should come as no surprise that it has evolved in mysterious ways and is essentially incoherent on many points. Logical inconsistencies may permeate the law generally, but in dealing with health care, the legal system seems unusually capable of harboring and selectively employing incompatible decision-making principles.

In seeming at different times to favor different horns of an important dilemma, health care law reflects similar confusion in the larger society. Indeed, cognitive dissonance is particularly prevalent in respect to matters related to health care. Guido Calabresi and Philip Bobbit have observed how society often suspends one or another disbelief in coping with "tragic choices"—that is, situations in which society's need to put its scarce resources to efficient use is in direct conflict with its natural desire to see everything possible being done to avert a specific peril or hardship.[6] The public's occasional psychological need to suppress its awareness of the scarcity of resources is illustrated most poignantly by its ability to tolerate tragedies that are revealed only through statistics while at the same time mobilizing virtually unlimited resources to save a single human life.

Because the legal system shares the public's ambivalence about counting costs in health care situations, its choices are not reliably aimed at getting the industry to strive for efficient outcomes. For example, the public's lack of realism about health care matters can create severe political, legal, or other risks for decision makers who, facing difficult trade-offs in potentially tragic situations, may go out of their way to avoid so-called Type I errors—that is, errors whose adverse consequences, if any, are apt to be tragic, highly visible, and easily traceable back to the decision maker. Avoiding Type I errors, however, may entail running an increased risk of less palpable Type II errors, the consequences of which may be more serious statistically or economically but cannot so easily be laid at the decision maker's door. In general, a kind of moral hazard makes efficiency a common casualty in decisions that society entrusts to policy makers and the courts. After all, legislatures, judges, and juries are in a position to commit others' resources to uses that reflect their own predilections or interests rather than thoughtful comparisons of benefits and costs or reasonable estimates of how consumers would rationally choose to spend their limited incomes.[7] The combination of this moral hazard and the tragic-choice element in health care decisions, all reinforced by the symbolic politics of health care, ultimately accounts for most of the contradictions in the legal system's approach to certain issues that are discussed below.

Decentralization and Competition, Yes! Freedom of Contract, No!

National policy with respect to privately-purchased health care purports to entrust health care choices to the competitive marketplace, apparently on the usual theory that allowing consumers to choose how their dollars are spent ensures an efficient allocation of resources. Yet, in reality, the law itself supplies most of the normative rules under which care is provided, leaving few significant decisions to be made by private parties. Indeed, the law's role in prescribing consumers' entitlements is such that health care is still far from being a typical consumer good about which people routinely make trade-offs and economizing choices. The legal system is very much at the heart of this contradiction. The difficulty lies largely in the limited role that the legal system allots, both de facto and de jure, to private contracts as instruments by which consumers can specify their health care preferences.[8] Not only are many important aspects of health care transactions prescribed by explicit regulation, but today's health care contracts do not even attempt to specify in customized terms the desired character, quantity, and quality of the services that consumers purchase. Such matters are left to be resolved under norms ultimately supplied by law.

It is conventional in health care law for courts to consult custom and consensus in the medical community, not specifications in private contracts, for the standards they use in defining the duties of providers in tort suits or the payment obligations of health plans in benefit disputes. These professional standards have rarely been examined, however, to see whether they represent good public policy or reflect realistic comparisons of benefits and costs. To be sure, legal prescriptions based on professional standards might make sense as default rules that apply in the absence of a contrary agreement among the parties. But professional standards are usually viewed as binding norms, not as merely a starting point for private bargaining. Moreover, even if such standards could in theory be varied by contract, there are reasons to believe courts would often refuse to enforce contractual departures agreed to *ex ante* against patients who regretted such agreements *ex post*.

Judicial attitudes toward private health care contracts allow private decision makers little discretion in contracting. Courts naturally question the extent to which consumer-plaintiffs exercise informed choice when selecting their health plans, doubting that consumers clearly understand the details of their coverage options or accurately anticipate their future needs. This skepticism about the quality of consumer choices may make a court reluctant to enforce even a clear limitation on coverage if it means denying a patient a service sanctioned by professional standards. Doubts about the contracting process also foster generous interpretations of contracts. Indeed, a time-honored principle of contract interpretation allows courts to construe ambiguous contract terms against the drafter (*contra proferentem*). This principle applies even when ambiguity is unavoidable, as would almost always be the case with health care contracts seeking to limit coverage on cost/benefit grounds. Because health plans cannot count on the courts to respect even their best efforts to authorize economizing, today's health care contracts are largely silent about the precise content of the service packages being purchased and instead define service commitments in terms of medical necessity, a standard incorporating costly professional standards by reference.

Like health-plan subscriber contracts, contracts between patients and providers offer little opportunity for consumers to agree to a different set of entitlements and rights than are prescribed for them by law. Indeed, under the prevailing paradigm of medical care, provider/patient relationships are not generally seen as a matter of contract at all. A North Carolina court has said, for example, that an agreement between a patient and a physician "creates a status or relation rather than a contract."[9] Thus, a doctor's obligations to his or her patients are usually deemed to be inherent in the relationship—a matter of law, not private agreement. To the extent that this antiquated view persists, consumers' freedom of contract is impaired.[10]

There are reasons to think, therefore, that despite the seeming triumph of market-oriented policies in the health care sector, American health care law remains wedded in many respects to the medical profession's preferred paradigm of medical care. Under this paradigm, economically significant decisions are characterized as technical and thus deemed inappropriate subjects for consumer choice or for resolution through private contracts. It is ironic that the same legal system that with one arm launched an antitrust initiative which successfully challenged overt efforts by the medical profession to impose its authority has, with its other arms, given medical interests a monopoly over the most important economic decisions affecting American health care.

Corporate Responsibility for Health Care, Yes! Corporate Practice of Medicine, No!

HMOs and other managed health plans have assumed major responsibility for controlling the cost of care, and they have achieved impressive results, causing health care's share of GDP, which had previously risen every year at burdensome rates, to remain stable (at around 13.6%) for six consecutive years, from 1993 to 1998.[11] However, at the same time that the public was realizing these cost-savings, it was becoming apprehensive about the effects of managed care on quality. Yet the law still treats quality of care as primarily a professional, not an organizational, responsibility. Only in limited circumstances has a health plan been held legally accountable for the actual quality of care delivered to a patient, and most plans are able to arrange things so that the physicians whom they select to treat their enrollees are viewed legally as independent contractors, to whom patients must look exclusively for compensation in the event of mishaps. This state of affairs persists in large part because the law still embodies the tenet of the old professional paradigm of medical care that holds that corporations don't practice medicine, only licensed individuals do. But there is an inconsistency in allowing corporate health plans to assume responsibility for the cost of care while making it easy for them to exempt themselves from more than nominal responsibility for its quality.

There is little evidence that managed care has lowered the overall quality of health care.[12] But there is certainly room for disappointment that the new arrangements for financing, delivering, and managing care have led to so few improvements in health status and patient outcomes.[13] Most of today's health plans are financers of care, not organizers of it, and few are actually managing care to ensure its quality or ensuring that their subcontractors do so. Indeed, managed care today means little more than subcontracting and capitation, techniques by which health plans can lower their costs by exercising their purchasing power over providers and by shifting financial risk to them.[14] Health plans routinely select their subcontractors based on low cost, not demonstrated skill in treating patients, and compensate them in ways that can induce neglect or undertreatment. Yet plans still successfully maintain that decisions about clinical matters are the responsibility of their subcontractors and the physicians they select. A close look at the managed care revolution thus reveals that we may have created the worst situation possible: corporate power being exercised to reduce costs and increase profits without significant legal responsibility for patient care.

The law has so far generally failed to entertain the idea that health plans should be presumptively liable for their physicians' torts. At least in the absence of an explicit contractual arrangement under which enrollees agree to look only to plan subcontractors for compensation in the event of negligent treatment, the law might reasonably impose "vicarious liability" on health plans, demanding that they stand behind the work of the agents they employ, whatever the private contractual arrangement between providers and plans.[15] To be sure, one court has recently held that an HMO may be held vicariously liable for the torts of independent physicians if it exercises enough control over their behavior to justify finding an implied agency.[16] But that holding seemed to impose vicarious liability on the health plan only as a penalty for influencing medical decisions in the interest of cost containment and not as an inducement to encourage plans to take a more active and constructive role in improving quality. Unfortunately, the message sent to health plans was the wrong one: Conform your conduct to the old professional paradigm and take less, not more, responsibility for the quality of care.

Accountability, Yes! Legal Liability, No!

The political backlash against managed care has generated renewed interest in making health care providers and health plan designers and administrators accountable to consumers. Some observers believe that additional regulatory legislation making health plans accountable to public officials will suffice, while others hope that new methods being developed to measure quality of care and to report the performance of individual health plans and providers will make it easier for consumers or employers to demand quality improvements. There is ambivalence in the legal system, however, about relying on ordinary tort liability as a significant instrument of accountability in the health care sector. Indeed, in recent years "malpractice reform" has mostly meant not improving the liability system to make it an effective deterrent of bad practices, but cutting back patients' legal remedies against health care providers. Lack of confidence in liability as a tool for holding private actors accountable to consumers has also been evident in Congress in connection with proposed managed-care reforms. Not only is the idea of vicarious liability not being considered as a possible source of incentives to improve quality, but many in Congress are skeptical about proposals to amend ERISA to let patients sue health plans for personal injuries that result when plans breach their payment obligations.

Admittedly, there are severe problems in the current tort liability system. Because medical practice evolves in a market in which consumers do not regularly compare benefits to costs, the law's reliance on professional custom and practice as the principal source of standards for defining provider negligence in malpractice cases may be driving providers away from efficient practices. Similarly, the practice of referring to professional standards in determining health plans' payment obligations may discourage appropriate comparisons of benefits and costs. In particular, the legal system's principal method of establishing standards—letting juries choose between the conflicting opinions of partisan experts—invites further skepticism over whether the law reliably pushes health plans or providers in the right directions. The fact that medical care accounts for such a high percentage of U.S. GDP suggests that efficient economizing is indeed discouraged by unreasonable expectations built into the legal system.

There are other reasons, too, why policymakers might doubt that tort liability could improve matters. For example, the Harvard Medical Practice Study not only presented evidence of a disturbingly high incidence of negligence in hospitals but also found that very few of the potential malpractice claims were ever brought to the attention of liability insurers or the legal system.[17] Moreover, litigation entails high transaction costs: about half the total insurance premiums paid for malpractice liability insurance goes to paying lawyers, experts, and liability insurers. Policymakers might reasonably resist incurring these costs if they lack confidence that the legal system is capable of holding providers appropriately accountable for their torts or of promoting optimal health care quality.

Instead of denying remedies to injured patients, however, the legal system might seek to improve its liability regimes so as to effectively discipline providers and induce affordable quality improvements. The earlier suggestion that health plans (or their subcontractors) might bear vicarious liability for physician torts reveals one possible way that the legal system might be redesigned. Allowing health plans to modify the law's traditional remedies by contract is another way by which the tort system might be made more responsive to consumers' needs.[18] Although a health plan would normally have little reason to lower an enrollee's cost of bringing a lawsuit, it might agree to a more efficient, contract-based method of dispute resolution if such a change could be coupled with one or more substantive changes, such as a modification of the legal standard of care or a limit on punitive or noneconomic damages. Earlier proposals to impose strict liability for selected adverse outcomes also deserve new policy attention.[19] Finally, it should be possible to fashion health-plan liability for errors in benefit determinations in such a way—without punitive damages, for example—as to induce plans not to be cavalier in denying claims while still enforcing plan-subscriber contracts to curb moral hazard.

It is unfortunate that the efficacy of liability has come into question just when the marketplace has the greatest need for incentives to deter quality shortfalls. Under earlier, more generous payment systems, there was little risk that quality would be intentionally stinted, and the tort system had a relatively small role to play in quality assurance. Now that managed care has introduced new risks of undertreatment, the legal system should actively strive to make liability an effective force for improving quality and ensuring patient welfare. Arguably, however, health care law would be more helpful if it focused less on enforcing rights and entitlements of its own devising and more on facilitating efforts by private parties to define their own reciprocal rights and obligations by contract—and on ensuring that those rights and obligations are evenhandedly enforced.

Financial Incentives, Yes! Conflicts of Interests, No!

The managed care revolution introduced new kinds of financial incentives into health care decision making. In the earlier era, providers had a strong incentive to offer more services than were optimal, and they could rationalize such overspending as serving their patients' interests as well as their own. Once payers developed the ability to select providers and to craft new ways of paying them, however, incentives began to run in the opposite direction. Although this was initially viewed as a desirable development, it was inevitable that public attention would eventually focus on the conflicts of interests that physicians face in making clinical choices, including referrals to other providers.

The legal system has generally approved the new incentive arrangements, but it also has a long tradition of opposing conflicts of interests, especially when they affect relationships between professionals and their clients. The law is thus pulled in two directions and is therefore arguably ill-equipped to determine the acceptability of managed care and the incentives cum conflicts of interests on which it depends. Likewise, as discussed earlier, fraud-and-abuse law has taken a highly literal, arguably unrealistic approach to the mere existence of inducements to physicians to refer patients, even in situations where referral may be the best clinical option. The legal system thus has begun to bring its natural hostility to conflicts of interests to bear on essential features of modern health care, with consequences yet to be determined.

Many thoughtful physicians have concluded that physician incentives, if properly designed and implemented, should be a part of any health plan.[20] In truth, any payment system or organizational structure creates conflicts of interests of some kind, necessitating reliance on physicians' ethics to prevent abuses. The legal system appears to be wholly at sea in knowing how to evaluate compensation arrangements aimed ostensibly at countering moral hazard. Fortunately, the Supreme Court in a recent case wisely declined an invitation to regulate incentive arrangements under ERISA.[21]

Entitlements, Yes! Public Financing, No!

Even though the American public has not seen fit to fund a universal entitlement to health care, the legal system regularly gives patients legally enforceable rights to receive certain health services or to receive care of a particular quality or kind. Often these entitlements and legal rights are created at the expense of private providers (and ultimately of those who must pay their charges). In other cases, public financing is provided but in a very selective way, creating a patchwork of entitlements that demonstrate compassion for certain afflicted persons but that also, if viewed from a distance, highlight the absence of universal coverage for other equally-indicated care.

A leading example of an unfunded entitlement to health services at private providers' expense is the Emergency Medical Treatment and Active Labor Act of 1986 (EMTALA). This law amended the Medicare act to require hospitals participating in Medicare to provide their usual emergency screening to any patient appearing in the emergency room (not just Medicare beneficiaries) and to stabilize any emergency medical condition discovered—all without regard to a patient's ability to pay. To be sure, emergency care has a powerful appeal, and the entitlement created by EMTALA has not been an overwhelming burden for private hospitals, most of which had already assumed similar responsibilities in their communities. But legislation making hospital charity mandatory—even when the hospital in question is a proprietary, tax-paying enterprise—ought to raise some eyebrows. Nevertheless, even though the notion of compulsory charity is an oxymoron, the nation has apparently adopted a policy of relying on hospitals' widespread ability and willingness to cross-subsidize uncompensated care for the uninsured as a principal safety net for those who fall through the gaps in private coverage. Congress's decision in EMTALA to prevent occasional holes from appearing in this safety net therefore has a certain expedient appeal, since it makes the policy of relying on private charity more responsible than it otherwise would be.

Other unfunded mandates to the private sector are less defensible. Congress is considering, for example, whether to implement a so-called bill of rights for patients vis-à-vis managed care plans. The regulatory requirements in that legislation will necessarily entail some increase in private costs—how much is hotly debated—that will price even more consumers out of the market for private coverage. Unfortunately, policymakers frequently seek political credit for their good intentions by advocating the best in health care. In so doing, they make the best the enemy of what many might regard as good enough for themselves.

Some moves by the political system toward providing health care for disadvantaged individuals or groups are exercises in the magician's art of misdirection—that is, ostentatious flourishes diverting attention from what is truly consequential (in this case, continuing major gaps in access to care). Thus, even though the Medicaid program was enacted in an admirable burst of generosity, the liberality of the coverage it extends to a subset of the underserved population is probably not optimal public policy, since the same resources could be better used to care for more people. Medicaid's apparent generosity serves policymakers well, however, as a demonstration of their good will toward the poor. At the same time, inadequate payment for services often diminishes de facto what seems so generous de jure. Similar misdirection is also notable with respect to Medicaid coverage of long-term care. In this case, Congress's visible hand holds out a generous entitlement, while hidden regulatory hands at the state level erode that entitlement by limiting the supply of nursing home beds under certificate-of-need requirements. Similarly, in the early days of liver transplantation, when efficacy was in doubt, costs extremely high, and private coverage very limited, some state Medicaid programs garnered good publicity by generously covering transplants for the few who needed them while at the same time neglecting greater but less obvious needs.[22] The end-stage renal disease program under Medicare is an example of an entitlement that earned political credit for an earlier Congress but that contrasts strikingly with the lack of universal coverage for other needs.

Needed: a permanent forum on legal issues in health care

Although the vagrancy of American health care law and its many contradictions are interesting, the practical aim of this chapter is to suggest the potential value of creating a new private forum in which insiders from both sides of the medical/legal divide can freely and openly discuss both broad and narrow issues. The forum's main concern should be the law affecting the financing, delivery, and quality of personal health services, not all law affecting individual or public health or regulating biomedical research or biotechnology as such. Although the forum might strive initially only to issue reports surveying problem areas and the relevant literature, it might aspire in the long run to fill a role similar to that of the American Law Institute or the National Conference of Commissioners on Uniform State Laws, seeking common ground and issuing authoritative model statutes and pronouncements on what the law should be. The overriding goal of the forum would be to assist the legal system in adapting legal thinking and doctrine to the new health care environment.

The need for a forum of the kind visualized arises in part because, as this chapter demonstrates, nowhere in the legal system is there a single governmental authority responsible for making law and policy to govern the health care industry in all of its interrelated aspects. Indeed, the industry is too large and diverse to enable rationalizing the law through the legislative process without a complete federal takeover. As things now stand, Congress and state legislatures each have major, somewhat overlapping, but largely complementary roles in developing health care law. In addition, lawmaking in a number of legal fields affecting the health care sector is largely in the hands of courts acting in a common-law mode, often with even less policy-making awareness and flexibility than legislatures bring to the exercise. In some health policy spheres, law is created, at least initially, by federal and state administrative agencies. The legal system also regularly gives the force of law to customary standards and to standards developed by professional or other private associations to guide or dictate the conduct of health care providers. In a number of instances, important legal regimes have been created not by legislatures, agencies, or courts but through negotiated settlements of litigation.

A private, nonprofit entity with a broad perspective could perform a useful synthesizing and coordinating function in health care law. Not only are Congress and state legislatures often inclined to see only one aspect of an issue—such as the possible benefits of legislation and not its true costs—but they typically lack responsibility for, or control over, many aspects of the health care system that their decisions affect. Both legislatures and courts are also influenced by special interests—lobbyists or litigants, as the case may be—and by overarching conventions and paradigms that, lacking plenary power, they cannot easily reexamine or alter. In these circumstances, an independent private forum could provide both valuable overviews and appropriate oversight for the legal system, at least occasionally going outside the bounds of conventional thinking. Such a forum should be above the political fray and well positioned to examine objectively how the law is influencing the health care industry's overall performance. It should seek to engage the most thoughtful persons in the medical profession and the health care industry, as well as equally leading lights from the legal world. The prestige of such an enterprise and the eminence of those who participate in its deliberations, should draw attention and lend authority and influence to its work products. The involvement of thoughtful representatives of the health care and legal establishments in the reexamination and reformulation of policy should not only improve the quality of thinking on legal issues in health care but also facilitate the education and reeducation of lawyers, judges, physicians, and other industry participants on difficult legal matters—perhaps through short courses and other educational endeavors.

Because of its combination of scientific prestige, stature in the eyes of policymakers, and ability to bring the findings of health services research to bear on legal and policy questions, the Institute of Medicine (IOM) of the National Academy of Sciences is uniquely positioned to convene the forum I propose.[23] The goal of the projected forum should be to take a genuine systems approach in evaluating legal rules in the health sector and in guiding the performance of courts and legislatures. As a prestigious convener of experts, finder of facts, and distiller of wisdom, the IOM could be a vital source of new insights and principles to which legislators, judges, officials, advocates, and academics could turn in thinking about and shaping law for the health care industry in the twenty-first century.

Acknowledgment

Adapted with permission from an article published by *Health Affairs*. Clark C. Havighurst, American Health Care and the Law—We Need to Talk! *Health Aff.* 84–106 (July/August 2000).

Notes

1. J. Sheils and P. Hogan, Cost of Tax-Exempt Health Benefits in 1998, *Health Aff.* 176–81 (March/April 1999).
2. G.F. Anderson et al., Health Spending and Outcomes: Trends in OECD Countries, 1960–1998, *Health Aff.* 150–157 (May/June 2000).
3. 421 U.S.773 (1975).
4. A much earlier antitrust case, by vindicating an early HMO in Washington, D.C., against efforts by organized medicine to drive it from the market, kept alive the possibility of creating alternative delivery systems, thus preserving the possibility of effective price competition in health care. *AMA v. United States*, 130 F.2d 233 (D.C.Cir.1942), *aff'd*, 317 U.S.519 (1943).
5. 211 N.E.2d 253 (Ill. 1965)
6. G. Calabresi and P. Bobbit, *Tragic Choices* (New York: W.W. Norton, 1978).
7. Public decision makers regularly eschew making rational trade-offs on consumers' behalf, assuming instead that consumers want nothing less than the best health care, whatever the cost. This defeats a central purpose of substituting public choices for private ones. Public regulation is usually justified, after all, on the ground that the "bounded rationality" of consumers makes them less capable than public decision makers of sending reliable signals to market actors. See R. Korobkin, The Efficiency of Managed Care Patient Protection Laws: Incomplete Contracts, Bounded Rational-

ity, and Market Failure, 85 *Cornell* L. Rev. 1–88 (1999). Nothing could be clearer, however, than that the signals that voters (consumers wearing a different hat and having less reason to think rationally or fully inform themselves) send to their political representatives do not invite rational consideration of difficult trade-offs.

8. See C.C. Havighurst, *Health Care Choices: Private Contracts as Instruments of Health Reform* (Washington: AEI Press, 1995).

9. *Kennedy v Parrott*, 90 S.E.2d 754, 757 (N.C.1976).

10. Gordon Wood has observed that in pre-Revolutionary America, all contracts "were regarded as evidence that the parties . . . had mutual rights and obligations established in custom. Such patriarchal contracts did not create these rights and obligations; they merely recognized their existence." G.S. Wood, *The Radicalism of the American Revolution* (New York: Vintage Books, 1993).

11. K. Levit et al., Health Spending in 1998: Signals of Change, *Health Aff.* 124–132 (Jan/Feb 2000).

12. See, for example, R.A. Dudley et al., The Impact of Financial Incentives on the Quality of Care, *76 Milbank Q.* 649–686 (1998).

13. New questions have lately been raised about the general quality of care. See *Institute of Medicine, To Err Is Human: Building a Safer Health System*, ed. L.T. Kohn, J.M. Corrigan, and M.S. Donaldson (Washington: National Academy Press, 1999). See also M.R. Chassin, Is Health Care Ready for Six Sigma Quality? *76 Milbank Q.* 565–591 (1998); M.A. Schuster et al., How Good Is the Quality of Health Care in the United States? *76 Milbank Q.* 517–563 (1998).

14. *See* W.A. Zelman and R.A. Berenson, *The Managed Care Blues and How to Cure Them* 12 (Washington: Georgetown University Press, 1998) ("The most recent trends suggest that . . . managed care plans may wind up watering down their products to such a degree that the potential for real coordination and cost- and quality control may be lost. Today much of managed care . . . is beginning to look and act ominously like the old fee-for-service system, only with lower provider reimbursement rates.")

15. *See* C.C. Havighurst, Vicarious Liability—Relocating Responsibility for the Quality of Medical Care, 26 *Am. J. L. Med.* 7–30 (2000) (including draft statutory language to establish vicarious liability as a default rule); C.C. Havighurst, Making Health Plans Accountable for the Quality of Care, 31 *Georgia L. Rev.* 587–647 (1997); W.M. Sage, Enterprise Liability and the Emerging Managed Health Care System, *Law and Contemporary Problems* 159–210 (Spring 1997).

16. *Petrovich v Share Health Plan, Inc.*, 719 N.E.2d 756 (Ill.1999).

17. P.C. Weiler, H.H. Hiatt, and J.C. Newhouse, *A Measure of Malpractice: Medical Injury, Malpractice Litigation, and Patient Compensation* (Cambridge: Harvard University Press, 1993).

18. See Havighurst, Health Care Choices; and Symposium, Medical Malpractice: Can the Private Sector Find Relief? *L. and Contemp. Probs.* 143–303 (Spring 1996).

19. See, for example, L.R. Tancredi, Designing a No-Fault Alternative, *L. and Contemp. Probs.* 277–86 (Spring 1986); C.C. Havighurst and L.R. Tancredi, Medical Adversity Insurance—a No–Fault Approach to Medical Malpractice and Quality Assurance, 51 *Milbank Q.* 125–52 (1973).

20. S.D. Pearson et al., Ethical Guidelines for Physician Compensation Based on Capitation, 339 *N. Eng. J. Med.* 689–92 (1998).

21. *Pegram v. Herdrich*, 530 U.S. 211 (2000).

22. C.C. Havighurst and N.M.P. King, Liver Transplantation in Massachusetts: Public Policy as Morality Play, 19 *Indiana L. Rev.* 955–987 (1986).

23. In fact, the IOM already has such a proposal under consideration, having explored it at a July 1999 workshop entitled "Creating in the IOM an Ongoing Interface between the American Health Care Industry and the American Legal System." This chapter is adapted from an essay prepared for that workshop. Although the proposal received widespread support from the workshop participants, the necessary funding has not yet been obtained.

2

ONE STEP AHEAD OF THE LAW: MARKET PRESSURES AND THE EVOLUTION OF MANAGED CARE

M. Gregg Bloche

During the last two decades of the twentieth century, market forces recast both the politics and the institutions of American medical care. Managed health plans emerged as large players in the politics of health care provision, able to shape policy debate and regulatory decisions. The terms of mainstream debate over cost-control policy shifted fundamentally, from the comparative merits of price controls, supply-side regulation, and competition among providers to the appropriate scope and design of regulatory constraints on competition among health plans and provider networks. Politically plausible discussion over expanding access to care shifted from European-style public provision of medical services or insurance to the merits of alternative government subsidy schemes for the purchase of private coverage.

American health care policy today thus presumes the primacy of markets. It frames, as its main subject of debate, the role of government in remedying market failures through selective regulation and targeted subsidies. But this debate itself presumes a government able to so act—a public sector able to specify social objectives, identify market failures, and craft interventions matched to current circumstances. Since the 1960s, government has failed to so act.[1] Some have concluded that government is inherently incapable of intervening effectively in the health sphere.[2] I am skeptical of this view and inclined toward the belief that a more fortuitous alignment of leadership and circumstances in the 1990s might have accomplished much that today remains undone.[3] But be that as it may, the central storyline in American health care policy over the past 20 years has been the ability of markets to adapt the institutions of health care provision to expressed consumer needs more quickly than have the cumbersome processes of regulation and law.

This agility is my focus here. The story I shall tell, however, is not a paean to free market successes. Rather, I will argue that markets have done well at adapting health care institutions to patients' concerns in large part *because* of the looming presence of law and politics. Despite daunting information and agency problems, market-driven actors have kept a step ahead of courts and regulators in responding to paying consumers' concerns. They have done so to some degree because of the inherent advantages of markets as media for transmission of information about consumer preferences. But their success has stemmed as well from something that has received much less attention—their exquisite sensitivity to the mere *prospect* of legal or regulatory intervention and to public perceptions shaped by press coverage and political debate. Market-driven actors have repeatedly adjusted to anticipated change in their legal and regulatory environments—and corrected their own excesses—before such change has occurred. They have been equally quick at anticipating and adjusting to shifts in public opinion. This has helped them to both deflect political clamor for robust regulation and restructure their products and services to satisfy shifting consumer preferences. This agility, on the other hand, has contributed to the paradox of rising numbers of uninsured Americans at a time of unprecedented national prosperity. Market-driven relaxation of constraints on health plan spending has allowed medical costs to resume rising ahead of overall inflation, pushing marginal insurance purchasers out of the market for medical coverage. Purchaser-driven development of custom-tailored benefits packages and diverse provider networks has increased the segmentation of insurance markets by medical risk and socioeconomic class, reducing the affordability of coverage to those with the greatest clinical need.

I will consider these developments, and the interplay between market pressures and the law and politics of health care provision, with an eye toward potential lessons for legal and political decision makers. In addition to suggesting some lessons to be learned about the potential and the limitations of the medical marketplace, I will offer some unconventional thoughts about the role of law and politics as agents of change. In brief, I will argue that legal and political conflicts shape market behavior at least as much through their impact on consumer preferences and providers' and payers' perceptions of risk and opportunity as through their end results. Analysis of prospective legal and regulatory measures that considers only their effects if implemented neglects the crucial role of interplay between ongoing legal and political processes and the perceptions and judgments of market actors. Those who weigh the potential effects of legal and regulatory proposals need to take much greater account of this interplay.

Political failure and the primacy of the marketplace

The collapse of comprehensive health care reform in 1994 not only left most medical care provision and financing to the market by default; it also accelerated the process of market-driven change by erasing the threat of large-scale regulatory interference. Capital investment in new facilities and organizational schemes, long-term contractual commitments among providers and payers, and devotion of entrepreneurial energy toward innovation in health services design were rendered less risky by the lifting of the looming prospect of federal reordering of the medical marketplace. To be sure, regulatory initiatives targeting the managed care industry in many states[4] have been a continuing source of risk and constraint. But as has been extensively chronicled elsewhere,[5] the sweeping federal preemption of state law read into the Employee Retirement Income Security Act (ERISA) by its judicial interpreters has shielded the industry from much of the potential impact of these initiatives. ERISA's preemption of state laws mandating particular health benefits[6] and regulating benefits administration and provider network design has left self-insured health plans largely free to custom-craft benefits structures, administrative procedures, and networks of doctors and hospitals.[7] The ability of employers to *exit* state regulation by self-insuring has in turn constrained the states' regulatory ambitions.

Several federal regulatory schemes govern specialized aspects of health care organization and financing, but they have not greatly constrained health services entrepreneurship. To participate in Medicare, managed health plans must accept the government's schedule of premiums and meet a variety of financial, administrative, and coverage requirements, but Medicare managed care constitutes a small fraction of the market for private medical coverage.[8] Medicare's fraud and abuse regulations bar myriad business arrangements that reward health care providers for making referrals, but the regulations create broad "safe harbor" exceptions for provider risk-bearing that limit Medicare program costs.[9] The 1973 HMO Act has fostered managed care entrepreneurship through its requirement that all employers providing medical insurance and employing 25 or more workers offer a federally qualified HMO, if locally available, as a coverage option.[10] The Act's preemption provisions, moreover, immunize federally qualified HMOs from a variety of state laws that historically posed obstacles to prepaid health plans. The Act, to be sure, has considerable regulatory content: it conditions federal qualification on standards encompassing fiscal stability, assumption of risk for the cost of care, quality assurance and subscriber grievance procedures, and restrictions on risk selection.[11] The Act also sets forth, in general terms that give individual HMOs wide latitude, the "basic health services" a plan must provide to become federally qualified.[12] Some have criticized these substantive prerequisites for federal qualification as too onerous, but major industry players have not had difficulty meeting them. Moreover, insofar as federal qualification constitutes a benefit conferred, not a baseline entitlement, these prerequisites represent an entrepreneurial opportunity, not a regulatory barrier.

The net result of these federal statutory schemes has been a remarkably permissive regulatory environment. Employers and health plans have been largely free to tailor benefits packages, establish coverage limits and exclusions, fashion provider networks and payment methods, and make rules for the management of coverage disputes. ERISA preemption has generally immunized plans from state tort liability for refusal to preauthorize care.[13] This has limited claimants in such cases to their ERISA remedies, which do not include compensatory or punitive damages.[14] Health plans have been free to devise their own administrative appeals procedures for subscribers dissatisfied with coverage denials, though growing numbers of states have enacted statutes calling for independent outside review when heath plans decline to pay. Medical care providers remain subject to state tort liability, but research has established that only small proportions of medical errors result in malpractice suits, let alone damage awards or settlements.[15] Identification of clinical error is itself often an uncertain enterprise due to variable medical practice patterns and the paucity of empirical evidence behind most clinical decisions.[16] The fact that courts assess medical liability based on professional norms of practice not only translates clinical uncertainty into legal uncertainty; it allows drift (downward or upward) in legal standards of care as market mechanisms reshape medical practice.

Aside from the Medicare fraud and abuse regulations and state tort liability, no legal or regulatory mandates impose serious nationwide constraints on physician collaboration with health plans or on plans' efforts to influence physicians. State proscriptions against the "corporate practice of medicine," which for much of the 20th century kept enterprises not owned or run by physicians from exercising managerial authority over clinical decision making, were largely eviscerated by the 1980s.[17] Neither federal nor state law clearly charges physicians with a duty to act as patient advocates vis-a-vis health plans or otherwise bars physicians from entering into arrangements that oblige them to weigh health plans' economic interests when making patient-care judgments. Although the Hippocratic ethical tradition imposes upon physicians a duty of undivided loyalty to their patients, the law has not incorporated such a duty.[18] Nor does federal or state law clearly require physicians to tell patients about non-covered therapies.

Health plans have similar legal latitude to influence their doctors. They are largely free to try to shape physicians' clinical behavior by profiling their practice patterns, linking plan participation and referrals to economic performance, and offering financial rewards for clinical frugality. Although some states ban explicit *gag* clauses (barring disclosure of costly clinical options) in plan-provider contracts, health plans rarely resorted to this crude strategy before these bans were enacted.[19] Health plans have a panoply of more subtle means of influencing what physicians tell their patients. These include aligning physicians' and plans' financial interests by rewarding clinical frugality; discouraging more costly options through correspondence, meetings, and other non-contractual channels; and monitoring physicians' practice patterns and patients' complaints.[20]

Plans that offer financial rewards for frugal practice face some regulatory hurdles, albeit none that pose a serious threat to the use of such incentives. In *Pegram v. Hendrich*, decided in 2000, the U.S. Supreme Court refused to construe ERISA's fiduciary duty provision to limit these incentives.[21] The Court, though, suggested that this provision might require health plans to disclose these incentives to subscribers.[22] In 1997, an 8th Circuit Court of Appeals panel held that ERISA does impose a duty on health plans (but not physicians) to inform subscribers of physician incentives to withhold services.[23] A much-publicized settlement between the Texas Attorney General and Aetna-U.S. Healthcare imposed a similar disclosure obligation,[24] as do statutes and regulations in several states.[25] But managed health plans in most jurisdictions have not been legally required to disclose physician financial incentives to withhold care,[26] and disclosures submerged in the "small print" of voluminous plan descriptions do little in practice to alert subscribers to the conflicts of interest these incentives create. Federal law does bar Medicare HMOs from paying physicians "as an inducement to reduce or limit medically necessary services," and statutes in 25 states[27] contain similar language. But in practice, these provisions *permit* health plans to reward doctors for withholding services, since they are accompanied by statutory language explicitly authorizing compensation schemes that put physicians at financial risk for the cost of care.[28] This risk plainly encourages the withholding of services.[29]

In this permissive regulatory environment, managed systems of medical care provision and financing steadily supplanted classic fee-for-service coverage. By 1994, when the Clinton administration's reform plan failed, managed care in its protean forms had achieved a dominant position in the market for employer-sponsored medical coverage. Some 128 million of the 146 million Americans insured through the workplace subscribed to some type of managed health plan.[30] Employer enthusiasm for managed care as the long-sought answer to the medical cost dilemma was peaking just as popular confidence in the political system's ability to assure quality care at affordable cost had reached a nadir. Investors bid up the prices of managed care stocks, and initial public offerings of physician practice management companies and other integrated organizational forms fared extremely well.[31] Commentators predicted that the unrestrained power of the medical marketplace would force the continuing vertical integration of hospital systems, medical practices, other outpatient services, and health care financing. Many argued that such integration was an optimizing response to the problem of "moral hazard" created by the emergence of third-party payment for medical services. Vertical integration, they contended, was the most efficient organizational means for keeping clinical spending within the limits set by what health plan purchasers were willing to pay for medical coverage—and for allocating available resources so as to maximize their clinical impact.[32]

Market skeptics in the early- and mid-1990s countered with dire warnings of profit-driven refusals to preauthorize lifesaving and other "necessary" care, retreat from hard-won principles of patient autonomy, and increasing socioeconomic stratification of health care provision. Without tight regulation of coverage standards and benefits administration, skeptics admonished, consumers' medical ignorance and market powerlessness would permit health plans to skimp recklessly on care. Absent tight regulation of benefits design and plan-provider contract terms, employers' and health plans' market power would enable them to foreclose therapeutic choices by selecting providers inclined toward cheaper alternatives and by pressuring these providers to refrain from recommending (or even disclosing) costly options. Predictions of ongoing vertical integration and eventual affiliation of most physicians with one or a few health plans[33] heightened market skeptics' concerns about foreclosure of choice between therapeutic alternatives (as clinicians adopted their plans' practice-norms) and socioeconomic stratification of health services. Market enthusiasts' open advocacy of multiple tiers of medical quality[34] was hardly reassuring in this regard. Market skeptics, and even some competition advocates, also worried that without the regulatory constraints on health plan risk selection that were part of the various "managed competition" proposals, segmentation of insurance markets by medical risk would grow worse, swelling the ranks of the uninsured.

The Market's Agility

To an extent unanticipated by market skeptics—and in ways that have dismayed many proponents of competition—the medical marketplace has proven responsive to these concerns. To be sure, market-driven accommodation to these concerns has been imperfect and has occurred in fits and starts. Information problems that have long beset medical markets, including knowledge asymmetries between patients and providers[35] and the lack of empirical data about the efficacy of most medical interventions, have been compounded by the agency problems that inhere in employer decision making about medical coverage for workers and their families. Yet one of the more remarkable health policy stories of the 1990s was the responsiveness of medical markets to concerns about quality of care, patient autonomy, bureaucratic power, and the trustworthiness of clinical caretakers. Repeatedly over the decade, these concerns translated into market pressures and thereby forced behavioral and organizational change while political and legal institutions failed to act. But political and legal mechanisms were hardly irrelevant to this process. To the contrary, political and legal advocacy by consumer and industry groups and public debate over proposed regulatory and legal action played large roles in shaping consumer understanding and thus begetting market pressures. The prospect of regulatory and legal action, in turn, influenced industry responses to these pressures. Actual regulatory or legal intervention, when it came, was often after the fact and beside the point.

Managed health plans' efforts to influence medical decisions illustrate both the market's responsiveness and the impact of political and legal conflict on market actors' understandings and expectations. Because doctors' decisions drive medical spending,[36] health-plan managers (and their critics) perceived early on that influencing these decisions was crucial to the management of medical costs. Since the demise of the "corporate practice of medicine" doctrine, which in general barred health plans from trying to manage clinical decision making, plans have been *legally* free to try to shape doctors' decisions by conditioning payment, plan participation, and referrals on doctors' adherence to plans' clinical-practice norms. Although efforts by health plans to influence medical judgment have received wide publicity, plans have done much less in this regard than the law allows. Rather than specifying, in their contracts with providers and subscribers, plan-wide cost–benefit trade-off rules to be followed as conditions for provider participation and subscriber coverage, they have typically promised to pay for "medically necessary" services. By so doing, they have deferred to professional understandings of appropriate care.[37] Health plans, to be sure, have tried to shape clinical decision making at the margins, by basing their medical necessity determinations on more frugal practice norms when a variety of professionally accepted approaches coexist and by otherwise encouraging physicians to choose more frugal options. But they have not tried to rewrite clinical practice norms to pursue greater parsimony than existing professional practice permits.

The market, not the law, explains this reticence. It is often asserted that the medical profession's market power prevents health plans from contracting with providers for standards of care that fall below professionally-accepted minima.[38] Whether offered up as an argument for robust antitrust policing of physicians[39] or as reason for *preserving* the profession's market power so as to protect patients from clinical skimping,[40] this claim finds support in abundant evidence of physician distaste for intrusion by health plans into matters of medical judgment.[41] Less often discussed is consumer resistance to the idea of coverage terms that push clinical standards below professionally-accepted minima.[42] What is *necessary*, in any society, is a matter of communal preference,[43] and American society continues to look to physicians to specify standards of needed care.[44] Coverage that economizes to the point of failure to meet professionally-accepted minima thus does not measure up to the communal sense of what is necessary. It is thus no wonder that such coverage has not appeared on the market. To survive in a competitive environment, health plans must accommodate to consumer demand, whether expressed directly by plan subscribers or mediated by employee benefits managers. Health plans have done so, and market skeptics' fears of contractually-driven erosion of clinical standards to below professionally-accepted minima have not thus far been realized.

Market pressures have also been a hindrance to less visible efforts to influence physicians. The mid-1990s controversy over so-called *gag* clauses—provisions in plan-physician contracts barring physician disclosure of costly therapeutic options—is illustrative. Reports of such provisions[45] attracted wide popular attention in 1995, and the absence of clear-cut legal proscriptions against gag rules led to calls for federal and state legislation to ban them. As a cost-control strategy, these contract terms had an obvious logic: patients typically learn about their clinical options from their physicians and usually follow their doctors' advice, so non-disclosure of expensive options should translate into cheaper patterns of practice. Yet follow-up research revealed that such contract terms were extremely rare,[46] suggesting (in view of the absence of legal barriers) that non-legal factors discouraged health plans from writing them. The most likely factors: expected physician resistance (whether arising from commitment to the ethic of informed consent, Hippocratic loyalty to patients, or financial self-interest) and the prospect of hostile consumer reaction (arising from the clash between patients' expectations of professional honesty and loyalty and the "don't ask, don't tell" deceit gag rules require). Health plan managers, in other words, probably anticipated physicians' and patients' negative *market* responses to this *lawful*, otherwise attractive cost-control strategy. Laws later enacted to ban explicit gag clauses[47] were beside the point, aside from rare cases. On the other hand, plan managers' anticipation of the possibility that popular anger over use of gag clauses could prompt legislative action may have contributed to their avoidance of such provisions.

The market's influence has also made itself felt in the area of provider choice. During the early 1990s, many competition theorists argued that the managed care paradigm would work most efficiently if each health plan selected only a small subset of the available providers and, conversely, each physician participated in only one or a few plans.[48] These theorists predicted that health–plan purchasers—employers and subscribers—would accept the resulting constraints on choice of physician in return for cost reductions won through deeply discounted fees and increased provider responsiveness to plans' policies and expectations. But this world of competing, vertically integrated plans with limited, only minimally overlapping panels of providers did not come to pass. Instead, consumers insisted on greater choice from among providers, eschewing tightly-managed HMOs with small physician panels in favor of plans with large, overlapping clinical panels, easier access to specialists, and out-of-network options. These more costly plans proliferated and grew in the mid- and late-1990s while plans that put tight restrictions on patient choice fared poorly.[49] Physicians today typically participate in several or more plans,[50] making them less responsive to any one plan's cost con-

trol pressures and incentives. Managed care companies offer employers and subscribers multiple coverage products with differing provider panels and levels of
access to specialized and out-of-network services.[51] Since, all else equal, employers would presumably prefer cheaper, more restrictive plans, consumer demand
appears to have pushed employers to select plans allowing more choice than market enthusiasts envisioned.

The managed care industry's retreat, since the mid-1990s, from prior authorization requirements for tests, treatments, and referrals was likewise driven by
market pressures, albeit with an extra push from the political process and the
mass media. The managed care horror stories that became routine television news
fodder in the mid- and late-1990s were typically about remote bureaucrats' refusals to preapprove payment for costly services that, in retrospect, might have
saved lives. These stories resonated with consumers' (and physicians') personal
experiences of frustration with long telephone waits, insensitive bureaucrats, and
administrative nay-saying. Although health plans enjoyed immunity from suit for
their preauthorization decisions (thanks to ERISA preemption of state tort liability for administration of employee benefits), they faced rising consumer resentment and the prospect of congressional intervention to permit suits for harm ensuing from prospective denial of benefits. They responded by backing away from
aggressive preauthorization review. By the late 1990s, several studies suggest,
health plans were approving the vast majority of physicians' prior authorization
requests.[52] When, in 1999, United Healthcare announced with much media fan-
fare that it would cease all preauthorization review of physicians' orders for tests,
treatments, and referrals, it cited its own, in-house 99% preapproval rate in arguing that prior authorization procedures cost more than the value of the savings
they yielded.[53] As Congress, in the years 2000 and 2001, worked toward compromise legislation that would give patients a limited right to sue health plans for refusal to preauthorize care, health plans rushed to abandon preauthorization requirements.[54] To what extent this abandonment of an axiom of managed care was
a market response to consumer demand versus a response to the prospect of Congressional intervention is impossible to say. What is clear, though, is that Americans' hostility toward remote bureaucratic nay-saying shaped both their preferences as health-plan subscribers and their attitudes as voters. As prospective
subscribers, they made their preferences felt in the medical marketplace, through
the mediating role of employers and contrary to market skeptics' beliefs that em-
ployee-benefits managers were insensitive to workers' health care preferences. As
voters, they commanded congressional attention through the prospect of an angry
electoral response to legislative inaction, despite the political clout of the managed care industry.[55]

By the end of the 1990s, even federal courts were showing signs of responsiveness to popular concerns about administrative nay-saying. ERISA's preemption of

state tort actions against health plans rests on a judicially-crafted distinction between provision of medical care, for which plans are subject to state malpractice
liability, and administration of benefits, for which plans are immune from suit.[56] In
several late 1990s opinions, the 3rd Circuit Court of Appeals narrowed the ad-
ministration-of-benefits category, recharacterizing health plans' preauthorization
determinations as quality-of-care decisions subject to state tort liability and treating HMO physicians' clinical frugality as a quality-of-care matter, beyond
ERISA's preemptive scope.[57] Although these decisions did not explicitly retreat
from prior holdings that remote, preauthorization review is immunized by
ERISA, they hardly reassured the industry, which may have retreated from such
review in part because of the prospect of a judicial shift. If indeed a doctrinal shift
was in the works,[58] the industry's quick move away from prior authorization once
again illustrates the ability of medical markets to stay a step ahead of the law.

   I do not mean to suggest that markets have been anything close to a panacea for
what ails managed care. To the contrary, the market pressures I have mentioned
worked slowly and incompletely to counter health-plan behaviors troubling to
subscribers or problematic on ethical grounds. Information and agency problems
in medical markets create myriad chances for opportunism, and the industry has
creatively exploited them. Managed care horror stories can be dismissed as anec-
dotal,[59] but their resonance among Americans suggests pervasive unease about the
industry's performance. Health plans' adaptations to consumer preferences do not
necessarily improve matters. A case in point is the industry's shift from aggressive preauthorization review to financial rewards for physicians who eschew
costly services.[60] Proponents of such incentives argue that by aligning the economic interests of physicians and health plans, they encourage cost control without engendering wasteful conflict between clinical caretakers and health care payers.[61] Beyond this, it is argued, physicians motivated by such incentives are better
situated than remote reviewers to eliminate the least cost-effective services, since
they know more about their patients' medical conditions.[62] These advantages,
however, come at the price of pitting physicians' and patients' interests against
each other at the moment of clinical decision.[63] To the extent that patients expect
their physicians' undivided loyalty and would experience mistrust, even betrayal,
were they to learn about this conflict of interest,[64] financial rewards for withholding care impose countervailing costs. The risk of opportunistic skimping by
physicians below levels of care promised by health plans adds to these costs.

   Information and agency problems that inhere in health care markets impede the
emergence of market pressure on health plans to take account of these costs.
Health plans often fail to inform subscribers about their financial arrangements
with physicians, and when such disclosure does occur, it tends to be in the *small
print* of legalistic plan descriptions. Physicians likewise tend not to tell their patients about how they are paid; indeed their fear of provoking patients' distrust is

itself a disincentive to financial disclosure. Employers are no more inclined to reveal physicians' incentives to do less, so long as these incentives restrain costs. It is thus not easy for patients to learn about their doctors' financial incentives. It is also difficult for patients to make sense of the limited information they are given. Not only do patients lack the knowledge needed to translate disclosures about their doctors' financial incentives into meaningful assessments of these incentives' impact on medical outcomes;[65] patients' feelings of trust in their caretakers as fonts of support, comfort and credible explanation are affected in impalpable, even unconscious ways by the discovery that their caretakers are being rewarded for what they withhold.

Perhaps, as press reports reveal that physicians are being rewarded for what they withhold, harsh consumer reaction will push health plans away from reliance on such incentives, just as popular backlash against nay-saying by remote bureaucrats pushed plans away from aggressive preauthorization review. But this prospect hinges on the future interplay of press accounts and public understanding, something notoriously unpredictable. Moreover, it is hardly clear that the troublesome features of financial rewards for withholding care outweigh their efficiency advantages as cost control tools. There may be no ready means for either market or government actors to pursue the cost-control sought by purchasers of medical coverage without troublesome consequences for subscribers. Health plans are caught between Americans' contradictory desires—for only the best when illness strikes and for affordability when they weigh medical coverage in the abstract against other needs and wants. By whatever means, plans must mediate between these unreconciled expectations, rendering consumer dissatisfaction inevitable. Perhaps, at best, plans can shift periodically among tools for budgetary reconciliation of the psychologically irreconcilable, sticking with each tool until mounting dissatisfaction forces a shift to a method not yet tainted by disillusion.[66]

If so, then medical markets do at least a tolerable job of managing their paying customers' competing expectations. In the 1990s, markets regularly responded more quickly and flexibly to consumers' evolving concerns than did regulatory and legal mechanisms. Stimulated by news accounts and their own (and friends' and family members') personal experience, consumers sought greater choice from among physicians, fewer administrative obstacles, standards of care set by reference to professional norms, and limits on health plans' power over what doctors tell their patients. Tightening labor markets in a prosperous economy empowered skilled workers to press these demands upon employers. An unprecedented economic boom made it easier for employers to respond favorably. By the end of the 1990s, as firms shifted toward health benefit packages with fewer restrictions and more choice, American medical spending had resumed its upward movement as a proportion of GDP, ending five years of stability.[67] Yet cost-control has thus far not reemerged as the high-profile national concern it was for the two decades that preceded those five years.

The Law's Rigidity

Americans' concerns about restrictions on choice of doctor, bureaucratic barriers to tests and treatments, downward pressure on standards of care, and efforts to limit what doctors tell patients also found voice in the political arena. Proposed *patients' bill of rights* legislation and *patient protection acts* were pushed by providers but became high-profile matters because they reflected popular passions. These passions, however, came up against the superior political staying power of the managed care industry and its corporate allies, principally large employers. Reform programs animated by popular feeling tend not to sustain themselves in the face of opposed, entrenched interest groups. Popular feeling is evanescent and often easy to assuage through rhetorical gesture and symbolic legislation, while entrenched interests sustain their focus on the crucial details of legislative drafting and regulatory implementation.[68] Such was the case with the congressional patients' bill of rights debate. By September 11th, 2001, when health care temporarily dropped off the national political agenda, both Houses had repeatedly passed comprehensive regulatory schemes governing managed care, only to see their attempts at compromise fail at the conference stage amidst intensive lobbying by managed health plans, providers, and other affected groups.

In retrospect, this failure was hardly a surprise. Managed care horror stories and growing public discontent pushed the legislative process forward. But through the latter half of the 1990s and the early years of this decade, the interested parties pursued sharply conflicting visions of managed care reform. Providers, especially physicians, sought, above all, to preserve their clinical and economic autonomy. To this end, they sought to rein in managed health plans' power to set clinical standards of care, professional fees, and other conditions of plan participation. Consumer advocacy groups forged a *strange bedfellows* alliance with the medical profession in support of the latter's authority to define medical need, but they took a more skeptical view of the profession's efforts to prop up medical fees. Advocates for the poor pursued the same strategy. They saw professional authority to define medical need as a buffer against market pressures to create multiple tiers of clinical quality for patients of different socioeconomic status. Accordingly, they joined forces with providers and consumer advocates to press for resolution of coverage disputes by independent medical panels. Providers, consumer groups, and advocates for the poor also forged a coalition to fight for the right to sue health plans for denials of coverage.[69] But the leading physician trade group, the American Medical Association, resisted consumer advocates' efforts to put tight limits on financial incentives to withhold care.[70] AMA leaders saw such incentive schemes as essential to *physicians'* ability to create their *own* managed care plans—and to thereby preserve a measure of professional autonomy while profiting from insurance risk-bearing.

This fractured constituency for reform could not match the managed care industry's superior financial resources,[71] political sophistication and staying power, ability to bridge internal fissures,[72] and political alliances with large employers concerned about medical costs. The industry used these strengths to press for "reform" that would secure its authority over coverage matters, its freedom to fashion financial incentives and other managerial tools for influencing medical decisions, and health plans' ability to employ their purchasing power to restrain provider fees. The most visible consequence of the industry's political strength was its success at forestalling amendment of ERISA to make it easier to sue for denial of benefits. But congressional inability to reach agreement on multitudinous details[73] prevented the law-making process from producing more than a long-running opportunity for legislators on all sides to proclaim their commitment to patients' rights in the rhetorical abstract. Even where Congress reached agreement-in-principle, as a House–Senate conference committee did in spring 2000 on patient access to review of coverage denials by independent physician panels,[74] intractable conflicts over small details froze legislative progress.

Similarly intractable conflict has stymied progress within the federal agencies responsible for oversight and regulation of managed care under existing law. Thorough review of these agencies' efforts is beyond my scope here, but major disappointments include the Health Care Financing Administration's failure to issue regulations specifying the role of cost and efficiency concerns in Medicare coverage determinations[75] and the Department of Labor's failure to make rules, under ERISA, specifying health plans' duties to disclose physician financial incentives and other cost management policies.[76]

The upshot has been the political system's remarkable failure to act on one of the highest-profile, most impassioned concerns of the electorate—the perceived power and abuses of managed health plans. Yet the threat of robust, consumer-oriented managed care reform held industry executives' attention through the late 1990s and beyond, and the patients' bill of rights debate reinforced popular concern about the industry's power over the practice of medicine. Health plan managers anticipated the possibility of consumer-oriented reform and incorporated it into their strategic planning.[77] Media coverage of the struggle over managed care reform shaped Americans' concerns as health care consumers, focusing their attention on competing plans' utilization management policies, dispute resolution procedures, and restrictions on patient choice.[78] In this circuitous manner, the protracted battle over managed care reform pushed the industry toward organizational arrangements that permit broader patient choice and impose fewer bureaucratic controls on physician decision making.

Lawyers interested in giving voice to Americans' anxieties about managed care did not lack for doctrinal opportunities in the 1990s to challenge the industry in the courts. But the glacial pace of the legal process, the sluggish responses of judges to rapid change in medical markets, and the fragmented nature of case-by-case judicial decision making on policy questions of national scope limited the impact of the courts. As noted earlier, through the early and mid-1990s federal judges construed ERISA's preemption provisions to safeguard health plans against state tort and contract liability for their administrators' decisions to deny coverage. By the late 1990s, when courts began to shrink the scope of ERISA preemption by recharacterizing such coverage decisions as *medical*, not merely administrative (and thus subject to state tort law),[79] health plans were already moving away from the utilization management practices that had occasioned this litigation. By delegating utilization management to treating physicians (and motivating them with financial rewards for withholding care), health plans could avert the risk of liability for negligent denial of benefits.

A new generation of lawsuits is challenging the industry's shift from utilization management by remote bureaucrats to financial rewards to physicians for furnishing fewer services. Attorneys General in several states are weighing actions against health insurers alleging that such incentive schemes violate state consumer protection and insurance laws.[80] In the federal courts, creative class action attorneys are painting such schemes as violations of both the Racketeer Influenced and Corrupt Organizations Act (RICO) and ERISA's fiduciary duty provisions.[81] To be sure, such suits face large legal obstacles. State attorneys general confront ERISA preemption problems, ambiguous statutory language, and large insurers' ability to put vast resources toward legal defense. Barriers to federal class action success include the difficulty of certifying, as a "class," health plan subscribers with different medical (and utilization) histories and the challenge of assaying, in monetary terms, the damages ensuing from rewards to doctors for withholding care.[82] Yet this litigation has already had a seismic impact upon the medical marketplace. The filing of the first federal class action, against Humana in 1999, triggered a 20% one-day drop in the company's stock,[83] and the specter of this litigation depressed managed care share values more generally.[84] The high profile the press has given to class action and other court filings against HMOs has alerted consumers to plans' use of financial incentives to encourage physicians to practice more cheaply. There are signs that these market pressures are pushing the industry to retreat from aggressive use of such incentives rather than mounting an all-out legal campaign to preserve them. An April 2000 settlement between Aetna-U.S. Healthcare and the Texas Attorney General committed Aetna to high-profile disclosure of physicians' financial incentives to withhold care, to limits on the magnitude of these incentives, and to physician compensation arrangements that reward disease prevention and patient satisfaction.[85] More significantly, Aetna announced that it would adopt the Texas agreement's terms nationwide on a voluntary basis. Aetna and other industry executives predicted that by acting along these lines to moderate their use of physician incentives (and to make other consumer-oriented changes), managed health plans could diminish the influence of the pending litigation on stock prices and consumer confidence.[86] Although putting physicians at financial risk for the cost of care remains common, the state-of-the-art in physician compensation is moving toward more nuanced approaches that reward quality of care, health promotion, and patient satisfaction, as well as clinical frugality.[87]

In short, public policy has been poorly responsive to consumers' concerns about the course of the managed care revolution. Interest group power and the sundry infirmities of legislative, administrative, and judicial decision making have combined to forestall system-wide, decisive government interventions. Yet government's inchoate engagement with Americans' anxieties about managed care has had large, indirect effects. By shaping the perceptions and market behavior of consumers and investors, it has pushed health plans away from cost-control methods that inspired subscriber resentment. These methods remained legal, or at least not clearly beyond the pale. Yet they became untenable, in part because political and legal developments recast the market more than they changed the law.

Market Responsiveness and Distributive Inequity

The truism that market allocation reflects preexisting distributive inequities found troubling expression in the health sector as the managed care industry responded to paying consumers' anxieties and expectations. Nominally, the industry's near-universal reliance on the "medical necessity" test for coverage, coupled with the courts' reluctance to vary standards of care in medical malpractice cases based on insurance status, preserved the precept of a unitary standard of care. But in practice, employees' differing skill levels, scarcity, and wealth led to the emergence of coverage options marked by wide variation in choice from among providers, access to elite doctors and hospitals, and bureaucratic restrictions. Upper-end professionals and managers won coverage with multiple fee-for-service features, including access to out-of-network providers on demand (albeit often at greater out-of-pocket cost). Near the other end of the spectrum, unskilled workers and others with little labor market power could count themselves lucky to be insured at all, in plans with daunting bureaucratic obstacles and tight limits on choice of provider. Many states moved Medicaid recipients into even more restrictive, often Medicaid-only plans.[88] Savings from the shift to Medicaid managed care financed some expansion of public insurance for the poor,[89] and employers' continued provision of lower-cost, tightly-managed coverage to unskilled and other low-wage workers probably slowed growth in the number of uninsured Americans.

The paucity of comparative data on the clinical outcomes of care provided within more and less tightly-managed health systems makes it impossible to say to what extent, if at all, the widening social stratification of health care provision has engendered variation in health outcomes. Close correlations between measures of health and socioeconomic status further confound efforts to compare clinical outcomes. Subscribers to tightly-managed health plans tend to be less well-off financially—and thus independently less likely to be in good health[90]— than subscribers to loosely-managed plans with multiple fee-for-service features. On the other hand, the growing social stratification of medical care is clearly widening the gap between well-off and poor patients' subjective experiences. Differing degrees of choice of treatment and provider, access to elite subspecialty care, conversation time with clinical caretakers, and confidence that caretakers put patients' needs ahead of plan officials' expectations are byproducts of medical market segmentation by economic status. Whether or not low-end plan subscribers experience lower quality of care in a technical sense, they probably experience lesser regard as persons.

Moreover the market's responsiveness to upper-end and middle-class consumers' dislikes about managed care may be contributing to the paradoxical rise in the number of uninsured Americans in an era of unprecedented prosperity. During the 1990s, estimates of the number of uninsured people soared from just over 30 million[91] to more than 45 million.[92] Cutbacks in welfare benefits and corresponding reductions in Medicaid enrollment[93] have been identified as one cause, but market-driven relaxation of constraints on clinical spending has probably played a large role, by permitting standards of care—and ensuing costs—to creep upward. Well-off consumers' upward pressure on standards of care has raised clinical standards and costs for all Americans, even the poorest, since ethical, legal, and cultural norms limit health care providers' conscious willingness to deliver different levels of care to patients from different socioeconomic strata.[94] This increase in costs at the low end of the medical coverage market has driven marginal group and individual insurance purchasers out of the market, adding to the ranks of the uninsured. In addition, insurers' movement toward myriad, differently-designed benefits packages; custom-tailored provider networks; and varying mechanisms for accessing tests and referrals[95] has increased the segmentation of insurance markets by medical risk as well as socioeconomic class. This, in turn, has reduced the affordability of coverage to individuals and groups with the greatest clinical needs. Through artful design of benefits and administrative features, health plans can avert regulatory proscriptions against risk selection by appealing to young, fit consumers[96] and discouraging subscribers with mental illness, HIV infection, and other chronic disorders.[97]

The buying power of well-off and middle class consumers, in short, has made health care provision a more stratified endeavor and pushed large numbers of Americans out of the market for medical coverage. Managed health plans' exquisite sensitivity to paying consumers' concerns comes with moral strings attached. Medical care today is probably more reflective of the distribution of wealth in America than it was, say, 15 years ago. Popular unwillingness to support generous public subsidies for care for the least well-off portends a future of widening clinical inequality and outright exclusion of more and more people from levels of care that insured Americans demand for themselves.

Conclusion: lessons from the medical marketplace

Health care markets, it would appear, adjust to widespread popular dissatisfaction more quickly than does the law, whether fashioned by courts, legislatures, or administrative regulators. This, at least, was the case through the 1990s and the early years of the current decade. Market-mediated adjustment requires that a considerable proportion of consumers be able to exercise choice between institutional mechanisms. In the 1990s, increasingly tight labor markets made this possible. Yet the judicial, legislative, and regulatory processes played crucial roles as agents of change. They did so not by refashioning the rules of the game but by directing the attention of key market actors—from consumers to investors—toward features of managed care that participants in these legal processes deemed troublesome. Litigation, political debate, and regulatory maneuvering influenced the perceptions of subscribers, physicians, health plan managers, and investors by supplying both information and message-bearing narratives. These changed perceptions, in turn, transformed these actors' market behavior—e.g. inducing consumers to eschew health plans that give bureaucrats broad veto power over clinical decisions. For health plans and providers, judicial, legislative, and regulatory proceedings created new business risks and potential opportunities. Risk averse institutional leaders tended to anticipate possible legal change and to adjust their organizational practices and structures accordingly. Synergies between different market actors' perceptions (and behavior) occasionally emerged, as when health plan executives, worried about Wall Street's skittish response to legal attacks on aggressive utilization management, moved to shift utilization decisions from plan bureaucrats to primary care physicians. Legal change, when it came, often seemed after-the-fact.

Academic commentary, in health policy and other spheres, that focuses on legal and regulatory *intervention* as a means of adjusting for market failures overlooks the large role of legal and regulatory *processes* in shaping market actors' perceptions and decisions. The legal end results of these processes are often beside the point. This has important implications for strategic thinking—by both policymakers and private actors—about use of regulatory and legal means. It suggests that policymakers and private actors who fashion regulatory or legal strategies should think at least as much about these strategies' interim impact upon interested parties' perceptions and (thus) market behavior as about legal outcomes. A case in point may be the controversy over health plans' shifting of insurance risk to treating physicians. Those who find the resulting incentives troubling on ethical or other grounds might do well to attack them through legal means that draw public attention to rewards to doctors for denying care, in the hope that consumer resistance and consequent investor skittishness will push health plans to limit such risk-shifting before courts or regulators act.

Whether, absent the tightening labor markets of the 1990s, the medical marketplace would have proven as responsive to consumers' concerns as it has is unanswerable. But the privatization of health care reform makes this an important question. The American health system's sensitivity to consumers' concerns now rests largely on the ability of labor markets to translate plan and provider behavior. A prolonged recession (or worse) could erode the power of labor markets to do this. A softer economy (and rising unemployment) might make the medical marketplace less sensitive to poor and middle-class consumers' anxieties while leaving its responsiveness to wealthy subscribers largely untouched. This would widen the socioeconomic stratification of health care provision, especially if, as appeared to be happening by 2001,[98] medical costs resume their historic rapid rise.

The failure of health care markets to diminish distributive inequity is hardly surprising, since market allocation inevitably reflects such inequity. But the widening stratification of health care provision by class in the 1990s, as power over clinical resources moved from medical professionals to the market, highlights something that has received insufficient attention from health policy commentators—the role of professional norms in attenuating economic inequality's impact at the bedside. To be sure, professional judgments have been shown to incorporate covert race,[99] gender,[100] and class[101] discrimination, and a paean to blind deference to physician judgment as a redistributive tool would be naive. But it is not surprising that in recent years advocates of redistributive health care policy have urged broad deference to treating physicians' judgments about resource use,[102] while commentators more accepting of the current distribution of wealth as a basis for allocating medical services have been leading critics of professional authority.[103]

If our market-driven health care system is to offer a decent minimum of care, as a matter of right rather than charity, to Americans unable to express their preferences through their buying power, political intervention is essential. It is a national embarrassment that at a time of unprecedented prosperity, we are nowhere near to being able to marshal popular support for public subsidies that would give the worst-off Americans the needed buying power. A politics that aspires to deepen our empathy for the other to the point of national willingness to rechannel the resources necessary to do this may be the highest moral imperative of health care policy.

Acknowledgments

The author thanks participants in faculty workshops at Georgetown University Law Center and Vanderbilt University School of Law for their comments and suggestions, as well as Elizabeth Jungman and Erica Pape for their research assistance. Preparation of this chapter was supported in part by a Robert Wood Johnson Foundation Investigator Award in Health Policy Research.

Notes

1. To be sure, there have been small steps toward expanded access—most notably the Children's Health Insurance Program (CHIP), 42 U.S.C. § 1397aa (2000), and the Mental Health Parity Act 42 U.S.C. §§ 201 et seq. (2000)—but multiple loopholes and less-than-robust implementation have severely limited these programs' effectiveness.
2. See Henry Butler & Jonathan Macey, Health Care Reform: Perspectives From the Economic Theory of Regulation and the Economic Theory of Statutory Interpretation, 79 *Cornell L. Rev.* 1434 (1994); Clark C. Havighurst, The Changing Locus of Decision Making in the Health Care Sector, 11 *J. Health Polit. Policy Law*, No. 4, 697, 709 (1987) ("Even when the government tried to impose specific checks on the industry's spending impulses, it found that it was politically impossible to make much difference.") Cf. Stuart H. Altman & Marc A. Rodwin, Halfway Competitive Markets and Ineffective Regulation: The American Health Care System, 13 *J. Health Polit. Policy, Law*, No. 2, 323 (1988) (arguing that political paralysis has prevented effective regulation).
3. See Theda Skocpol, The Rise and Resounding Demise of the Clinton Health Plan, in *The Problem that Won't Go Away: Reforming U.S. Health Care Financing,* Chap. 3 (Henry J. Aaron ed., 1996), and Haynes Johnson and David S. Broder, *The System: The American Way Of Politics At The Breaking Point* (1996) for rich accounts of how alternative leadership strategies and styles might have made a large difference in the health care reform battles of the early- and mid-1990s.
4. See Carey Goldberg, The 2000 Campaign: For Many States, Health Care Bills Are Top Priority, *The New York Times*, January 23, 2000, at 1,1.
5. See Richard Briffault & Sherry Glied, The Implications for Federalism for Health Care Reform (Chapter 3 of this book); Peter D. Jacobson and Scott D. Pomfret, Form, Function, and Managed Care Torts: Achieving Fairness and Equity in ERISA Jurisprudence, 35 *Houston L. Rev.* 985 (1998).
6. See *Metropolitan Life Ins. Co. v. Massachusetts*, 417 U.S. 724, 739.
7. ERISA's preemption of state laws that "relate to" employee benefit plans, Employee Retirement Income Security Program (ERISA), 29 U.S.C. § 1144(a) (2000), combined with (a) ERISA's so-called "insurance savings clause," 29 U.S.C. § 1144(b)(2)(A), which withholds this preemption from state laws that specifically target insurers, and (b) ERISA's so-called "deemer clause," 29 U.S.C. § 1144(b)(2)(B), which states that no employee–benefit plan shall be deemed an insurer for preemption purposes, has been construed to preserve only state law that meets two conditions: (*1*) the law must govern insurance in particular rather than being law of general applicability that only incidently covers insurance, *Pilot Life Ins. Co. v. Dedeaux*, 481 U.S. 41 (1987), and (*2*) the objects of regulation must be entities that contract with employers to bear insurance risk (as opposed to employee

benefit plans that retain their own risk). Application of these conditions to diverse economic arrangements has engendered much litigation.

8. In 1998, 234 million Americans subscribed to private managed care plans. See Ken McDonnell & Paul Fronstin, Employee Benefit Research Inst., EBRI Health Benefits Databook, 53 (1999). Approximately 38.8 million people were enrolled in Medicare and, of these, 5.6 million were enrollees in Medicare managed care. See HCFA, 1998 Data Compendium 83 (1998). Even if all Medicare beneficiaries were in managed care, they would constitute only 16% of subscribers to private health plans.

9. See James F. Blumstein, The Fraud and Abuse Statute in an Evolving Health Care Marketplace: Life in the Health Care Speakeasy, 22 *Am. J. Law Med.* 205 (1996).

10. 42 USC § 300e-9(A). To trigger this requirement, a federally-qualified HMO must serve an area where at least 25 of the firm's employees live. State and local government entities that provide health insurance coverage to their workers are subject to the same requirement. 42 USC § 300e-9(B).

11. 42 USC § 300e(c).

12. 42 USC § 300e(b).

13. See, e.g., Recent developments suggest that this immunity is narrowing, and may even disappear, in response to signals from the U.S. Supreme Court to lower courts to construe ERISA prreemption more narrowly. See *Pappas V. Asbel*, 768 A2d 1089. (Pa.Sup.Ct. 2001); Peter J. Hammer, Pegram v. Herdrich: On Peritonitis Pre-emption and the Elusive Goal of Managed Care Accountability, 26 *J. Health Polit. Policy Law* 767 (2001); M. Gregg Bloche & Peter D. Jacobson, The Supreme Court and Bedside Rationing, 284 J. Am Med. Ass'n. 2776 (2001). *Corcoran v. United Healthcare*, 965 F.2d 1321 (5th Cir. 1992) cert. denied, 506 U.S. 1033 (1992).

14. See Corcoran, 965 F.2d at 1335–36 (construing ERISA to permit only recovery of the value of benefits improperly denied by a plan).

15. See Paul C. Weiler, et al., A Measure Of Malpractice: Medical Injury, Malpractice Litigation, And Patient Compensation (1993); Patricia M. Danzon, Medical Malpractice: Theory, Evidence, And Public Policy, (1985). The studies reviewed in these sources also document that large proportions of malpractice claims made are "false positives" (based on independent review of medical records by panels of researchers).

16. See John E. Wennberg, Understanding Geographical Variations in Health Care Delivery, 340 *New Eng. J. Med.* 52–53 (1999); Dartmouth Atlas Of Health Care In The United States (1998). See also M. Gregg Bloche, *The Invention of Health Law*, Cal. L. Rev. (forthcoming) (discussing legal and economic implications of clinical practice variation and uncertainty) (hereinafter Invention of Health Law).

17. See generally, Dominick C. DiCicco, Jr., HMO Liability for Medical Negligence of Member Physicians, 43 *Vill. L. Rev.* 499, 501–03 (1998); Jeffery F. Chase-Lubitz, Note, The Corporate Practice of Medicine Doctrine: An Anachronism in the Modern Health Care Industry, 40 *Vand. L. Rev.* 445 (1987).

18. See M. Gregg Bloche, Clinical Loyalties and the Social Purposes of Medicine, 281 *JAMA* 268–74 (1999). (hereinafter Clinical Loyalties).

19. See Government Accounting Office, Managed Care: Explicit Gag Clauses Not Found in HMO Contracts, But Physician Concerns Remain, Letter Report, GAO/HEHS-970175 (August 29, 1997).

20. If plan physicians speak to patients in positive terms about more costly options, patients will be more inclined to demand them, leaving physicians with a Hobson's choice between more profligate practice styles and less-satisfied patients. Physician self-censorship avoids this problem.

21. 120 S.Ct. 2143 (2000).

22. *Id.* at 2153, n.8.

23. See *Shea v. Esensten*, 107 F.3d 625, 629 (8th Cir.), cert. denied, 522 U.S. 914 (1997).

24. *Texas v. Aetna U.S. Healthcare*, No. CV000584, settlement (Tex. Dist. Ct., Travis County, Apr. 11, 2000), Compliance Agreement, doc. #31–000414–104.

25. See, e.g., Ariz. Rev. Stat. § 20–2323(A)(6) (2000); Minn. Stat. § 256B.77, Subd. 9(b) (2000); Mo. Rev. Stat. § 354.443 (2000); N.D. Cent. Code § 26.1-36-03.1(k) (2000). Cf. Ind. Code § 27-13-15-1(a) (noting that an HMO "may not prohibit [a] participating provider from disclosing" financial incentives).

26. Thus far, no other federal circuit has followed the 8th Circuit's lead in construing ERISA to require disclosure. See *Weiss v. CIGNA Healthcare*, 972 F. Supp. 748 (S.D.N.Y. 1997) and *Ehlmann v. Kaiser Fund Health Plan*, 198 F.3d 522 (5th Cir. 2000) (declining to impose disclosure duty under ERISA). See also William Sage, Regulating Through Information: Disclosure Laws and American Health Care, 99 *Colum. L. Rev.* 1702, 1750 (1999) (discussing challenges to financial incentives in managed care brought under the Federal Racketeer Influenced and Corrupt Organizations statute (RICO) and under state law).

27. See Health Policy Tracking Svc., Fact Sheet: Bans On Financial Incentives (July 1999). The following states have banned financial incentives for physicians to provide a lesser standard of care: AK, CA, NV, IA, ID, ND, SD, MN, NM, TX, LA, FL, GA, KS, NE, IL, OH, WV, MD, DE, PA, NJ, RI, VT, MO. For a sample statute, see Tex. Ins. Code Ann. § 20A.14(k) (West 2000); Tex. Ins. Code. Ann. Art. 3-70-3c, sec. 7(d) (West 2000).

28. See SSA, Title XVII, s. 876 (g) and (h).

29. Federal law does require the Secretary of Health and Human Services to develop standards limiting physician financial risk and to compel health plans to provide stop–loss protection to keep physician risk within these limits. See SSA, Title XVIII, s. 1876 (42 U.S.C. 1395mm) (1)(8)(A)(ii).

30. See *Ebri Issue Brief*, no. 170, February 1996.

31. Physician Practice Management: Investors Eye Growth, *Am. Health Line*, November 15, 1994.

32. In so arguing, they could draw upon several decades of economics commentary that presented vertical integration and the employment relationship as superior to both spot contracting and longer term, administered contracting between independent firms (and/or individuals) under circumstances characterized by: (*1*) uncertainty about future contingencies, (*2*) recurring transactions, and (*3*) specialized human and physical assets. See, e.g., Benjamin Klein, Robert G. Crawford, and Armen A. Alchian, Vertical Integration, Appropriable Rents, and the Competitive Contracting Process, 21 *J. L. & Econ.* 297 (1978); Oliver E. Williamson, Markets And Hierarchies: Analysis And Antitrust Implications (1975); Ronald H. Coase, The Nature of the Firm, 4 *Economica* 386 (1937). Health care provision, especially by combinations of providers who pursue distinctive cost–benefit trade-off and other policies, tends to have these characteristics.

33. See Lisa Bransten, Aetna Purchase Highlights a Growing Trend: Acquisition of US Healthcare May Create National Managed Care Group, *Financial Times*, April 3, 1996.

34. See generally, E. Haavi Morreim, Redefining Quality by Reassigning Responsibility, 20 *Am. J. L. & Med.* 79 (1994). See also Blumstein, Health Reform and Competing Visions on Medical Care: Anti-Trust and State Provider Cooperation Legislation, 79 *Cornell L. Rev.* 1459, 1468 (1994) [hereinafter Competing Visions].

35. See Kenneth Arrow, Uncertainty and the Welfare Economics of Medical Care, 53 *Am. Econ. Rev.* 941 (1963).

36. See Victor Fuchs, *Who Shall Live? Health, Economics, And Social Choice* 56–58 (1974).

37. See Clark C. Havighurst, *Health Care Choices: Private Contracts As Instruments Of Health Reform*, 190–200 (1994).

38. See Competing Visions, supra note 34, at 1464–66.

39. See id. at 1486.

40. See John Fairhall, Clash of the Titans: Doctors, HMOs, Insurers on Health Care, *Balt. Sun*, July 3, 1994, at 1E.

41. See Marsha Gold, The Changing US Health Care System: Challengers for Responsible Public Policy, Vol. 77, No. 1 *Milbank Q.* 1, 18 (1999).

42. See Richard A. Epstein, *Mortal Peril: Our Inalienable Right To Health Care*, 45–52 (1997).

43. *See* Michael Walzer, Spheres Of Justice: A Defense Of Pluralism And Equality, 64–68 (1983).

44. That Americans still generally defer to physician judgment about what constitutes medical need is consistent with politicians' frequent focus group-tested promises to keep medical decisions in the hands of doctors, not "bureaucrats," and with poll results indicating that Americans have much more confidence in their physicians than in health plan managers. The Gallup Organization, "Gallup Poll: Honesty and Ethics in Professions" (available at http://www.gallup.com/poll/indicators/indhnsty ethics.asp). See also David Mechanic & Mark Schlesinger, The Impact of Managed Care on Patients' Trust in Medical Care and Their Physicians, 275 *JAMA* 1693 (1996).

45. See Mark A. Rodwin, Conflicts in Managed Care, 332 *New Eng. J. Med.* 604, 605 (1995); Jerome P. Kassirer, Managed Care and the Morality of the Marketplace, Editorial, 333 *New Eng. J. Med.* 50, 50 (1995); Robert Pear, Doctors Say H.M.O.s Limit What They Can Tell Patients, *The New York Times*, December 21, 1995, at A1.

46. See Government Accounting Office, *Managed Care: Explicit Gag Clauses Not Found in HMO Contracts, But Physician Concerns Remain*, Letter Report, GAO/HEHS-970175 (Aug. 29, 1997).

47. See John F. Harris, President Backs Measure to Ban 'Gag Rules' Affecting Health Plan Physicians. *The Washington Post*, February 21, 1999, at A09; Unmuzzling H.M.O. Physicians; State and Federal Bills Aim at Treatment Option 'Gag Rules'. *Los Angeles Times*, July 2, 1996, at B6.

48. See Alain C. Enthoven, A Consumer-Choice Health Plan for the 1990s: Universal Health Insurance in A System Designed to Promote Quality and Economy. 320 *New Eng. J. Med.* 94, 95 (1989).

49. James Robinson, *The Corporate Practice of Medicine: Competition and Innovation in Health Care* 79–80 (1999).

50. See J. M. Mitchell et al., Perceived Financial Incentives, HMO Market Penetration and Physicians' Practice Styles and Satisfaction, 34 *Health Serv. Res.* 307, 308 (1999); F. Hellinger, The Impact of Financial Incentives on Physician Behavior in Managed Care Plans: A Review of the Evidence, 53 *Med. Care Res. Rev.* 294 (1996).

51. See Robinson, supra note 49, at 47.

52. See, e.g., T. M. Wickizer and D. Lessler, Effects of Utilization Management on Patterns of Hospital Care Among Privately Insured Adult Patients, 36 *Med. Care* 1545 (1998) (reporting that fewer than 1% of patients in a fee-for-service plan with prospective utilization management were denied care on hospital admission or required to obtain outpatient instead of inpatient care, but that concurrent review did constrain inpatient lengths-of-stay); T. M. Wickizer, D. Lessler, and K. M. Travis,

Controlling Inpatient Psychiatric Utilization Through Managed Care, 153 *Am. J. Psychiatry* 339 (1996) (reporting that prospective utilization management approved psychiatric hospitalization in almost 99% of cases but that only a third of the inpatient days requested were authorized); D. S. Lessler and T. M. Wickizer, The Impact of Utilization Management on Readmissions Among Patients with Cardiovascular Disease, 34 *Health Serv. Res.* 1315 (2000) (reporting that cardiovascular disease patients were rarely denied approval for hospitalization but that prospective utilization management both decreased inpatient lengths-of-stay and increased the likelihood of subsequent rehospitalization).

53. See Milt Freudenheim, Big H.M.O. to Give Decision on Care Back to Doctors, *The New York Times*, Nov. 9, 1999, at A1; United Healthcare Puts Docs in Drivers Seat, *Medical Industry Today*, December 2, 1999 (available at www.medicaldata.com).

54. See Steven Wilmsen, HMOs Seen Likely to Follow UnitedHealth's Lead, *Boston Globe*, November 10, 1999, at C5; Carol Gentry, UnitedHealth Move on Reviews is Seen as Industry Watershed, *Wall Steet Journal*, November 10, 1999, at B6; M. Gregg Bloche, Look Out! That's the Wrong Way to Patients' Rights, *Washington Post*, July 22, 2001, at B2. By the summer of 2001, just before the events of September 11th swept health care legislation off the political agenda, congressional debate over competing proposals for a limited right to sue health plans was largely beside the point. Id.

55. Vigorous lobbying efforts by organized medicine and the plaintiffs' personal injury bar has been a countervailing force.

56. See *Corcoran v. United Healthcare*, 965 F.2d 1321,1331–34 (5th Cir. 1992).

57. See *In re U.S. Healthcare, Inc*, 193 F.3d 151, 162–63 (3rd Cir. 1999) (holding that state law claims of medical negligence targeting an HMO's policy of discharging newborns within 24 hours of birth was not preempted by ERISA); *Dukes v. U.S. Healthcare, Inc.*, 57 F.3d 350, 356 (3rd Cir. 1995) (holding that medical malpractice claims were not claims for benefits and thus were not preempted by ERISA). See also, *Pacificare of Okla., Inc. v. Burrage*, 59 F.3d 151, 155 (10th Cir. 1995); Rice v. Panchal, 65 F. 3d 637, 645 (7th Cir. 1995).

58. By the summer of 2001, a large doctrinal shift seemed likely as courts began to back away from wholesale immunity for remote pre-authorization review. *See supra* note 13.

59. See David Hyman, Managed Care at the Millennium: Scenes from a Maul, 24 J. *Health Polit. Policy Law* 1061 (1999).

60. See Thomas Rice, Physician Payment Policies: Impacts and Implications, 18 *Ann. Rev. Pub. Health* 549, 551–54 (1997).

61. Walter A. Zelman and Robert A. Berenson, The Managed Care Blues and How to Cure Them 80–81 (1998).

62. In information economics terms, *information-impactedness*—the difficulty of extracting information from a particular context and conveying it to remote observers, Oliver E. Williamson, The Economic Institutions of Capitalism 51 (1985),—is an inherent feature of medical care and thus an obstacle to administrative review of clinical decisions.

63. Proponents of rewarding physicians financially for clinical frugality sometimes argue that, viewed from the patient's perspective when she subscribes to a health plan (prior to the onset of her illness), there is little or no such opposition of interests, since such incentives encourage physicians to practice in accordance with the cost constraints to which the patient subscribed.

64. See Clinical Loyalties, supra note 18, at 272.

65. Patients are hardly alone in this regard: the relationship between physicians' incentives and clinical outcomes is ill—understood by health services researchers. See Thomas Rice, supra note 60.

66. M. Gregg Bloche and Peter D. Jacobson, The Supreme Court and Bedside Rationing, 284 *J. Am. Med. Ass'n* 2776, 2779 (2000). Cf. Guido Calabresi and Philip Bobbit, *Tragic Choices*, (1978) (invoking idea of "tragic cycling" to convey mounting dissatisfaction with and abandonment of successive methods for making allocative choices that demand the sacrifice of values we hold to be sacred and beyond compromised, such as preservation of life).

67. Sheila Smith, Mark Freeland, Stephen Heffler, David McKusick and the Health Expenditures Projection Team, The Next Ten Years of Health Spending: What does the Future Hold? *Health Aff.*, 128 (September/October, 1998); Reed Abelson, Hard decisions for Employers as Costs Soar in Health Care, *The New York Times*, April 18, 2002, at C1. To what extent the shift to less restrictive plans with more provider options is responsible for this renewed rise is not empirically known. Other, confounding potential factors include the insurance underwriting cycle and exhaustion of opportunities for one-time-only cost reductions accruing from shifts to managed care as managed health plans completed their penetration of the market for medical coverage.

68. See Daniel A. Farber and Philip P. Frickey, *Public Choice in Practice and Theory: Law and Public Choice* (1991); Mancur Olson, *The Logic of Collective Action: Public Goods and the Theory of Groups* (1965); George Stigler, A Theory of Economic Regulation, 2 Bell *J. Econ. & Mgmt. Sci.* 335 (1974). For a review of public choice literature intended for lawyers see Daniel A. Farber and Philip P. Frickey, Law and Public Choice—A Critical Introduction, 3–5 (1991); Symposium—Public Choice Theory and the Law, 74 *Va. L. Rev.* 167 (1987).

69. They were joined by the most unlikely of provider allies, the plaintiffs' medical malpractice bar, which became the principal public target for managed care and other trade groups opposed to a new right to sue health plans.

70. See Brief of Amicus Curiae American Medical Association in Support of Petitioner Lori Pegram, *Pegram v. Herdrich*, 1999 WL 0154917, *25–29 (Nov. 19, 1999). See also Statement of the American Medical Association, H-285.951 (available at www.ama-assn.org) (asserting that "[p]hysicians should have the right to enter into whatever contractual arrangements with health care systems they deem desirable and necessary").

71. Managed care providers have joined with interested business groups to form the Health Benefits Coalition (for more details see the HBC website available at www.hbc.com). From 1993 through the spring of 2000, HBC members contributed over $27 million to Congress through PACs, soft money, and contributions to individual candidates. This figure includes over $9 million in contributions during the 1998 election cycle and over $6 million in the 2000 election cycle (as of 6/1/00). In 1998 the HBC spent $144, 000 on lobbying. Two other associations representing managed care interests had larger lobbying budgets in 1998; the Health Insurance Association of America spent almost $4.5 million on lobbying and the American Association of Health Plans spent over $2 million. See Center for Responsive Politics (available at www. opensecrets.org)(visited June 15, 2000).

72. See Johnson & Broder, supra note 3, at 199–200. (describing the split between the HIAA and five of its largest insurers—Prudential, Cigna, Travelers, Metropolitan Life, and Aetna).

73. Alissa J. Rubin, Fine Lines Drawn in Health Care Debate, *Los Angles Times*, July 15,

1999, at A12; Robert Pear, 2 Patients' Rights Bills Take Divergent Roads, *The New York Times*, July 4, 1998, at A9; Battle Lines on Patients' Rights, *The New York Times*, July 16, 1998, at A18.

74. See Robert Pear, House and Senate Agree on Patient Rights Plan, *The New York Times*, April 14, 2000, at A8. But see Robert Pear, Negotiators Stall on Patients' Rights Bill, *The New York Times*, May 26, 2000, at A17.

75. HCFA (recently renamed the Center for Medicare and Medicaid Services) considered incorporating cost-related concerns into Medicare coverage decisions in 1989, 54 FR 4302, but then withdrew this proposed rule. 64 FR 22619.

76. On the other hand, HCFA has developed and promulgated regulations governing physician risk–bearing within Medicare and Medicaid managed health plans. See 61 FR 69034; HCFA Releases Final Rule Governing Medicare, Medicaid Incentive Plans, 6 *BNA Health L. Rep.* 25 (January 27, 1997). In general, if a managed care organization puts 25% of a physicians potential payments at risk it must disclose this, conduct a member satisfaction survey, and provide stop–loss protection. See HCFA, Overview of the Physician Incentive Plan Regulation (available at www.hcfa.gov/medicare/physincp/pip-gen.htm). See also HCFA Reminds Medicare Contracting HMOs to File Physician Incentive Plans by March, 7 *BNA Health L. Rep.* (December 24, 1998).

77. See Utilization Review Decrease Just a Step Along the Path to a Mature Managed Care Industry? 18 *Health Care Strategic Mgmt.* 4 (January 1, 2000).

78. See Does Your Doctor Put Money Before Medicine?, *Consumer Reports on Health* (October 1999); Examining Your Health Plan, *Consumer Reports on Health*, (November 1997); How Good is Your Health Plan? *Consumer Reports* (August 1996); Rita Rubin, Rating the H.M.O.s: A National Survey, *U.S. News & World Reports* (September 2, 1996); Center for the Study of Services, *Consumers Guide To Health Plans* (1995); How to Avoid Mismanaged Managed Care, *Consumer Reports on Health* (April 1994).

79. See supra note 13 and text accompanying notes 57–58.

80. Following Aetna's settlement of the Texas Attorney General's suit alleging that the HMO illegally compensated physicians who limited medical care to patients, see *Texas v. Aetna US Healthcare, Inc.*, Tex. Dist. Ct., No. 98–13972, settlement April 11, 2000, attorneys general in California, New York, and North Carolina began "scrutinizing" HMO financial incentives. See Aetna Hopes Texas Deal Will Spread, as Attorneys Analyze Settlement Details, 9 *BNA Health L. Rep.* 18 (May 4, 2000).

81. E.g. *Patricia Freyre v. Humana, Inc.*, Complaint (United States Dist. Ct. for the Southern Dist. FL, No.00–01429, Miami, FL).

82. Because ERISA has been construed to disallow the awarding of consequential damages, e.g. pain and suffering, plaintiffs can recover under ERISA only for the costs of services wrongfully withheld. For example, if a $250 CT scan, wrongfully denied, would have led to early diagnosis and cure of a malignant tumor that caused a patient's death, the patient's estate could recover the $250 but not compensation for wrongful death. Determining the aggregate costs of services *wrongfully* withheld *as a result of* financial rewards to physicians for withholding care presents intractible problems. Deciding what has been wrongfully withheld requires reference to standards of appropriate treatment in individual cases. Such standard-setting is an uncertain, conflict-laden endeavor in individual cases and an intractibly complex task for large clinical populations. Bloche, Invention of Health Law, supra note 16. Assessing which services deemed wrongfully withheld would have been provided but for financial incentives to withhold care is equally uncertain and subjective.

83. See Milt Freudenheim, Humana Sued in Federal Court over Incentives for Doctors, *The New York Times*, October 5, 1999, at C7; Herman Middleton Files Nationwide Class Action Against Humana, *Business Wire Inc.*, May 1, 2000; Plan Liability: Class Actions Against HMOs Climb as 'REPAIR Team' Physicians File More Suits, 8 *BNA Health L. Rep.* 1887, December 2, 1999.

84. See Health Insurer Shares Fall on Threat of Suits, *The New York Times*, October 1, 1999, at C5; H.M.O. Stocks Take Hard Falls Amid the Threat of Class Actions, *Los Angeles Times*, October 1, 1999, at C1.

85. See *Texas v. Aetna Healthcare*, No. CV000584, Settlement (Tex. Dist. Ct. Travis County, April 11, 2000) (Text of settlement available at http://www.oag.state.tx.us. notice/avc=_fin.1.pdf).

86. Industry officials voiced hopes that other state attorneys general would settle their cases along similar lines, that investors would see the pending class action suits as less of a threat to current and future industry practice, and that consumers would regain confidence in managed care. See Laura Benko, Aetna Settles with Texas; Agreement Could Become The Standard, Observers Say; Class-Action Suits Still Pending, *Modern Healthcare*, April 17, 2000, at 30; Managed Care: Report Cites Shift by Health Plans Away from Aggressive Cost Containment, *BNA Health Care Daily Report*, August 29, 2000 (describing a report by the Center for Studying Health System Change); Rebecca Lentz, Building Blocks: Aetna's Settlement in Texas is a Step in Improving Relations, *Modern Physician*, May 1, 2000, at 3.

87. See Different Approaches, *Modern Physician*, March 1, 2000, at 60.

88. See Bruce Landon & Arnold Epstein, Quality Management Practices in Medicaid Managed Care: A National Survey of Medicaid and Commercial Health Plans Participating in the Medicaid Program, 282 *JAMA*. 1769 (1999). See also MS Sparer, Medicaid Managed Care and the Health Reform Debate: Lessons from New York and California, 21 *J. Health Polit. Policy Law* 433, 455–56 (1996).

89. James Blumstein, Health Care Reform Through Medicaid Managed Care: Tennessee (TennCare) as a Case Study and a Paradigm, 53 *Vand. L. Rev.* 125, 243–245 (January 2000).

90. See P.M. Lantz et al., Socioeconomic Factors, Health Behaviors, and Mortality: Results From a Nationally Representative Prospective Study of U.S. Adults, 279 *J. Am. Med. Ass'n.* 1703 (1998); P.D. Sorlie, et al., U.S. Mortality by Economic, Demographic, and Social Characteristics: The National Longitudinal Mortality Study. 85 *Am. J. Pub. Health* 949 (1995); H. Hemingway et al., The Impact of Socioeconomic Status on Health Functioning as Assessed by the SF-36 Questionnaire: the Whitehall III Study, 87 *Am. J. Pub. Health* 1484 (1997); J.W. Lynch et al., Cumulative Impact of Sustained Economic Hardship on Physical, Cognitive, Psychological, and Social Functioning, 337 *N. Eng. J. Med* 1889 (1997).

91. See Paul J. Kenkel, Faced With Inaction in Washington, States Forge Ahead With Plans to Cover Uninsured, 20 *Modern Healthcare* 32, 32 (August 6, 1990).

92. See James Dao, Bradley Presents Health Plans for Almost All the Uninsured, *The New York Times*, September 29, 1999, at A1.

93. Because the welfare reform legislation that raised the eligibility requirements for Aid to Families with Dependent Children (AFDC) decoupled Medicaid eligibility from AFDC eligibility (Medicaid eligibility was previously tied to AFDC eligibility), welfare reform did not, as a formal matter, affect Medicaid eligibility. Medicaid eligibility remained linked to income thresholds independent of AFDC requirements. However, the uncoupling of Medicaid and AFDC eligibility resulted in practice in decreased Medicaid enrollment because the separate qualification processes con-

fused potential beneficiaries, increasing the number of people who are eligible for Medicaid but not enrolled.

94. See American Medical Association, Code of Medical Ethics (Chicago: American Medical Association, 1994): at xiv. But see Bernard Friedland, Managed Care and the Expanding Scope of Primary Care Physicians' Duties: A Proposal to Redefine Explicitly the Standard of Care, 26 *J. L. Med. & Ethics* 100 (1998).

95. James Robinson, supra note 49, at 83–87 and 227–228.

96. Free and discounted sports and fitness club memberships and generous obstetrical and well-baby care coverage are typical examples.

97. Bureaucratic barriers to specialized care, limited choice among specialized providers, long waiting times, poor amenities, and inconvenient clinic locations are typical methods. The proscriptions against explicit discrimination contained in such statutes as the Americans with Disabilities Act 42 U.S.C. §§ 12101 et seq. (2000), and the Mental Health Parity Act, 42 U.S.C. §§ 201 et. seq. (2000), are no obstacle to these more subtle approaches.

98. See supra note 66.

99. Institute of Medicine Committee on Understanding and Eliminating Racial and Ethnic Disparities in Health Care, *Unequal Treatment: Confronting Racial and Ethnic Disparities in Health Care* (2002).

100. See generally Barrie Zevin, Transgender Health in the New Millennium, 354 (9192) *Lancet* 1828 (1999); Lisa A. Hayden, Gender Discrimination within the Reproductive Health Care System: Viagra and Birth Control, 13 *J. L. & Health* 171 (1998–99).

101. See generally Kevin Fiscella, et. al., Inequality in Quality: Addressing Socioeconomic, Racial, and Ethnic Disparities in Health Care, 283 *JAMA* 2579 (2000).

102. E.g. Sara Rosenbaum, et al., Who Should Determine When Health Care is Medically Necessary?, 340 *N. Eng. J. Med.* 229 (1999).

103. See, e.g., James F. Blumstein, The Application of Antitrust Doctrine to the Healthcare Industry: The Interweaving of Empirical and Normative Issues, 31 *Ind. L. Rev.* 91 (1998); Mark A. Hall, Rationing Health Care at the Bedside, 69 *N.Y.U. L. Rev.* 693 (1994); Epstein, *Mortal Peril: Our Inalienable Right to Health Care* (1997).

3

FEDERALISM AND THE FUTURE OF HEALTH CARE REFORM

Richard Briffault and Sherry Glied

An important theme in the ongoing health care reform debate is federalism. During the battle over the Clinton Health Plan in 1993–94, the question of which level of government—federal or state—should take the leading role in health policy was almost as contentious as the particular proposals for extending access to quality health care and controlling health care costs. With the failure in 1994 to achieve comprehensive legislation at the national level, many policymakers and commentators gave fresh attention to the states as potential agents for health care reform.

Theories of federalism provide support for a significant state role in health reform. As we will argue in this chapter, however, the current arrangements for the financing and delivery of health care are likely to impede effective action at the state level. This is because most private health insurance in the United States is provided through the workplace. Our constitutional structure and federal law together restrict the ability of states to regulate employment-based health insurance. Indeed, they provide employers with an opportunity for a *"double exit"* from state regulation. First, as with most forms of policy-making, state decision making is constrained by the possibility of *"external exit,"* that is, the ability of an employer to relocate to another the state to avoid cost-imposing regulation. Second, with respect to health care, many employers enjoy immunity from state regulation without having to physically exit the state. This is due to the federal Employee

Retirement Income Security Act (ERISA),[1] which, to a considerable degree, pre-empts state regulation of employment-based health plans. This "internal exit" is far cheaper than "external exit" and, thus, greatly expands the exit option. Conse-quently, state regulatory powers are particularly limited when it comes to health reform.

This employer double exit has several implications. States are restricted in their ability to compel employment-based plans to provide specific benefits or to con-tribute to health care for the uninsured. They also find it difficult to apply cost containment strategies to employer-provided health care, or to control the effects of employer-provided health care on the costs of public and other privately-pro-vided health care delivery systems.

Other effects of the double-exit option may be more subtle. With exit readily available, employers—particularly larger employers—may have less incentive to engage in *voice*, that is, in political participation in state legislative and regula-tory activity with respect to health issues. As a result, state health care policy making may be more susceptible to domination by provider interests than it might otherwise have been. Instead of pursuing cost containment, state laws dealing with privately-provided health insurance may actually drive up health care costs by mandating certain benefits. This, in turn, can fuel employer interest in escaping from state regulatory authority, and reinforce employer opposition to federal legislation that would enhance the capacity of the states to engage in health reform.

ERISA's preemption of state law is not a complete barrier to state regulation of employer-provided health care. The statute is complex, and its preemptive scope indeterminate and changing. As the Supreme Court once tartly noted, ERISA is "not a model of legislative drafting,"[2] and the zigs and zags of judicial interpreta-tion have contributed to what one federal appeals court labeled a "veritable Sar-gasso Sea of obfuscation."[3] In 1995, following a decade of expansive readings of the statute's preemptive effect, the Supreme Court changed course and signaled a narrower reading of ERISA's preemption language and a greater tolerance of state measures regulating health care providers. Nevertheless, the Court did not repudi-ate any of its earlier preemption decisions, and ERISA continues to limit the prospects for action at the state level. The uncertainty of ERISA's scope and the complexity of the strategies needed to overcome its preemptive effect are them-selves barriers to action that reinforce other federalism constraints on states.

This chapter has four parts. The first examines the general principles of feder-alism that affect the role of the states in determining health policy, as well as the implications for the federalism debate of the central role of employer-provided health insurance in the American health care system. Next the major components of health care financing and delivery are summarized, with particular attention to the division between private and public providers of health insurance and the cross-cutting roles of the federal and state governments. The third part develops our thesis of employer double-exit by examining the impact of ERISA on the states' capacity and willingness to engage in the traditional regulatory and financing activities necessary for extending coverage and containing costs. Finally, the last part examines alternative scenarios for dealing with the double exit option, such as limiting ERISA's preemptive effect, or increasing substantive federal regulation of employer-provided health plans. Our analysis suggests that without changes in federal law, state-level action is unlikely to achieve comprehensive health reform.

Federalism principles and health care reform

Traditional principles of federalism support a substantial state role in the provision and regulation of health care. As a general rule, decentralized regulation is appropriate when relevant conditions or public preferences vary significantly from place to place, the activity regulated is primarily local, and there are few savings to be derived from centralized administration. Decentralization, then, rather than uniform national regulation, increases the likelihood that public policy will more nearly match the circumstances and satisfy the preferences of the people affected by it.

Theorists of federalism argue that regulation at lower levels of government increases opportunities for public participation in shaping policy, for experimentation, and for the consideration of a greater variety of solutions to common problems. As Justice Sandra Day O'Connor stated it, decentralized government "will be more responsive to the diverse needs of a heterogeneous society," "allows for more innovation and experimentation in government," and "increases opportunity for citizen involvement in democratic processes."[4]

Health care seems a proper subject for state regulation. Utilization practices, institutional arrangements, costs, and demographic conditions affecting health vary significantly from state to state, as do preferences concerning the role of government and the structures of health care delivery. So, too, many aspects of health care administration, such as the interaction of patients with doctors, clinics, or community hospitals, are intensely local, with few extra-local, let alone interstate, ramifications. Much information concerning access to and quality of health care "may be specific to a particular time, place, and circumstance and may be virtually useless outside a local area."[5] Decentralization of administration may also improve the ability of regulators to monitor outcomes and revise policies in light of their effects. And, as many participants in the health reform debate of the last several years have emphasized, the high level of uncertainty over the way various reform proposals would work in practice suggests that state-level experimentation with a variety of options for cost containment and expansion of coverage would be beneficial for the nation as a whole.[6]

Similarly, some exponents of federalism have suggested that state, rather than federal, responsibility may increase the likelihood of assistance to the poor. As Professor Michael McConnell observed, "the natural spirit of benevolence, which lies at the heart of public spiritedness, is weaker as the distance grows between the individual and the objects of benevolence."[7] Communities are more likely to *take care of their own* than to look after the needs of strangers. In this view, people may be more likely to define the residents of their own locality or state as *their own* than to feel responsible for the health insurance needs of people who live on the other side of the continent.

Consistent with these principles, states have traditionally taken a leading role in health care. They have long regulated the licensing of physicians and other health care providers, the practice of medicine, and the operation of private hospitals. States and localities have administered public health programs and operated public hospitals to assure availability of care for the local poor. Protected by the McCarran-Ferguson Act,[8] the states have played a leading role in regulating health insurance.

In many states, consumer protection laws address aspects of the insurance relationship—insurer solvency, premium rates, disputes over claims, the content of coverage and the terms upon which insurance is offered and renewed. Many states have pursued cost-containment strategies through certification-of-need programs and regulation of the rates that hospitals and other providers may charge. States have taken the lead in attempting to enable the uninsured to obtain private insurance coverage through such insurance market reforms as small-employer pooling and restrictions on denial or nonrenewal of coverage.[9]

Principles of federalism, however, also flag some of the difficulties that constrain state-level health reform initiatives. State fiscal resources are far more limited than those of the federal government. Unlike the federal government, the states cannot print money. Moreover, the states enjoy no constitutional entitlement to federal fiscal support. A state can raise funds only by taxing people, property, or activities with a nexus to the particular state, or by borrowing on the strength of these revenues. As a result, states have a considerably smaller revenue base than the United States. The states may find it more difficult to finance the costs of extending health care to the uninsured.

In addition, state resources vary considerably. Poorer states may simply be unable to do as much for their residents, particularly the poor, as can more affluent states. Exclusive reliance on state funds to assure access to health care is likely to result in very different levels of health care, reflective of the very different levels of state wealth across the United States.

The limited nature of state resources is compounded by the openness of state borders. The constitution creates an American common market, securing the flow of capital, goods, and labor throughout the United States relatively free from state or local interference. Firms are free to move from state to state without fear of losing access to markets in the state they left behind. With states dependent on firms within their borders to provide jobs and the tax base crucial for state revenues, business's ability to relocate limits the capacity of any individual state to take action. With its much greater territorial scope and its greater legal authority to control its borders, the federal government, by contrast, is much less vulnerable to taxpayer or business exit.

Business or taxpayer exit—and the fear of such exit—limits the capacity of states to adopt top-down redistributive policies, such as programs to extend health care coverage to the poor.[10] Firms or households required to pay more in state taxes, or subjected to more state regulatory costs, are free to leave for other states that have lower taxes or less-burdensome regulation. As the Supreme Court observed more than 60 years ago in discussing why, during the Great Depression, most states failed to tax local businesses to fund state unemployment insurance schemes prior to the enactment of a federal system: "Many held back through alarm, lest in laying such a toll upon their industries, they would place themselves in a position of economic disadvantage as compared with neighbors or competitors."[11] As a result, federal action was necessary. A state's fear that if it adopts a generous social program people will come to or remain in that state to take advantage of the program—and that taxpayers will leave to avoid shouldering the costs—can further constrain state redistributive initiatives.[12]

To be sure, physical relocation to another state can be costly. Not all firms or households are mobile. Some are tied to particular jurisdictions, and some jurisdictions have strong attractions that offset the costs of regulation and taxation. So, too, state policy-making is driven by factors other than the single-minded pursuit of jobs and tax base. Some state political actors are concerned less with the size of the economic pie and more with the allocation of the slices; they may have the incentive and the political muscle to get state government to impose taxes or regulation that drive up costs, notwithstanding the impact on potentially mobile constituents. Nevertheless, at the margin, the constitutional guarantee of the exit option, coupled with states' dependence on in-state resources, creates a prisoners' dilemma in which interstate competition for tax base and economic development limits state policy options.

State-level regulation may also burden interstate commerce by creating variable and possibly conflicting requirements across the states. Although health care delivery may be a local matter, health care markets are shaped by the social and economic contours of metropolitan areas that often do not respect state boundaries. Some health care providers are active in more than one state. So, too, people may commute across state borders, or move from one state to another. More importantly, employers play a critical role in financing health care for their employees and their employees' dependents, and many employers, particularly larger ones, maintain operations in more than one state. Compliance with different state rules imposes costs for health care payers and providers who act in interstate commerce and are thereby subject to multiple and potentially conflicting state regulatory regimes.

The weaknesses of state-based policy-making, therefore, flow from two factors: limited (and unequal) state resources; and the potential for interstate variation or non-uniformity. As a theoretical matter, the states' fiscal shortcomings could be addressed by federal financial support that preserves state policy-making autonomy. Limited state resources, unequal state resources, and the effect of interstate competition on the ability of the states to engage in redistributive social programs have since the New Deal served to justify federal action. Federal funding could assure the states of the revenues necessary to extend coverage to the uninsured, mitigate the inequalities in state resources, and avoid the constraint on state redistributive activity imposed by the interstate competition for jobs and taxpayers. As a matter of practical politics, federal funding is often accompanied by conditions that limit state discretion—as with Medicaid—or, indeed, by a complete federal takeover of a field, as with Medicare. Nevertheless it is possible to couple federal funding with state policy-making autonomy.

The costs flowing from interstate variation are more difficult to address since such variation is inherent in state-level action. State policies reflect interstate differences in needs, preferences, conditions, and political participation. Whereas federal financing to mitigate state fiscal weakness can be reconciled with state policy-making, federal regulation to reduce the burden of conflicting state laws necessarily reduces the ability of states to respond to their particular preferences, conditions and constituencies.

The potential for interstate variation is both a cost and a benefit of state-level decision-making. The costs will turn on the extent of interstate policy variations and the significance of multistate actors, and of activity that crosses state lines. For health care, a central factor is the critical role played by employers in the financing of health care. As will be discussed more fully below, most Americans receive their health insurance from their employer or the employer of a family member. Health care financing and delivery are, thus, not solely questions of health policy or insurance policy—two areas traditionally dominated by the states. They are also a matter of employment policy. Since the New Deal, employment policy has been the subject of extensive federal regulation—including such measures as the Wagner Act,[13] the Fair Labor Standards Act,[14] the Taft-Hartley Act,[15] and the laws against discrimination in the workplace.

To be sure, employment law has not been entirely federalized. Some matters, such as workers compensation, remain exclusively subject to state regulation, while others, such as occupational health and safety and anti-discrimination law involve both federal and state responsibilities. States generally tax and regulate the firms that operate within their borders. Nevertheless, the federal role in regulating the workplace, and displacing state regulation, is substantial—far greater than its role with respect to privately-provided health care or health insurance.

Federal regulation of employer-employee relations is not limited to large, multistate employers. Nor is it justified exclusively in terms of the avoidance of duplicative or inconsistent state laws or the effects of interstate competition on state regulatory capacity. The growth of federal employment law reflects a vision of the economy as a national one, not a collection of state and local economies. From this perspective, most economic activity, including activity occurring entirely within one state, has implications for interstate commerce. Even smaller firms, whose operations are limited to one state or who trade primarily within local markets, may be subject to federal regulation because the aggregate of workplace relations even at smaller, locally-oriented firms, affects, at least indirectly, the national economy. Not all federal employment law preempts state law, but state regulation of even relatively local aspects of the employment relationship may be displaced when it interferes with federal policy.

The close association of health care with employment has profound consequences for the states' role in health reform. ERISA's preemption provision has created a substantial federal presence in the area of health reform, but it is a presence which proceeds from federal involvement in the regulation of employment, not in insurance or health care itself. Much of the impetus for ERISA preemption was the avoidance of different rules in different states for employers with activities in more than one state, but ERISA is not limited to the large, multistate firms for whom compliance with the laws of different states would be uniquely burdensome. Rather, it applies to employer-provided health benefits generally. It directly displaces the ability of states to regulate health care financed by employers. Indirectly, it affects the ability of states to address the health care costs and needs even of those state residents who do not receive health benefits from the workplace.

Yet, unlike most other federal employment laws, such as those regulating wages and hours or governing collective bargaining, ERISA itself imposes almost no substantive requirements with respect to employer-provided health benefits. ERISA's federal "presence" thus tends to create an "absence," a regulatory vacuum that leaves the scope of employer-provided health care to employer decision or employer-employee bargaining.

The precise scope of ERISA's displacement of state law is variable and uncertain. The statute is general in its terms. The courts have labored to reconcile federal regulation of employment benefits with the states' traditional control over health care and insurance. The result has been a wavering pattern of decisions that includes both broad and narrow readings of the statute's purpose and of its preemptive effect. The struggle over ERISA preemption not only shapes the allocation of federal and state roles in health reform, it also nicely mirrors the broader federalism debate concerning the costs and benefits of state decision-making and interstate variation in matters that affect both the national economy and traditional areas of state regulatory authority.

The organization and dynamics of the health care delivery system

The current health care financing and delivery system can be thought of as organized along two crosscutting axes: the source of health care coverage, and the source of governmental regulatory authority or financial support.

The *source of coverage* axis consists of three major components. Employer-provided health plans constitute the single largest source of health insurance coverage in the United States. In 2000, 59% of all Americans had insurance from an employment-based plan—either the insured's employer (or union) or the employer (or union) of a member of the insured's family.[16] Non-employment based government programs were next in size; 20% of health coverage was provided by two government programs—Medicare (13%) and Medicaid (7%).[17] Finally, Americans who are not insured through either employment-based or government plans either buy their own insurance (5% of the population) or are among the 39 million without health insurance in 2000 (14% of the population). Many of the uninsured are employed—but their employers may not provide insurance to any of their employees, or may not have offered it to *them*, or the contribution expected from the employee renders the insurance unattractive.

With respect to *source of government authority*—that is, the level of government, federal or state, that regulates or funds the source of care—the federal role looms large for those who receive insurance through public programs. Medicare is a wholly federal program; the federal government funds it and determines all of its components, such as eligibility, services and providers covered, and benefit levels. It supersedes state regulatory authority with respect to providers of health care services to Medicare beneficiaries, although the cost of Medicare will be affected by local conditions which may be shaped by state regulation.

The costs of Medicaid are shared by the federal government and the states, with the federal government bearing about 60% of the costs and the states the remainder—the split varies from state to state according to a formula that factors in the per capita income of the state.[18] Historically, the federal government determined the principal features of Medicaid, but the 1990s witnessed an increase in the states' regulatory role. The federal government has been willing to permit states to experiment with new methods of providing insurance to Medicaid recipients. The Clinton administration provided many states with waivers from federal Medicaid requirements. The 1997 Balanced Budget Act eliminated the requirement that a state receive federal permission before directing most Medicaid beneficiaries to enroll in managed care programs, and it increased state discretion to set payment rates for hospitals, nursing homes, and federally qualified community health centers.[19]

The increased discretion is intended to enable states to do more with the same funds—to redeploy existing federal and state dollars to increase the number of people insured.[20] The ability of the states to utilize their discretionary authority to extend coverage to the uninsured will turn on whether the projected savings from managed care can be achieved. Early results indicate that "savings will be more modest than previously indicated."[21] Without additional funding there is a limit on what regulatory flexibility alone can accomplish. Indeed, new state discretionary power is often coupled with federal efforts to cut costs, as in the disproportionate-share hospital program.[22] Where Congress makes new funds available, as with the State Children's Health Insurance Program—which is intended to encourage states to extend coverage to children in families with incomes above the traditional Medicaid ceiling—it may adopt new programmatic requirements or require the commitment of state matching funds, thereby affecting state budgetary decision-making.[23]

Health care needs of the self-insured and uninsured have traditionally been the responsibility of the states. State laws regulating insurance affect whether (and on what terms) private insurance will be offered to this group, and whether it will be adequate to their needs. State licensing of doctors, state regulation of hospitals and the practice of medicine, statewide and local health payments that include direct support of public hospitals and public health programs, even state contract and tort law will affect the delivery of health care. Apart from anti-discrimination laws, such as the Americans With Disabilities Act, federal law until recently had little direct regulatory impact on the ability of this group to obtain insurance. Payments by the self-insured for health insurance come from income subject to federal income tax, and payments are normally not deductible from taxable income.[24] The Internal Revenue Code's subsidy for employment-based health benefits which—as we shall see—provides critical federal support for employment-based coverage, is less helpful to low-wage workers who are in a lower tax bracket. And Medicare and Medicaid are not available to the non-elderly, non-disabled, and non-poor uninsured. Those people unable to obtain employer-provided health insurance are thus a burden primarily for the states.

Recent state initiatives have focused on insurance market reforms that could make it easier for low-wage workers or employees at small firms to move from the uninsured to the employment-based sector, although, as we shall see, ERISA has been an obstacle to these initiatives.[25]

With respect to those who receive health insurance through the workplace, the interplay of state and federal roles is particularly complex.[26] On the one hand, federal legislation—the Internal Revenue Code—has helped stimulate the enormous role of employment-based private health insurance. Like wages, employer contributions to health insurance plans are deductible as a business expense and thus are not subject to corporate taxation. Moreover, workers are not required to pay income tax on payments employers make to buy them health insurance. The federal tax expenditure attributable to the special treatment accorded employer-provided health insurance was worth $111 billion in 1998.[27]

But, until recently there was little substantive federal regulation of employer-provided health benefits. ERISA mandates certain reporting, disclosure and fiduciary responsibilities, but does not address the terms or structures of employer health plans. Private health insurance has traditionally been the province of state regulation; both the provision of insurance and the regulation of health care are longstanding state concerns. Yet, although ERISA contains few substantive requirements it has powerfully curtailed state regulatory authority over employment-based health insurance. Indeed, ERISA preemption and the consequent regulatory weakness of the states may ultimately be responsible for a federal role—which has only just started to emerge—in regulating the terms and conditions of privately provided health insurance.

The impact of ERISA on the states' role in health care reform is discussed below.

ERISA preemption and prospects for state-level health reform

ERISA Preemption

As the "Employee Retirement Income Security" phrase in the short title of the statute suggests, ERISA was enacted primarily in response to concerns about the security of employer-based pension plans. It imposed participation, vesting and funding requirements for pension plans, and established a system of pension plan termination insurance. Although congressional deliberations leading up to ERISA focussed on pension plans, the statute's scope is far broader. It addresses *employee welfare benefit plans* generally; these are defined to include employer health plans.[28] As a result, all health plans established and maintained by an employer[29] (other than a government or church employer) for its employees[30] are covered by ERISA.

ERISA imposes few substantive requirements on health or other employee welfare benefit plans. Unlike pension plans, health plans are not subject to participation, vesting or funding requirements. ERISA mandates no health benefits or health benefit plans, nor does it regulate changes in—or the elimination of—benefits or plans. With respect to health benefits, ERISA's requirements are limited to the periodic filing of forms concerning plan participation and finances with the Department of Labor; disclosure of summary descriptions of plans to beneficiaries; fiduciary standards to protect beneficiaries from mismanagement and conflicts of interest; the requirement that employers establish claims procedures; and remedies for violations of the Act's minimal requirements.[31]

ERISA imposes far fewer substantive federal standards for employee welfare plans—including health plans—than for pension plans, but the same sweeping preemption provision applies to *all* employee benefit plans. To the extent that ERISA supersedes state regulatory authority without providing for substantive federal regulation of health plans, the Act empowers employers. Indeed, much of the law of ERISA preemption has developed out of the efforts of employers to nullify state laws intended to protect employees or the beneficiaries of employee health plans.[32]

ERISA's preemption provision has three components. The *preemption clause* provides that ERISA "shall supersede any and all state laws insofar as they may now or hereafter relate to employee benefit plans."[33] The *savings clause* excludes from preemption state laws that regulate insurance.[34] The *deemer clause*, in turn, limits the effect of the savings clause by providing that an employee benefit plan shall not itself be "deemed" an insurer or "engaged in the business of insurance."[35]

The scope of ERISA preemption turns on two questions of interpretation: which state laws *relate to* employee benefit plans? And how much state regulation is preserved by the savings clause as modified by the deemer clause?

State laws relating to health benefit plans

As the Supreme Court has noted, "the preemption clause is conspicuous for its breadth."[36] In its early preemption decisions, the Court found that Congress intended "the words 'relate to' . . . in their broad sense" to displace any state law, including state common law, "if it has a connection with or reference to" an employee benefits plan.[37] The Court rejected the argument that ERISA should be read to preempt only those laws specifically aimed at employee benefit plans or dealing with matters regulated by ERISA—reporting, disclosure, fiduciary responsibility and the like.[38] Instead, the Court has repeatedly held that ERISA preempts state laws that require employers to provide their employees with certain benefits—whether a package of basic benefits,[39] or benefits relating to a specific condition, such as pregnancy.[40] In 1992, the Court held that a state law requiring employers to continue providing benefits to employees out on workers compensation "relates to" employee health plans within the meaning of the preemption clause.[41]

ERISA preemption has had a powerful impact on general state laws, including common-law doctrines, intended to protect employee rights to contractually-provided health or insurance benefits. In *FMC Corp. v Holliday*, the Court determined that a Pennsylvania law that generally prohibited "any program, group contract, or other arrangement" from seeking subrogation of reimbursement from a beneficiary's tort recovery in a motor vehicle accident case relates to employee health plans within the meaning of ERISA.[42] Similarly, the Court found that state common law contract or tort doctrines *of general application,* such as breach of contract, breach of fiduciary duty, or fraud, "relate to" employee health plans within the meaning of ERISA and are subject to preemption in cases involving claims over the denial of employee health benefits.[43] Indeed, the Court held that ERISA preempts a state common law wrongful discharge claim in a case where an employee alleged he was unlawfully discharged to prevent his attainment of benefits under a plan covered by ERISA.[44]

Some lower federal courts have gone further, holding that state medical malpractice or negligence claims against utilization review agencies or managed care organizations for denial of coverage for particular health care treatments or procedures relate to employee health plans and are subject to preemption—even though ERISA itself provides no remedies against such third-party organizations for denial of coverage.[45] To be sure, not all lower courts have adopted such an expansive view of ERISA preemption. The applicability of medical malpractice law to ERISA plans is particularly uncertain.[46] The emerging distinction appears to be that malpractice claims brought to establish the vicarious liability of a health maintenance organization for the *quality* of care provided by a physician employed by the HMO are not preempted, but malpractice claims which challenge the denial of coverage in a utilization review or precertification process and thereby attack the administration of the plan and the *quantity* of benefits are preempted.[47]

At one point, even state health care taxes and provider reimbursement schemes that affected ERISA plans were held to relate to those plans within the meaning of the preemption clause. The Fifth Circuit Court of Appeals found that a Texas tax on fees for the administration of health plans was subject to preemption.[48] The Second Circuit found that ERISA preempted New York's inpatient hospital reimbursement scheme, which permitted hospitals to impose surcharges for patients covered by health plans other than those of non-profit health service corporations, such as Blue Cross/Blue Shield.[49] The surcharges were intended to compel patients covered by commercial health plans not open to the entire community to subsidize the nonprofits, which practiced open enrollment and community rating, and thus were providing coverage to more costly risks. Most, but not all, of the patients affected by the higher charges were in ERISA plans, and the Second Circuit determined that because the surcharges "impose a significant economic burden on commercial insurers . . . they have an impermissible impact" on ERISA plans.[50] In a case involving the application of a New York state tax on the gross receipts from patient care services to a medical center run by an employee health plan, the Second Circuit implied that a tax that "targets only the health care industry" presumptively relates to ERISA plans "[b]ecause this industry is, by definition, the realm where ERISA welfare plans operate."[51]

Ultimately, the two Second Circuit decisions were reversed by the Supreme Court in cases that indicate that ERISA preemption may have reached its highwater mark. In 1995, in *New York State Conference of Blue Cross & Blue Shield Plans v Travelers Insurance Co.*,[52] a unanimous Court upheld the New York hospital rate-setting scheme despite the impact on ERISA plans. Placing a new emphasis on respect for the state role in "fields of traditional state regulation,"[53] *Travelers* took a very different approach to the meaning of ERISA's "relate to" provision. As Justice Souter noted, "[i]f 'relate to' were taken to extend to the furthest stretch of its indeterminacy, then for all practical purposes, preemption would never run its course."[54] "Relate to" had to be treated as "words of limitation" rather than as a basis for potentially limitless preemption.[55]

Reviewing ERISA's legislative history, the Court concluded that "[t]he basic thrust of the pre-emption clause . . . was to avoid a multiplicity of [state] regulation in order to permit the nationally uniform administration of employee benefit plans."[56] ERISA would thus preempt state laws "that mandated employee benefit structures or their administration" or that "provid[e] alternate enforcement mechanisms."[57] Preemption of those state laws would protect ERISA plans from the threat of conflicting and inconsistent state regulation. But the mere fact that state laws regulating health care or other traditional areas of state concern impose costs that might influence ERISA plan decisions—and that the laws of different states might impose different costs—was not itself sufficient to make those laws relate to ERISA plans. Such costs and differentials are an unavoidable consequence of differences in state policies and regulatory regimes, and thus a necessary aspect of federalism. In the absence of a showing that the economic impact of the tax was so acute as to effectively "force an ERISA plan to adopt a certain scheme of substantive coverage or effectively restrict its choice of insurers,"[58] a tax or other regulation that does not target ERISA plans specifically[59] but merely drives up ERISA plan costs or creates interstate cost variation is not subject to preemption.

Travelers upheld the reimbursement scheme even though the state intended it to have an impact on health care policy. By providing for lower charges for patients covered by Blue Cross/Blue Shield, compared to commercial insurers or HMOs, the New York law sought to make the Blues "more attractive (or less unattractive) as insurance alternatives and thus have an indirect economic effect on choices made by insurance buyers, including ERISA plans."[60] But an indirect economic influence "does not bind plan administrators to any particular choice and thus function as a regulation of an ERISA plan itself. . . . Nor does the indirect influence of the surcharges preclude uniform administrative practice or the provision of a uniform interstate benefit if a plan chooses to provide one."[61]

Travelers put an end to the expansion of ERISA preemption that had marked the Supreme Court's decisions of the 1980s and early 1990s.[62] Two years later, in *DeBuono v NYSA-ILA Medical & Clinical Services Fund,*[63] the Court underscored its new respect for state regulation—and the exclusion from preemption of general state laws that only indirectly impose costs on ERISA plans—by reversing the Second Circuit decision that had invalidated the gross receipts tax New York had imposed on all hospitals, residential health care facilities, and diagnostic treatment centers. The New York tax applied to a treatment center operated by a self-insured ERISA plan. The Second Circuit had held that by reducing the plan assets available to provide benefits, the tax directly "relate[d] to" an ERISA plan. The circuit court reiterated that conclusion even after *Travelers* because the gross receipts tax applied directly to ERISA plans, whereas the reimbursement scheme in *Travelers* affected only insurance carriers.[64] The Supreme Court, however, determined that the Second Circuit had failed to heed *Travelers'* directive to narrow the scope of "relate to."

Beginning by "noting that the historic police powers of the state include the regulation of matters of health and safety,"[65] *DeBuono* found preemption inappropriate given that the New York law neither addressed the benefits available under an ERISA plan, nor made the existence of an ERISA plan a "critical element" in the tax.[66] The tax applied to all hospitals, not just to those owned by ERISA plans. The plan's hospital was not singled out, nor were its benefits or administration constrained by the tax.[67]

More recently, in *Pegram v Herdrich*,[68] the Supreme Court held that "mixed eligibility and treatment decisions"[69]—that is, decisions that mix questions concerning an ERISA plan's "coverage of a particular condition or medical procedure for its treatment" with "choices about how to go about diagnosing and treating a patient's condition"[70]—by HMO physicians, are not fiduciary decisions subject to suit for breach of fiduciary duty under ERISA. Although concerned with ERISA's substantive requirements, not preemption of state law, *Pegram* relied in part on the Court's recognition of the traditional role of state law in regulating medical malpractice. The Court expressly sought to avoid the creation of a body of federal medical malpractice law that would preempt state malpractice. The Court expressly sought to avoid the creation of a body of federal medical malpractice law that would preempt state malpractice law.[71]

These cases indicate that state laws taxing and regulating health care may not be preempted despite their impact on ERISA plans. More generally, they suggest a greater respect for the traditional state role in health care and an effort to create some space for the states to act. But *Travelers* and *DeBuono* do not yet mark a rollback in the scope of ERISA preemption. The Court preserved its earlier ERISA case law[72] and confirmed that ERISA would continue to preempt even general state laws not specifically targeted on ERISA plans that prescribed specific benefits or sought to regulate plan administration or remedies. Even after *Travelers* and *DeBuono*, ERISA preemption is not limited to direct regulation of ERISA plans, as *Travelers* acknowledged it could not so limit ERISA preemption "with fidelity to the views expressed in our prior opinions on the matter."[73] The anti-subrogation law preempted in *FMC Corp. v Holliday*, for example, did not directly mandate or limit benefits available under a plan; rather, the basis for preemption was that plans in Pennsylvania might choose to calculate plan benefit levels differently in that state than elsewhere because Pennsylvania's tort law raised costs to plans in the state. *Travelers* or *DeBuono*, however, did not limit the opportunity to obtain preemption to multistate employers or multistate plans. State laws can be "conflicting or inconsistent" only when the laws of two or more states apply to the same plan, but that can occur only when an employer has operations or a plan has beneficiaries subject to the laws of more than one state. A one-state employer or one-state plan may not be threatened by conflicting or inconsistent state laws. Yet, the Court did not limit ERISA preemption to multistate employers. Rather, it left in place ERISA's preemption of the application of state laws regulating employee benefits, plan administration, or remedies even to small, one-state firms or plans.[74]

The savings and deemer clauses and the rise of the self-funded/insured distinction

In *Metropolitan Life Insurance Co. v Massachusetts*,[75] the Supreme Court held that ERISA's *savings* clause protects traditional state regulation of insurance, including insurance contracts purchased by employers for their employees.[76] Although Massachusetts could not require employers to provide employees with specific health benefits—that would be preempted by the clause barring state laws that "relate to" ERISA plans—it could require that insurance policies sold within the state include particular benefits and thus reach employer-provided benefits indirectly. An employer could not be required to provide health insurance, but if it chose to purchase insurance for its employees, the only insurance policies it would be allowed to buy would include the benefits mandated by the state. In addition, state laws that regulate the interpretation of insurance contracts and protect the interests of policyholders generally are saved from preemption by the "savings" clause and may be applied to ERISA plans.[77]

But, according to the Court, due to ERISA's *deemer* clause, the *savings* clause does not save insurance-type state regulation of an employee health-benefit plan that bears the risk of health benefit claims itself.[78] A health plan that bears the risk of health-benefit claims, rather than transferring that risk by contract to an insurer or other third party, is not in the business of insurance and is not subject to a state's insurance laws. Such a plan—called self-funded—is exempt from the state insurance regulation saved by the *savings* clause.

Metropolitan Life thus gives employee health plans the opportunity for internal exit from state insurance law. By structuring their plans to be self–funded, employers can immunize their health plans from state insurance laws, such as taxes on premiums, mandatory health benefits, financial solvency standards, and health insurance reforms affecting small employers.[79] Self-funding has great legal advantages, with few costs. Indeed, most self-funded plans do not actually set aside a separate fund to cover anticipated health claims, but, instead pay health benefits out of ordinary funds.[80]

At the time of ERISA's enactment, fewer than 5% of the employees and family members receiving insurance through the workplace obtained it from self-funded plans, and self-funding was practiced mostly by large, multistate employers, or multiemployer union-sponsored plans.[81] By 1996, according to the United States General Accounting Office, approximately 40% of those insured through private workplaces were in self-funded plans.[82] Self-funded plans were particularly common with larger employers; approximately 63% of employees in firms with more than 500 employees were in self-funded plans, compared with 34% of employees in firms with 101 to 500 employees, and 11% of employees in firms with fewer than 100 employees.[83]

Data on the extent of self-funding are uncertain in part because of ERISA it-self—ERISA preempts state efforts to require employers to provide health plan data, but does not require reporting to any federal agencies of the information necessary to determine the extent of self-funding.[84] More importantly, the scope of self-funding is unclear because the concept itself is, in practice, a fuzzy one. The distinction is "meaningless to beneficiaries"[85] and is blurred by a range of contractual arrangements between health plans and insurers or other entities, such as managed care organizations. As the GAO has observed, "[c]learly distinguish-ing between self-funded and fully insured plans is growing more difficult as the health market changes."[86] Many employers that provide a self-funded plan also provide insured coverage to some employees, by, for example, offering employ-ees a choice of one or more HMOs, through financing arrangements in which risk is spread among the employer, the plan, and the provider.[87]

Most importantly, most self-funded plans shift at least some of their risk to in-surance companies through the purchase of "stop–loss" or excessive risk cover-age.[88] Generally, courts have found these plans to be self-funded, and thus im-mune from state insurance regulation, despite the purchase of stop–loss insurance, and they have usually rejected the claim that the stop–loss insurance is itself health insurance subject to state insurance regulation, at least when the health plan is directly liable to participants for the benefits owed and the stop–loss insurance does not cover plan participants directly.[89] Yet, "particularly among smaller employers," stop–loss coverage may begin at a very low level of claims, so that most of the risk of loss is shifted to a third party insurer.[90] Stop–loss cover-age, along with the ability of smaller employers to contract for administrative services for their plans from insurance companies, has lowered the cost of self-funding for many smaller employers. Although smaller firms are less likely to offer their employees health insurance, a substantial proportion of those who do are able to do so through self-funded plans.

The distinction between "self-funded" and non–self-funded or "insured" plans has little to recommend it from the perspective of federalism. It no longer maps onto an important federalism distinction—whether the firm is a multistate orga-nization or whether its employees are located within one state—nor does it relate to other important federalism distinctions, such as whether the firm operates within one health care market. Moreover, given the rise of stop–loss coverage, it is not even clear whether there really is a distinction between self-funded and "in-sured" plans from an insurance perspective. If this distinction ever had substan-tive meaning it no longer does so. It is an illusive, if not illogical, basis for policy formulation.

The two prongs of ERISA preemption thus provide employers with a form of internal exit from state regulation that is nearly as potent as the traditional external exit but not nearly as costly. The preemption clause immunizes employers—including employers who provide no health benefits at all—from state laws mandating employers to provide health benefits, directly regulating benefits that employers choose to provide, or providing consumer protections for plan beneficiaries. The reigning interpretation of the interplay of the savings and deemer clauses virtually invites employers to structure their health plans as self-funded—an invitation that a steadily growing number of employers, including smaller employers, have taken—in order to exempt themselves from state regulation of insurance.

ERISA Preemption and State-Level Health Reform

ERISA preemption constrains state initiatives to extend access to health care for the uninsured and to contain health care costs in several ways.

Assuring health insurance coverage

ERISA limits several state strategies for providing health security. ERISA precludes state laws that would mandate employers to provide their employees with health benefits.[91] It preempts state laws protecting employees from the termination or nonrenewal of coverage, the reduction of previously-provided benefits or the exclusion of coverage for preexisting conditions, as well as laws that would require employers to continue coverage for former employees.[92] ERISA may displace other state "consumer protection" measures intended to protect the rights of beneficiaries under existing health plans. The precise scope of ERISA preemption is often uncertain; such legal uncertainty may itself discourage state regulatory innovation. For example, the fifth circuit court of appeals has held that ERISA preempts a state law requiring HMOs to provide patients with a mechanism to obtain an independent review of the HMO's determination that a treatment sought by the patient is not medically necessary or appropriate,[93] although the seventh circuit court of appeals reached the opposite conclusion and held that a state independent review law was saved by the insurance savings clause.[94] The question currently awaits Supreme Court resolution. Even if state independent review laws are held to be saved from preemption, the deemer clause may enable self-funded plans to escape such regulation.[95] More generally, ERISA limits the ability of states to mandate particular benefits or coverage for particular high risk groups through laws regulating health insurance contracts since employers can escape the effect of these laws by creating self-funded plans.[96]

ERISA places a cloud over the legality of *pay-or-play* plans, that is, requirements that employers either provide their employees with health benefits that satisfy a state's standards or pay a tax that would be used to pay for health care for the uninsured. Although pay-or-play leaves the terms and conditions of employer-provided benefits to the employer, and thus might be exempt from preemption as a law with only an indirect, economic effect within the meaning of *Travelers*, a *pay-or-play* plan that forced an employer to pay a tax equal to the full cost of health care for its employees might well be seen as presenting the employer with the sort of Hobson's choice that *Travelers* would treat "as imposing a substantive mandate" and thus preempted.[97]

Not only does ERISA significantly constrain the ability of states to regulate employer-provided health insurance or to use employers as the means for assuring insurance for employees and their dependents, ERISA also limits the ability of states to deal with the insurance needs of people who do not receive insurance from the workplace or who have no insurance at all. ERISA impedes the ability of states to raise funds to cover the costs of public health insurance programs, whether a universal health care system or subsidies for high-risk groups or the uninsured.

ERISA precludes direct taxation aimed at ERISA plans[98] as well as taxes on contributions to plans.[99] Employers, of course, remain subject to general state taxation, including payroll taxes and business income taxes, and these may be used to generate the funds necessary to provide funds to extend insurance to the uninsured—although one commentator has suggested that even such general taxes on employers might be preempted if they were used to fund a universal health care program that would effectively cause employers to discontinue their own plans.[100] The principal difficulty of relying on general taxation in this era of fiscal restraint and anti-tax philosophy is that general tax increases are unlikely to be adopted. Compulsory employer provision of health care and taxes on employer-provided health plans are a more politically palatable source of the dollars needed to extend coverage to the uninsured—yet ERISA puts these means beyond the reach of the states.

Following *DeBuono*, however, states may tax health-care providers to raise funds for state programs for the uninsured. Provider taxes thus may serve as the one means of financing the extension of insurance coverage out of funds generated from the health care sector itself, and may serve as an indirect tax on individuals with commercial insurance. Unlike mandates, pay or play, or other strategies targeted at employers, provider taxes are not borne exclusively by employers or persons insured through the workplace.

ERISA is thus not a complete barrier to strategies other than general taxation for financing coverage for the uninsured, but it does tend to limit the ability of states to make employers, or employment-based health plans, bear the brunt of the direct costs of paying for health insurance for the uninsured.

ERISA's other significant constraint on state mechanisms for extending access to insurance derives from its impact on insurance market reforms intended to make insurance less expensive, particularly for high-risk insureds. States cannot force employees insured through self-funded ERISA plans into pools with employees of other firms and uninsured individuals. Pooling is an essential mechanism for the spreading of risks and the performance of insurance's most basic function—the redistribution of income from those who do not suffer a loss (that is, those who are well) to those who do (those who are sick). Effective insurance requires pools that are large enough to reduce the burden of catastrophic loss to the participants. Moreover, *risk spreading*, as distinct from insurance, requires the pooling of those who have a high risk of incurring a loss with those who have a low risk of incurring loss. Without proper pooling—that is, pools that are heterogeneous in composition and that have the capacity to sustain large losses—insurance will not spread risks from the sick to the well, and the cost of health insurance will be higher for those who need it most.

Traditional insurance practices resist the wholesale pooling of risks. To combat the threat of adverse selection, insurers deploy risk-based rating and other mechanisms in order to create more homogeneous pools in which people with comparable risks are grouped with each other. In turn, an important feature of current state insurance regulation has been the effort to exert some control over premium pricing—such as community rating—in order to constrain insurer risk-based pricing, and thereby use the insurance mechanism to subsidize care for those at greatest risk of illness.

By immunizing self-funded plans from state insurance regulation—such as community rating; controls on deductibles, copayments, or exclusions from coverage; and inclusion in purchasing pools with small firms and individuals—ERISA undermines the ability of states to perform this traditional state function. ERISA plans simply cannot be forced into state risk-spreading mechanisms. As a result, any state pools that are created will be shallower, and less efficient at spreading risk, and less capable of buffering the risk of loss for high-risk people in them.[101]

Employees covered by self-funded ERISA plans may be healthier and at lower-risk than the uninsured whom the states are seeking to assist. As a result, the cost of insurance for those in state-sponsored community-rated pools will be higher than if the employees in self-funded plans were a part of the mix. This is likely to inspire further departure of healthier people from community-rated pools and thus even higher premium costs to those who remain behind.

If unable to include self-funded plans, state pooling policies may have perverse consequences. With many of the lower risks immune from state regulation, and presumably all of the uninsured high-risk people opting for coverage by the pool, community-rated premiums will be higher than otherwise. Low-risk people will, then, drop coverage, and community-rated premiums will be higher still.[102] States will be spreading risks across fewer, but more high-risk, people.

To be sure, states can provide for voluntary pooling and can use tax policy, such as tax deductions or credits, to encourage self-funded plans to participate in insurance purchasing pools.[103] Appropriately structured, these could serve as "modest but effective enrollment incentives."[104] But designing such incentives will take more sophisticated analysis, and may be more difficult to implement, than mandatory pooling of risks. More direct use of state tax powers to force employees into pools would "raise even greater ERISA problems."[105] The more state tax and regulatory actions directly impinge on employer decisions concerning the structure of their plans and the content of plan benefits the more state policies are subject to ERISA challenge. As we shall see, the states' inability to apply insurance reforms to self-funded ERISA plans contributed to Congressional enactment of the Health Insurance Portability and Accountability Act of 1996.

Cost containment

The exemption of ERISA plans from state regulation also limits the ability of states to pursue equitable forms of cost containment. Common cost containment strategies include limitations on health services or benefits available under insurance, limitations on payments by insurers to providers, caps on spending on behalf of insureds, and controls imposed directly on providers, such as certification of need requirements for new equipment or hospitals. With the exception of controls imposed directly on providers, ERISA would exempt self-funded plans from such state cost containment strategies.

It is unlikely that states would attempt to limit the availability of health care for one component of the privately-provided sector but not the other. Thus, state policies to restrict the purchase of health services would affect only those whose care is funded through the publicly-provided sector. Given Medicare's current exemption from state regulation, a state could reach only those who obtain their health insurance coverage through Medicaid.

Global budgets and health care rationing are controversial notions and debatable as cost containment strategies, but surely spending caps and rationing services are even more problematic if they are applied inequitably, with spending by only the poor controlled or the care available only to the poor rationed. Yet, due to ERISA and Medicare, a large proportion of the non-poor are immunized from state health care spending limitation or rationing plans. Federal exemptions from state regulation, thus, tend to preclude states from controlling spending by all segments of society. Indeed, when the effects of the Internal Revenue Code's subsidy for employer-provided health care are factored in, the current division of regulatory and fiscal powers among the states and federal governments could create a situation in which the states are restricting the health services available to the poor through publicly-funded programs while the federal government is subsidizing the care available through self-funded employer plans. Together, the interaction of such federal and state programs would foster the development of a two-tier system of rationed and unrationed care which many people find objectionable.

Not only does ERISA limit the ability of states to regulate the costs of privately-provided health care, in so doing it may increase the magnitude of the states' burden of attending to the needs of the uninsured. Health care needs are not absolute; rather, they are to a considerable extent defined in terms of the technologies, services and procedures available. If self-funded plans are more generous in the scope of their coverage—and with employer-provided care subsidized through the Internal Revenue Code that is certainly a plausible development—that stimulates the interest in such services generally and tends to raise the level of what is deemed an acceptable standard of care throughout society. As the Clinton Health Plan demonstrated, when many policymakers talk about providing a package of basic benefits to the uninsured, they do not mean minimal benefits but, rather, benefits comparable to those available through employer-provided health insurance.

To the extent that self-funded employee benefit plans set the standard for health insurance generally, the costs of those plans are not borne solely by employers and employees. Rather, they will drive up the costs of state programs for the uninsured, or, if the state is unable or unwilling to meet those costs, the standard set by ERISA plans will increase dissatisfaction with, and a sense of injustice about the more limited coverage available through state-assisted or state-provided plans. Self-funded plans are exempt from state regulation and state cost-containment but they may add to the financial and political burdens of state policy-makers with respect to the uninsured.

Employer Exit and Employer Voice

ERISA preemption, and the opportunity for internal exit from state regulation that it allows employers, may have a more subtle, indeed, perverse, effect on health reform, particularly cost containment. ERISA may unintentionally increase the political efficacy of health care providers in state deliberations, making it more likely that states will adopt rules requiring companies selling health insurance to cover specified health services or the services provided by specific providers. As a result, ERISA may lead to an increase in health care costs for those unable to take advantage of the Act's internal exit.

Many state-level health policy deliberations may be characterized as a struggle between provider and payer interests. Employers are the principal representative of payer interests. Large firms in particular are typically savvy and forceful participants in state politics and ordinarily they would play a major role in state policy-making. But employers, especially those with self-funded plans, are to a considerable extent immune from state regulation. As a result, they may have less incentive to get involved in state health policy debates or to join in opposition to proposals to require insurers to cover particular treatments or the services of particular provider groups. Participation in legislative or regulatory policymaking is costly in terms of firm time, money, and energy. Firms with self-funded plans might choose to husband their resources and devote themselves to those aspects of the state political agenda which have more direct implications for their interests, while forsaking the debate over matters, like state regulation of health insurance, that do not affect them. As a result, it would not be surprising if provider interests dominate state health care policy, or, at least, play a more powerful role than they would have in the absence of ERISA. The smaller firms and individual insureds who remain subject to state insurance regulation may be less capable of resisting provider demands than big firms would have been.

The relatively one-sided nature of the payer–provider battle in the health care setting may account for the proliferation of state cost-imposing, provider-oriented legislation, such as generous mandatory benefit and mandatory service requirements and any-willing-provider laws. By one count, states have adopted more than 700 separate benefits mandates, although many have identical or similar requirements.[106] Although the courts have divided over the application of ERISA preemption to any-willing-provider laws it seems likely that self-funded plans are exempt from coverage.[99] If the big firm employee benefit plans that have been able to escape state regulation via ERISA preemption were subject to these laws, it is hard to believe that so many of these laws would have been enacted or would remain on the books after their consequences in terms of health care costs had become known. By contrast, few states have been willing to finance the expansion of health insurance coverage through general taxation. The rejection of general taxation is no doubt overdetermined—in the current anti-tax climate, nearly all politically powerful groups resist general tax increases. But surely the resistance of the large firms that are immune from state insurance regulation but subject to general taxation has played a role in shifting states away from general tax support for insurance for the uninsured.

The impact of easy exit on the interest of larger firms to give voice to their concerns with respect to health policy at the state level may be more subtle than simply the non-participation of firms that sponsor self-funded ERISA plans in discussion of cost-enhancing regulation. Many large firms have successfully experimented with new forms of health care delivery, utilization review, wellness programs, and other innovations that contain costs while maintaining or improving quality. Given their immunity from state regulation—and the absence of substantive federal regulation—they have had little incentive to share their experiences with government. Indeed, given their exemption from even state reporting, disclosure and data collection requirements, states have little direct access to the expertise of these firms. State policy-making is simply less informed than it might otherwise be if self-funded firms had a larger stake in state decisions or could be required to provide information about their employee-benefit plans to state policy-makers.

Internal Exit and External Exit

Cost-imposing state health reform is also constrained by the possibility of external exit by employers or taxpayers who might be called upon to bear the fiscal burden of extending health care to the uninsured. ERISA does leave open the possibility of general taxation, or taxation targeted at health care providers and passed along to health care consumers and payers, as a basis for subsidizing coverage for the uninsured, but, as noted earlier, the threat of employer external exit has traditionally constrained state redistributive taxation. It is not simply that employers who have actually exited are able to escape state taxation. Rather, it is the threat of exit, including the threat to shift new investment outside the state, by those who remain within the state that tends to limit the adoption of state redistributive measures.

State governments engage in an ongoing competition for tax base and jobs. Costly regulatory and redistributive efforts "are vulnerable to erosion in political systems with many competing governments."[108] The threat of exit can be a clinching argument in a state policy debate.

Of course, the threat of external exit is not always available. Firms with substantial fixed capital invested in a place or with expertise in serving a local market may be relatively immobile. In the health care setting, however, the threat of external exit is supplemented by the possibility of internal exit. Although internal exit permits a state to reach a firm for some purposes, such as general taxation, and does not cost the state employment, it does reduce the state's regulatory authority. Together, external and internal exit uniquely restrain the ability of states to undertake comprehensive health care reform.

Alternative scenarios for federalism and the future of health care reform

The expansive effect of ERISA preemption on state policymaking has itself been the subject of a variety of proposals for reform. The scope of ERISA preemption could be narrowed. For more than a decade, individual states and organizations of state governments pushed for so-called ERISA "waivers"—which is really a misnomer since "waiver" implies administrative action to exempt a state from statutory requirements pursuant to authority already granted by Congress—as with Medicaid waivers. As no federal agency has the power to exempt states from ERISA preemption, any ERISA waiver would require congressional action. Alternatively, the federal government could exercise its authority over employer-provided health benefits by adopting substantive rules that protect or extend health benefits.

Either approach would tend to diminish the preferred position of employer-provided health plans and could eliminate the difficult-to-defend distinction between self-funded and non-self-funded plans. But the two approaches would have very different consequences. ERISA waivers would give states authority over employer plans. Combined with their traditional regulatory authority over health care providers and over insurance, state government would then have a much greater capacity to engage in health care reform, although limitations on state resources and the threat of external exit from more regulatory to less regulatory states would still constrain redistributive policy. Moreover, the empowerment of the states would increase prospects that differing state strategies would place particular burdens on multistate firms. By contrast, substantive federal regulation would shift power over privately-financed health care to the federal government. This would avoid the costs of state decision-making, but would also lose the benefits of decentralization. In the years since the demise of the Clinton Health Plan there has been little in the way of ERISA waiver but the beginning of substantive federal regulation of employer-provided health plans.

ERISA Waivers

ERISA waivers could eliminate the internal exit for self-funded plans thus enabling states to extend their insurance regulations to all employees and dependents insured through the workplace. By allowing a state to deal more comprehensively with those who are insured through the workplace an ERISA waiver would enhance state resources for addressing the problems of the uninsured. ERISA waivers could enable states to improve the spreading of risks, raise revenue, or contain costs in an equitable manner. If, due to adverse selection or the external effects of ERISA plans on the costs of health care, ERISA plans are a part of the problem of addressing the needs of the uninsured, then ending ERISA preemption may be part of the cure.

But ERISA waivers are not likely to solve that problem. First, it is unlikely that any exemption Congress would grant from ERISA preemption would allow states to regulate all firms within their borders. Although many of the current beneficiaries of ERISA preemption are not large, multistate firms, some of the benefitted plans are. Those firms can persuasively argue that they would be especially burdened by the financial and administrative costs of complying with multiple and potentially conflicting state laws, and that their employees' health security would be unsettled if their benefits were to change with each relocation. They are likely to argue for a special exemption from any waiver for multistate firms. As the special exemption for large firms contained in the Clinton Health Plan suggests, it is unlikely that Congress would ignore the interests of large multistate firms.

Second, it is not clear that Congress would ever raise the barrier of ERISA preemption for all forms of regulation. Opponents of ERISA waivers could point persuasively to the prevalence of mandatory benefits, any-willing-provider, and other cost-imposing state laws. Self-funded plans contend that they have been particularly successful at cost containment, and they argue that part of that success is attributable to exemption from state insurance laws. Surely there would be strong opposition to waivers that would subject well-run plans to provider-inspired cost-imposing state laws.

In the long-run the return of large firms to state regulatory jurisdiction might reduce the propensity of states to enact such laws. In the short run, however, the costs could be substantial, and concern about such costs means that any exemption from ERISA would probably be fairly narrow. Indeed, Congress might make an exemption contingent on state enactment of a comprehensive health reform with program components that address both cost containment and the needs of the uninsured. This would require close federal oversight of a particular state plan in the context of each request for a waiver—whether by Congress itself, or by a federal administrative agency pursuant to Congress' directive. The latter approach would, of course, require Congress to spell out exactly what it considered to be the basic elements of comprehensive health care reform—a task Congress has so far failed to accomplish. It would also require ongoing monitoring to assure that, in light of the possibility of provider capture of the state regulatory process and the impact of state regulation on federal interests, the state program as implemented comports with federal criteria.

Indeed, due to the federal subsidization of employer-provided health care through the Internal Revenue Code and the federal commitment to health care for the elderly, state programs that affect health care costs have significant implications for the federal fisc. Close federal oversight of state programs exempted from preemption would be a reasonable response to the federal fiscal interest. And, of course, a state would have to return to Congress, or to the administrative agency entrusted with waiver authority, if it sought to change its plan after a waiver is granted—as Hawaii, which received an ERISA exemption for the health plan it enacted in 1974 but not for modifications to the plan enacted thereafter,[109] has learned.

ERISA waivers thus would not resolve the state autonomy problem but transform it; rather than displacing state regulation of employer-provided health insurance, the federal government might oversee it as a condition for the retrocession of federal power. Close federal oversight of state regulation is not unprecedented; in other areas, such as environmental law, state administrative authority is contingent on compliance with federal regulatory standards. The difficulty here is the absence of clear federal criteria for reviewing state plans. Standardless oversight is likely to be far more offensive to state prerogatives and to a functioning federalism than a relationship governed by federal statutory criteria. But Congress has so far been unable to formulate the criteria that would define the terms of comprehensive guarantees of access to quality health care.

Moreover, an ERISA waiver approach would require *two* sets of complex political processes: congressional willingness to grant such a waiver tailored to the protection of federal interests, and a state's willingness to formulate a comprehensive health reform plan. Thus far few states have shown an interest in comprehensive reform—although, in fairness, given the limitations posed by ERISA preemption, many states might reasonably have concluded that comprehensive reform is beyond their capacities and might not have bothered to try. Moreover, to the extent that a state plan entails the significant top–down redistribution necessary to provide coverage for the currently uninsured, external exit might become a more significant federalism-based constraint on state action. By according states greater regulatory authority and leading employers to focus more of their attention on state policy, reducing ERISA's preemptive effect might increase the states' capacity and the willingness to pursue cost-containment strategies. But given the ongoing constraints of limited state resources and interstate competition for business and taxpayers, prospects for state-level and state-financed initiatives to expand access to health insurance for the uninsured remain uncertain.

In any event, Congress has so far demonstrated greater interest in new substantive regulation of employment-based health insurance than in giving the states greater regulatory authority in this area by reducing the preemption barrier created by ERISA.

Substantive Federal Regulation of Employer-Provided Health Benefits

The other way of dealing with the dilemmas posed by ERISA preemption is substantive federal regulation of employer-provided health plans. This would eliminate the disparate treatment currently affecting self-funded and insured plans, but it would also mark a substantial departure from the long-standing federal policy, codified in the McCarran-Ferguson Act, of leaving insurance regulation to the states. Whether combining ERISA's preemption of state laws with substantive federal regulation of employee health plans would result in comprehensive health reform depends on a number of factors.

Much of the impetus for federal action has been to provide greater protection for the already insured. Initial federal actions in this area—the Health Insurance Portability and Accountability Act of 1996, (HIPAA)[110] the Mental Health Parity Act of 1996,[111] the Newborns' and Mothers' Health Protection Act,[112] the Women's Health and Cancer Rights Act of 1998 [113]—are in some sense consumer protection measures for health plan participants and beneficiaries, or for individuals covered under one plan who would like to switch to another. Many of these measures grew out of state-level initiatives that had been partially frustrated by the ability of self-funded plans to use ERISA to immunize themselves from state regulation.[114] HIPAA, in particular, provides for greater portability and and imposes limitations on the use of preexisting conditions. The more recent effort to enact a "patient protection" law also reflects a consumerist tilt. So far Congress has been less sensitive than the states to pressures from providers. This could change—legislation that would expand a patient's treatment choices could be characterized as both consumer protection and provider protection—once providers have a greater incentive to concentrate their lobbying energies on Congress. Still, large employers who have no option to exit from federal legislation are likely to be major players in federal health policy-making, as they were in shaping the contours of—and the legislative reaction to—the Clinton Health Plan. Indeed, large employers have played a significant role in the protracted congressional struggle over whether to enact a federal patients' "bill of rights."

Existing state health care and insurance regulations are, in part, a consequence of the incentives for consumer, payer and provider political participation created by current federal measures, like the McCarran-Ferguson Act and ERISA preemption, that have structured the distribution of policy-making responsibility between the federal government and the states. Once that structure is changed, as by substantive federal regulation of health plans, the politics of policy-making is likely to change as well. As a result, it is difficult to extrapolate from the present distribution of political influence across consumers, payers, and providers to a future in which the stakes might be quite different.

Even if federal consumer-protection regulation reduces the cost and, thus, increases the availability of insurance at the workplace, it is unlikely to lower costs enough to induce employers to pay a significant portion of the insurance premiums of all their low-wage workers. "HIPAA guarantees the opportunity to purchase insurance, and at least some of those purchasers will be pooled with others who would have had access to insurance without HIPAA. [But] HIPAA does not guarantee that insurance will be affordable."[115] Nor is federal insurance regulation likely to make the non-employer-paid portion of those premiums affordable to low-wage workers. Unless accompanied by subsidies for low-wage workers and the unemployed, expanded federal regulation of employment-based health insurance is unlikely to help most currently uninsured workers, let alone the uninsured who are also self-employed or unemployed (or not poor enough or old or disabled enough to qualify for public insurance programs). Nor would a greater federal substantive role in insurance regulation do much to help the states compel employers and employee health plans to contribute to meeting the costs of expanding access for the uninsured. The states would remain responsible for meeting the needs of the uninsured, but the federal government would have both the regulatory authority over employer-provided benefits and the greater resources needed to implement programs for the uninsured.

Greater federal regulation of employer-provided benefits coupled with limited federal support for redistributive public programs and the ongoing role of the federal tax expenditure for employer-based health care would represent an inversion of traditional academic arguments for the allocation of federal and state roles in social policy. The federal government would displace state regulation of workplaces, including small, locally-oriented firms, and supplant the states in that long-standing state bailiwick, insurance regulation. The federal government would be regulating what the states are capable of regulating but not undertaking the greater redistributive role for which the federal government is particularly suitable.

Conclusion

The states can address the central problems of health care reform only if they have the regulatory authority and the resources adequate to the task. Currently, ERISA constrains state regulatory authority. Due to ERISA, states have limited powers over the employer-provided health plans which are the principal source of privately-financed health insurance, and their traditional powers over insurance are undermined by the ability of employer-provided health plans to obtain internal exit from state insurance regulation. By affecting the incentives for participation in state policymaking, ERISA may also indirectly affect the propensity of states to adopt policies that drive up health care costs. Although *Travelers* and *De-Buono* appear to mark an end to the expansion of ERISA preemption, and to reaffirm the legitimacy of the traditional state authority to regulate health care and especially health care providers, ERISA preemption remains a serious obstacle for many reform strategies.

Even if ERISA preemption were constrained, traditional federalism concerns—limited and unequal state resources, political opposition from multistate actors to the burdens that would result from differing state regulations, and especially the constraint on state redistributive policies posed by the threat of external exit—would remain. States would be able to pursue cost-containment initiatives; but without substantial federal financial support, it is unlikely that state-level action alone can deal comprehensively with the problems of the uninsured. Only a combination of federal subsidies—that would enhance state resources and, by shifting financing to the federal level, mitigate the external exit constraint—and broad state policy-making authority can optimize the mix of federal and state roles in health reform.

Notes

1. 29 U.S.C. § 1001 et seq.
2. *Metropolitan Life Ins. Co. v Massachusetts*, 471 U.S. 724, 739 (1985).
3. *Travelers Insurance Co. v Cuomo*, 14 F.3d 708, 717 (2d Cir. 1993).
4. *Gregory v. Ashcroft*, 501 U.S. 452, 458 (1991).
5. Susan Rose-Ackerman, *Rethinking the Progressive Agenda* 165 (Free Press 1992).
6. See, e.g., Jerry L. Mashaw and Theodore R. Marmor, The Case for Federalism and Health Care Reform, 28 *Conn. L. Rev.* 115, 116–17 (1995).
7. Michael W. McConnell, Federalism: Evaluating the Founders' Design, 54 *U. Chi. L. Rev.* 1484, 1510 (1987).
8. 15 U.S.C. § 1011–1015.
9. See Len M. Nichols and Linda J. Blumberg, A Different Kind of 'New Federalism'? The Health Insurance Portability And Accountability Act of 1996, 17 *Health Aff.* 25, 30 (May/June 1998) (47 states passed some small group or individual market reforms between 1989 and 1996).
10. As Deborah Stone has pointed out, "the corollary of the exit threat in a federal system is the 'magnet fear.' States fear that by offering more generous benefits to the poor than neighboring states they will actually induce more poor people to move into the state." Deborah S. Stone, Why the States Can't Solve the Health Care Crisis, 9 *The American Prospect* 53, 59 (Spring 1992).
11. *Steward Machine Co. v. Davis*, 301 U.S. 548, 588 (1937).
12. See, e.g., Paul E. Peterson, *The Price of Federalism* 27–29 (The Brookings Institution 1995).

13. The National Labor Relations Act of 1935, 49 Stat. 449 (1935), codified as amended at 29 U.S.C. §§ 151–69.
14. 29 U.S.C. §§ 201 et seq (as amended).
15. The Labor Management Relations Act of 1947, 61 Stat. 136 (1947), codified as amended at 29 U.S.C. §§ 141–97.
16. Tabulations of the 2001 March Current Population Survey. Some employment–based health insurance is provided by federal, state, and local government employers. Three million Americans (1.19% of the population) received health insurance from the Department of Veterans Affairs or the Civilian Health and Medical Program of the Uniformed Services (CHAMPUS) health plans.
17. Id.
18. Medicaid is the informal name for the Grants to States for Medical Assistance Program. Medicaid provides medical assistance to the poor, disabled and aged, as well as minor dependent children and their parents. The states establish minimum eligibility and medical service standards that must be consistent with federal guidelines. 42 U.S.C. § 1396 et seq.
19. See Michael Sparer, Devolution of Power: An Interim Report Card, *Health Affairs* (vol. 17, no. 3, May/June 1998) 7, at 9.
20. However, there is some evidence that some people previously covered by employer-provided insurance are now switching to Medicaid so that the growth in Medicaid enrollment may not represent an increase in the total number of people insured but simply a shift in the source of insurance from private to public funds.
21. See Sparer, supra, at 10. See also Robert Pear, Florida Struggles to Lift Medicaid Burden, *The New York Times*, April 24, 1995, at A12; Penelope Lemov, The Medicaid Numbers Game, *Governing* (vol. 8, no. 5, May 1995) at 27.
22. Sparer, supra, at 9.
23. Id. at 11–12.
24. Taxpayers whose payments for medical expenses, including health insurance costs, exceed a certain threshold of their gross income and who itemize deductions may deduct the excess over that threshold from their taxable income, but this tax break benefits very few individual purchasers of health insurance.

    The tax treatment of health insurance premiums for the self-employed lies between the treatment of individual and employer contributions. The self-employed are permitted to deduct a portion of the cost of their health insurance premiums from their taxable income.
25. Sparer, supra, at 12.
26. Each level of government is responsible for regulating and financing the health insurance of its own employees (and their dependents). See United States General Accounting Office, *Employer-Based Health Plans: Issues Trends, and Challenges Posed by ERISA*, GAO/HEHS-95-167 (July 1995)(hereinafter "1995 GAO Report") at 7.
27. See John Sheils and Paul Hogan, Cost of Tax–Exempt Health Benefits in 1998, 18 *Health Affairs* 176–181 (Mar/Apr 1999) See generally Sherry Glied, *Revising the Tax Treatment of Employer-Provided Health Insurance* (American Enterprise Institute 1994).
28. 29 U.S.C. § 1002. Employee welfare benefit plans include plans maintained for the purpose of providing participants or their beneficiaries "through the purchase of insurance or otherwise" "medical, surgical, or hospital care benefits, or benefits in the event of sickness, accident, disability, death or unemployment, or vacation benefits, apprenticeship or other training programs, or day care centers, scholarship funds, or prepaid legal services."

29. 29 U.S.C. § 1003(a).
30. 29 U.S.C. § 1003(b).
31. 1995 GAO Report at 30–31. In addition, the 1986 Consolidated Omnibus Budget
    Reconciliation Act amended ERISA to add provisions requiring group health plans
    covering over 20 employees to continue health coverage for 18 to 36 months follow-
    ing a termination of employment and certain other conditions. 29 U.S.C. § 1161 et
    seq.
32. See Catherine L. Fisk, The Last Article About the Language of ERISA Preemption?
    A Case Study of the Failure of Textualism, 33 *Harv. J. Leg.* 35, 38 (1996).
33. 29 U.S.C. § 1144(a).
34. 29 U.S.C. § 1144(b)(2)(A).
35. Id. at § 1144(b)(2)(B).
36. *FMC Corp. v. Holliday*, 498 U.S. 52, 58 (1990).
37. *Shaw v. Delta Air Lines, Inc.*, 463 U.S. 85, 96–97 (1983).
38. Id. at 98.
39. *Agsalud v. Standard Oil Co. of California*, 454 U.S. 801 (1981), affirming 633 F.2d
    760 (9th Cir. 1980).
40. *Shaw v. Delta Air Lines, Inc.*, supra.
41. *District of Columbia v Greater Washington Board of Trade*, 506 U.S. 125 (1992).
42. *FMC Corp. v. Holliday*, 498 U.S. 52, 58–59 (1990).
43. *Pilot Life Insurance Co. v. Dedeaux*, 481 U.S. 41, 47 (1987); *Metropolitan Life In-
    surance Co. v Taylor*, 481 U.S. 58, 62 (1987).
44. *Ingersoll-Rand Company v. McClendon*, 498 U.S. 133 (1990).
45. See, e.g., *Corcoran v. United Healthcare* Inc., 965 F.2d 1321 (5th Cir. 1992); *Kuhl v.
    Lincoln Nat'l Healthplan*, 999 F.2d 298 (8th Cir. 1993); *Spain v. Aetna Life Ins. Co.,*
    11 F.3d 129 (9th Cir. 1993).
46. See, e.g., Karen A. Jordan, *Travelers Insurance*: New Support for the Argument to
    Restrain ERISA Pre-emption, 13 *Yale J. Reg.* 255, 267–68 (Winter 1996); Fisk,
    supra, 33 *Harv. J. Legis* at 59.
47. See, e.g., *Dukes v US Healthcare, Inc,* 57 F.3d 350 (5th Cir. 1995). See Mulcahy,
    Comment: The ERISA Preemption Question: Why Some HMO Members are Dying
    for Congress to Amend ERISA, 82 *Marq. L. Rev.* 877, 886–88 (Summer 1999).
48. See, e.g., *E-Systems, Inc. v. A.W. Pogue*, 929 F.2d 1100 (5th Cir. 1991) (Texas Ad-
    ministrative Services Tax Act preempted by ERISA).
49. 14 F.3d 708 (2d Cir. 1993).
50. Id. at 721.
51. *NYSA-ILA Med. & Clin. Serv. Fund v Axelrod*, 27 F.3d 823, 827 (2d Cir. 1994).
52. 514 U.S. 645 (1995).
53. Id. at 655.
54. Id.
55. Id.
56. Id. at 657.
57. Id. at 658.
58. Id. at 668.
59. See also *California Div. of Labor Standards Enforcement v Dillingham Constr., N.A.,
    Inc.*, 519 U.S. 316 (1997) (California law dealing with apprenticeship wages on pub-
    lic works projects not preempted by ERISA's regulation of apprenticeship programs
    because California law not limited to formally separate ERISA apprenticeship
    plans).
60. *Travelers*, supra, 514 U.S. at 659.

61. Id.
62. See *California Div. of Labor Standards Enforcement v Dillingham Constr., N.A., Inc.*, 519 U.S. 316, 335 (1997) (Scalia & Ginsburg, JJ, concurring) ("the broad definition of 'relate to' was a project doomed to failure" and has been effectively abandoned).
63. 520 U.S. 806 (1997).
64. *NYSA-ILA Med. & Clin. Serv. Fund v Axelrod*, 74 F.3d 28 (2d Cir. 1996) (preempting application of New York Health Facility Assessment tax to medical centers directly operated by a health plan).
65. 520 U.S. at 814.
66. Id. at 815.
67. See also *Thiokol Corp. v Roberts*, 76 F.3d 751 (6th Cir. 1996) (upholding the inclusion of payments to employee–benefit plans covered by ERISA in the tax base of business-paid compensation subject to Michigan's Single Business Tax).
68. 530 U.S. 211 (2000).
69. Id. at 229.
70. Id. at 228.
71. Id. at 236 ("federal fiduciary law applying a malpractice standard would seem to be a prescription for preemption of state malpractice law, since the new ERISA cause of action would cover the subject of a state-law malpractice claim").
72. See also *California Div. of Labor Standards Enforcement v Dillingham Constr., N.A., Inc.*, supra, 519 U.S. at 335 (Scalia & Ginsburg, JJ, concurring) (criticizing the Court "because it does obeisance to all our prior cases").
73. 514 U.S. at 668.
74. See, e.g, *Turner v Fallon Community Health Plan, Inc*, 127 F.3d 196 (1st Cir. 1997) (state law claims for failure to provide benefits still preempted notwithstanding *Travelers* and *DeBuono*); *Community Health Partners, Inc. v Commonwealth of Kentucky ex rel Nichols*, 14 F.Supp2d. 991, 998 (W.D. Ky. 1998) (finding it significant that the Supreme Court in *Travelers* and *DeBuono* "has not disavowed its earlier decisions").
75. 471 U.S. 724 (1985).
76. See *Metropolitan Life Ins. Co. v. Massachusetts*, 471 U.S. 724 (1985).
77. See, e.g., *Unum Life Insurance Company of America v Ward*, 526 U.S. 358 (1999) (California's "notice-prejudice" rule, under which an insurer remains liable for a claim filed after the contractual deadline unless the insurer suffers actual prejudice from the delay, is saved from ERISA preemption as a law regulating insurance).
78. See, e.g., *FMC Corp. v. Holliday*, 498 U.S. 52 (1990); *Shaw v. Delta Air Lines, Inc.*, 463 U.S. 85 (1983). See also *Unum Life Insurance Co. v Ward*, supra, 526 U.S. 358, 367 n.2 ("Self-insured ERISA plans . . . are generally sheltered from state insurance regulation." Insurance savings clause applies "[b]ecause this case does not involve a self-insured plan").
79. United States General Accounting Office, Health Insurance Regulation: Varying State Requirements Affect Costs of Insurance, GAO/HEHS 96–161 (August 1996) (hereinafter "1996 GAO Report").
80. 1995 GAO Report, supra, at 3 n.2
81. Stone, Why the States Can't Solve the Health Care Crisis, supra, at 57.
82. 1995 GAO Report, supra, at 2–3, 9–14; United States General Accounting Office, Employer-Based Managed Care Plan: ERISA's Effect on Remedies for Benefit Denials and Medical Malpractice, GAO/HEHS 98–154 (July 1998).
83. 1996 GAO Report, supra, at 5.
84. 1995 GAO Report, supra, at 9.

85. Jeffrey G. Lenhart, ERISA Preemption: The Effect of Stop–Loss Insurance on Self–Insured Health Plans, 14 *Va. Tax Rev.* 615, 625 (Winter 1995).

86. 1995 GAO Report, supra, at 8.

87. Id.

88. In addition, many self-funded plans contract with insurers or other third parties for administrative services.

89. See *American Medical Security, Inc. v Bartlett*, 111 F.3d 358, 365 (4th Cir. 1997) (Maryland law regulating stop–loss insurance policies issued to self–funded ERISA plans preempted); *Thompson v Talquin Bldg. Prods. Co.*, 928 F.2d 649 (4th Cir. 1991) (plan self–funded despite purchase of stop–loss insurance applicable to individual claims exceeding $25,000); *United Food & Comm. Workers & Employers Ariz. Health & Welfare Trust v. Pacyga*, 801 F.2d 1157 (9th Cir. 1986) (plan found to be self-funded despite stop–loss policy where policy proceeds were payable only to the plan, and not to health-plan beneficiaries); *Brown v Granatelli*, 897 F.2d 1351 (5th Cir. 1990) (mandatory health insurance benefits law inapplicable to stop–loss insurance). But see *Michigan United Food & Comm. Workers Union v Baerwaldt*, 767 F.2d 308 (6th Cir. 1985) (mandated benefits law applicable to stop–loss policy that provided benefits directly to ERISA participants after the stop–loss trigger point was reached). For a critical evaluation of the judicial treatment of stop–loss coverage, see Note, Stop–Loss Insurance, State Regulation and ERISA: Defining the Scope of Federal Preemption, 34 *Harv. J. Legis.* 233 (1997)

90. 1995 GAO Report at 8.

91. The only exception to this rule is ERISA's exemption from preemption for Hawaii's Prepaid Health Care Act. 29 U.S.C. § 1144 (b) (5) (A). Hawaii was the only state that had adopted an employer mandate prior to ERISA's enactment. The exemption, added to ERISA in 1983, however, only protects the Hawaiian Act as it stood on September 2, 1974, the date of ERISA's enactment. Any later amendments to the Hawaiian Act are subject to preemption. Id. at § 1144 (b) (5) (B) (ii).

92. See *District of Columbia v Greater Washington Board of Trade*, supra.

93. *Corporate Health Insurance Inc. v Texas Dep't of Insurance*, 215 F.3d 526 (5th Cir. 2000).

94. *Moran v Rush Prudential HMO, Inc.*, 230 F.3d 959 (7th Cir. 2000).

95. See id. at 970 (deemer clause inapplicable because the plan "is not a self-funded plan; it is an insured plan").

96. Cf. *Washington Physicians Service Ass'n v Gregoire*, 147 F.3d 1039 (9th Cir. 1998) (rejecting ERISA preemption claim against Washington State law that requires HMOs and health care service contractors to cover acupuncture, massage therapy, naturopathy, chiropractic services and other "alternative providers" but noting that the statute does not apply to self-funded plans or to health carriers under contract to perform administrative services for self-funded plans).

97. *Travelers*, supra, 514 U.S. at 668. See also *DeBuono*, supra, 520 U.S. at 816.

98. 29 U.S.C. § 1144 (b) (5) (B) (i).

99. See Jesselyn Alicia Brown, ERISA and State Health Care Reform: Roadblock or Scapegoat?, 13 *Yale L. & Pol. Rev.* 339, 356 n.104 (1995) (citing cases).

100. See id. at 361. Presumably, universal health care plans funded by other general taxes, such as taxes on personal incomes or sales, would not be subject to challenge under ERISA.

101. See Sparer, supra, at 13 ("the main limitation" on state insurance reforms designed to make insurance more available to individuals and employees of small firms was ERISA).

102. Id. (noting press stories "profiling healthy young males who had received rate in-

creases of 100 percent (or more)" following Kentucky's adoption of a package of insurance reforms in July 1995).
103. See *Brown*, supra, at 372.
104. Id.
105. Id.
106. 1995 GAO Report, supra, at 56–61.
107. Most courts have found that any-willing-provider laws "relate to" ERISA plans by affecting plan benefits, but then disagree as to whether such laws are saved by the "insurance savings" clause. Compare *CIGNA Healthplan of Louisiana, Inc v State*, 82 F.3d 642 (5th Cir. 1996) (Louisiana law which requires that all licensed health providers who agree to terms of preferred-provider contracts must be accepted as providers in preferred-provider organizations (PPOs)"relates to" ERISA plans and is not saved from preemption from the insurance savings clause since its application is not limited to entities in the business of insurance) *Texas Pharmacy Ass'n v Prudential Ins. Co.*, 105 F.3d 1035 (5th Cir. 1997) (Texas law requiring health insurers or managed care plans to contract with any willing provider of pharmacy services "relates to" ERISA plans; is not "saved" by insurance savings clause since statute applies to entities other than insurers); *with Community Health Partners, Inc v. Commonwealth of Kentucky ex rel Nichols*, 14 F.Supp.2d 991 (W.D. Ky 1998) (any willing provider law "relates to" ERISA plans but is saved by insurance savings clause); *Stuart Circle Hosp. Corp. v Aetna Health Management*, 995 F.2d 500 (4th Cir. 1993). To the extent that any willing provider laws are saved by the "savings" clause, they are likely to be inapplicable to self–funded plans. Cf. *Washington Physicians Service Ass'n v Gregoire*, 147 F.3d 1039 (9th Cir. 1998) (rejecting ERISA preemption claim against Washington State law that requires HMOs and health care service contractors to cover acupuncture, massage therapy, naturopathy, chiropractic services and other "alternative providers" but noting that the statute does not apply to self–funded plans or to health carriers under contract to perform administrative services for self-funded plans).

See also *American Drug Stores, Inc. v Harvard Pilgrim Health Care, Inc.*, 973 F. Supp. 60 (D. Mass, 1997) (Massachusetts law requiring that access to pharmacy networks be open to all licensed providers does not "relate to" ERISA plans since the law regulates pharmacy networks, not health plans).
108. Rose-Ackerman, supra, at 169.
109. 29 U.S.C. § 1144 (b) (5).
110. Pub. L. 104–191, 110 Stat. 1936.
111. Pub. L. 104–204, 110 Stat. 2944.
112. Pub. L. 104–204, 110 Stat. 2935.
113. Pub. L. 105–340, 112 Stat. 3191.
114. See Nichols and Blumberg, supra.
115. Id. at 34.

4

THE MANAGEMENT OF CONFLICT OVER HEALTH INSURANCE COVERAGE

Gerard F. Anderson and Mark A. Hall

Conflicts over health insurance coverage are inevitable. Initially, there are conflicts over what range of services to include in the benefits package. Then there will be conflicts over the application of the benefits package to specific individuals. Since both types of conflict are likely to involve people with serious medical problems, it is not surprising that they can become very intense.

Though the philosophic, religious, social, and moral issues that surround many of the debates over what to include in health insurance benefits can't be easily settled,[1] it may be possible to develop a framework for resolving specific disputes over whether promised benefits will be covered in particular cases. This chapter begins with a brief overview of some of the broad issues that have influenced coverage determinations for both public and private insurers during the past several decades. We then focus on the litigation that has occurred when public and private insurers have interpreted coverage language to deny services to a specific individual, and we examine alternative methods to minimize the conflict between individuals and insurers. Drawing from our statistical analysis of reported court decisions, we evaluate various proposals for altering how courts resolve these disputes.

Defining benefits packages

Conflicts over insurance coverage usually begin when a public or private insurer seeks to design a benefits package. The design has three components: specification of covered categories of service, appropriateness criteria applied to these categories, and financial limitations. All three are contentious, but the second issue has generated the most conflict. Before exploring the debate over appropriateness criteria, however, it is necessary to explain how typical benefits packages are defined.[2]

Coverage categories are typically broad and are usually defined by types of institutions and by professional licensure status. The Health Security Act proposed by President Clinton,[3] for example, mandated that health plans cover "hospital inpatient services, services of physicians and other health care professionals, and outpatient diagnostic and laboratory services." Coverage categories can also be treatment- and condition-specific. The Clinton plan, excluded cosmetic orthodontia, cosmetic surgery, in vitro fertilization and other services. Preventive services were limited to those specifically mentioned and certain services—such as hospice care or home health visits—were limited by the number of days or visits that would be covered. These coverage categories were patterned after the benefit categories typically adopted by most large employers.

Whether to include or exclude broad categories of services is often controversial. Pressure from individuals with compelling medical problems (often encouraged by provider groups with a financial interest) makes it difficult for insurers or employers to exclude broad service categories. It is hard to argue that a broad category of service or type of medical provider offers no value to the patient. There are often concerns, however, about how much the service will cost and whether it is necessary to insure those costs.

These debates occur in both the public and private sectors. In the public sector, for example, it is often suggested that Medicare should cover long-term care and prescription drugs as part of its benefits package. Each time the government examines the various options for financing these services, however, cost considerations become paramount and comprehensive expansion of these benefits is stymied.[4] A similar type of debate has occurred at the state level. During the 1970s and 1980s, many states mandated that all private insurers cover certain services in their basic benefits package that were considered nonessential by employers and insurers. In response to employers' and insurers' complaints that state legislative mandates were forcing them to offer too many expensive and undesired categories of service, some states allowed insurers to offer *bare-bones* insurance to individual and small-group purchasers. This stripped-down insurance has been a failure in the marketplace because, when given a choice of plans, most consumers perceive these bare-bones policies as offering too little protection.[5] Finding the correct balance between medical needs and financial concerns is thus a difficult issue for both the public and the private sectors.

In an attempt to make the design of benefit categories more scientific, some commentators have, advocated developing practice guidelines to define benefits packages.[6] The precision of practice guidelines allows them to be targeted to the most compelling cases. Practice guidelines specify for each covered medical intervention the particular clinical conditions and indicators for which the intervention is appropriate. The difficulty with using practice guidelines to limit reimbursement is that, no matter how attractive they might be in theory, they are not yet available in sufficient numbers for practical implementation, and there is serious doubt that acceptable guidelines will ever be sufficiently detailed and comprehensive to serve as the primary basis for designing insurance coverage. Despite the commendable efforts of the Agency for Health Care Policy and Research and of various medical professional societies, we are still far from covering all major areas of medical practice with detailed guidelines. This is a seemingly impossible task, particularly considering that this encyclopedic effort would have to be continually updated to reflect changes in knowledge, technology, and disease patterns.

Appropriateness criteria

The approach to defining a benefits package that is now standard in the industry relies on broad categories of service, but it provides much greater specificity about the criteria and processes for determining the appropriateness of individual items of treatment within each category. Unlike the practice guidelines model, this approach does not necessarily make specific appropriateness determinations as part of the benefits package itself. Rather, particular coverage decisions are made by applying general appropriateness criteria to individual cases. These determinations can be made either by treating physicians or by various committee and review processes.

How appropriateness criteria are defined and interpreted has evolved considerably during the past 30 years.[7] At one time, most public and private insurers covered all care ordered by a physician within defined monetary and service limits. However, in the mid 1960s, insurers began to question physicians' decisions to order certain tests or procedures. For example, insurers balked at paying for lengthy hospital stays for patients convalescing from minor injuries or trying to lose weight. Because insurance policies were generally written to provide all services ordered by a physician, the insurer usually lost in court when the coverage denial was litigated.[8]

By the late 1960s and early 1970s, governments, corporations, unions and insurers had become concerned about rising health care costs. One potential method of cost containment is to require that care be *medically necessary*. Definitions of what is medically necessary have evolved over time. Even today, it is difficult to give a single definition that everyone accepts.[9] In general, the term *necessary* is not intended to connote a strict sense of life-or-limb urgency but instead means something like acceptable or appropriate. The stress on *medical* requires that the condition can be classified as an illness or injury that is addressed with a diagnostic or therapeutic service within generally accepted professional standards.[10] These conventional interpretations do not allow insurers to question the doctor's assessment of appropriateness or to set limits on which, among various appropriate treatments, is the most cost effective.

By the early 1970s academicians were publishing studies suggesting that we know very little about the appropriate use of many, if not most, medical treatments. There seemed to be no good justification for the considerable geographic variation in utilization rates for certain procedures.[11] At the same time, the Food and Drug Administration, National Institutes for Health and other government agencies were publishing studies showing that certain procedures in use were clearly not appropriate. The Food and Drug Administration, for example, issued regulations that laetrile and certain "immuno-augmentative" treatments were not "safe and efficacious" and therefore were not to be performed in the United States.[12] However, when private insurers tried to use these government findings to deny coverage to insured patients receiving care in Mexican clinics, their denials were sometimes overturned in court and they were ordered to pay.[13]

Responding to these judicial decisions, some insurers added two new contractual provisions to give them more authority to deny claims that they believed represented inappropriate, unnecessary, or perhaps even dangerous medical care. First, they specified that medical necessity is to be determined by the insurer, not the practicing physician. The second change was to exclude payment for *experimental* or *investigational* procedures. These exclusions responded to the concern that most medical procedures are adopted without rigorous testing and are therefore of unproven clinical value. By withholding coverage until it is better known how actual health outcomes vary according to patients' clinical conditions and different treatment regimens, it may be possible to prevent the adoption of ineffective treatments or ineffective applications of beneficial treatments.

Insurers have adopted a variety of criteria to define what is *non-experimental.* These criteria include regulatory approval, independent scientific specification of known risks and benefits, demonstration through health services research of a positive effect on outcomes, outcomes that are at least as favorable as those from alternative treatments, and favorable results that can be obtained in nonideal situations or everyday medical practice outside the research setting. However, precise definitions for each of these terms is difficult.[14]

To assess medical appropriateness under these general concepts, insurers next developed a process, known as utilization review, for reviewing individual claims. The federal government incorporated utilization review into the Medicare program with the introduction of Professional Standards Review Organizations (PSROs) in the mid 1970s, later modified to become Peer Review Organizations (PROs) in 1983. Both programs used retrospective utilization review to assess the appropriateness of medical care delivered to Medicare patients. By the mid-

1980s, most large insurers and self-insured corporations were instituting their own utilization review programs. A fundamental difference between the public and the private programs, however, was that the latter began to review many treatment decisions on a prospective or concurrent basis. The public sector continued to perform retrospective claims review, while most private insurers required expensive treatment decisions to be submitted for prior authorization or continuing review during treatment. This was done not only to better control costs, but also to avoid the perceived unfairness to a patient who accepts treatment relying on his physician's advice, and learns only later that insurance will not pay.

Insurers' success in court did not improve markedly as a result of these changes. For example, the *experimental* exclusions have been repeatedly litigated in a series of highly contentious cases over whether "autologous bone marrow transplants" are appropriate treatment for cancer and other life-threatening illnesses. In *Bradley v. Empire Blue Cross & Blue Shield*,[15] for instance, the court ordered an insurer to cover ABMT treatment for an AIDS patient despite evidence that his physician was the only one in the country who had ever used the treatment in this fashion and despite the patient's having signed an informed consent form that emphasized the experimental nature of the treatment.

Several thoughtful academic proposals suggest better ways to define appropriateness criteria. Brook and Hadorn propose a spectrum of assessment levels such as essential, appropriate, equivocal, and inappropriate, and defining the basic package as either all-essential care or all-essential-and-appropriate care.[16] Kalb would distinguish among safe, effective and cost-effective, and limit basic coverage to cost-effective.[17] Eddy calls for limiting coverage to treatment whose outcomes are documented through well-controlled, peer-reviewed studies to be cost effective compared to its alternatives.[18] Havighurst has articulated ideas similar to all of these in extensive model contract language.[19] Our own prior work, along with Earl Steinberg, offers the most complex scheme for defining appropriateness.[20] We have sketched a taxonomy that specifies hierarchical categories of medical technology assessment relating to each of five dimensions: (1) safety, (2) effectiveness, (3) cost, (4) level of confidence in empirical findings, and (5) the outcomes measures to be used in evaluating each of these. Using this scheme, one might limit the benefits package, for instance, to demonstrably safe treatments that are at least as effective as the available alternatives, with effectiveness defined in terms of outcomes measures such as quality-adjusted life years (QALYs), and costing no more than $50,000 per QALY gained. Ellman and Hall take a step further by outlining how subscribers could specify budgets for designated categories of service by selecting from a menu of cost-effectiveness options when they enroll.[21] Returning to the traditional approach, Rosenbaum and Frankford propose that treating physicians' judgment should govern, when consistent with locally prevailing standards of care.[22]

Individual coverage disputes

To investigate how these and other innovations might fare in the courts, we conducted a statistical analysis of all reported court decisions of potential relevance
since 1960. The following section describes this study and reports the findings
that bear on whether changes in the structure and definition of insurance coverage
will likely alter the way courts decide these disputes. Because we conclude that
these changes in substantive coverage terms alone will not have much effect, we
go on to outline changes in the dispute resolution process that are likely to have
greater impact. We conclude with an evaluation, drawn from this same study, of
the effectiveness of the current litigation process in protecting consumers.

The methodology of our statistical study is set forth in detail elsewhere.[23]
Briefly, we compiled a list of all published federal and state court decisions from
January 1960 to June 1994 involving health-insurance coverage disputes. We included all forms of standard health insurance, both public and private, such as
Medicare and Medicaid, the Federal Employees Health Benefit Program and
CHAMPUS, and self-insured employers. For a case to be included in this study,
the court's basis for decision had to turn on the appropriateness of the treatment
rather than on a procedural technicality or some other legal defect in the case. We
defined appropriateness disputes to include questions of whether the treatment
was *medically necessary, experimental, investigational, custodial* or other similar
terms. Where exclusions were more specific, we made a judgment about whether
the exclusion was possibly related to the appropriateness or experimental status of
the treatment, such as *no coverage for solid organ transplants* or *in vitro fertilization is not covered*. Examples of exclusions that are clearly not related to medical
appropriateness are those that merely define the type of insurance, such as exclusions of mental health or dental services. These selection criteria resulted in a
sample of 203 cases.

We then analyzed these cases using content analysis, a research technique
widely used in the social sciences that allows the objective and quantitative study
of qualitative data.[24] Three readers (two law students and a lawyer in medical
school) were trained to code these cases following a code book we developed
consisting of 37 questions, classified into the following general categories: case
description (date, court, type of insurance, outcome); legal and process factors
(source of law, contract language, type of insurer review); patient/treatment factors (patient demographics, type of treatment, seriousness of condition, results of
treatment); evidence of treatment effectiveness (sources of assessments, numbers
of expert witnesses, objections to assessments, process of review); and the court's
analysis (whether various factors appeared from the written decision to influence
the court; the most important factors as expressed in the courts' decisions).[25]

These coding data were analyzed, first using bivariate analysis (comparing one factor to only one other), and then using multivariate analysis. Throughout the analysis, the primary dependent variable (the factor we were trying to predict) was the outcome of the case, defined as coverage upheld or coverage denied.[26] There were 185 cases with a definitive outcome. For purposes of analysis and interpretation, we group our findings into three sets of issues: (*1*) appropriateness evidence and substantive contract factors; (*2*) legal and procedural contract factors; and (*3*) consumer protection.

Appropriateness Evidence

The dominant impression from our findings is that systematic assessments of medical appropriateness have little or no influence on the courts, nor does the language of the substantive criteria for insurance coverage contained in the contract or governing statute. We measured whether the case outcome differed according to the insurer's reliance on various sources of evidence about the appropriateness of the treatment in question. An identifiable assessment source existed in 124 of the total 203 cases.[27] We compared the 79 cases without any assessments with cases where the insurer relied on assessments from the following three categories of sources: (*1*) public sector agencies (Food and Drug Administration, National Institutes of Health, Agency for Health Care Policy and Research, Office of Technology Assessment, etc.); (*2*) private sector assessments (American Medical Association, RAND Corporation, academic institutions, etc.); and (*3*) assessments conducted internally by the insurer.[28] We found that the outcome of the cases was virtually identical regardless of the sector from which the assessment came or even whether there was any assessment source at all. In all events, the patient won about 50% to 60% of the time.

Whether an assessment was formal or informal came closer to having a statistically significant effect. A formal assessment was defined as any assessment by an external source (private or public sector) and any internal insurer's assessment that relied on a national expert or an extensive literature review, in contrast with informal assessments, which consisted of the ad hoc judgment of the medical director, a local expert, or a small-scale literature review. Patients won more often under informal assessments (57% vs. 36%), but this difference did not quite meet standard tests for statistical significance ($p = 0.073$).[29]

We attempted to analyze the types of objections to particular assessments that courts found convincing or unconvincing, but there were too few of each type to provide meaningful statistical analysis. The types of objections made most frequently were classified as: assessment did not consider enough sources of information, or information was a poor fit with the specific facts of the case (43 times); personnel involved in review were not sufficiently expert or knowledgeable (15 times); assessment relied on a biased source of information based on financial conflict of interest (14 times); and information in assessment was outdated (10 times).

We also reviewed a selection of these cases to determine in the courts' own words why formal assessments are not always convincing. This perspective provides a more qualitative insight into the quantitative findings described so far. Whereas the quantitative findings help us understand overall what in general is happening, a qualitative reading of the cases amplifies this understanding by revealing why or how these results obtain in the particular circumstances of individual cases.

We begin with the cases in which courts ordered coverage of treatments that were not approved by the FDA. In *Wilson v. Travelers* (1980),[30] a case involving laetrile, the court reasoned that "[t]he contract could have precluded payment for illegal drugs, experimental drugs or provided that all drugs must have been declared safe and effective by the FDA before they would be covered expenses under the contract. It did not do so." Another court expressed the concern that, for Medicare to make FDA assessments definitive of coverage would place too much of a drag on medical advances.[31] And another, more recent decision, ruled that an insurer had not clearly enough excluded payment for unapproved (*off-label*) uses of FDA-approved drugs.[32]

A review of the court decisions involving guidelines of external bodies—e.g., advisory groups such as the NIH and the AMA—suggests additional concerns. One series of cases involving liver transplants refuses to allow insurers to adopt external assessments, even when the contract specifies the particular source. These courts hold that it is unfair for insurers to bind patients to practice guidelines that are not available for them to inspect at the time they subscribe,[33] or that, for reasons related to government powers over public insurance, it is unlawful to effectively delegate authority to private third parties.[34] Other courts have ruled that private insurers may not rely on Medicare coverage policies to deny liver transplants where this source is not stated to be binding in the insurance contract.[35]

Still other courts held that private insurers may rely on various governmental assessments, especially where the specific source is stated as binding in the contract. Several courts have ruled that private insurers can rely on Medicare coverage rules, FDA regulations, or NIH consensus statements to deny coverage for autologous bone marrow transplants (ABMT).[36] Others have upheld reliance on private sector sources such as a prestigious medical school[37] or professional societies[38] to deny coverage for a variety of treatments. These courts did not find convincing the reasoning in cases discussed above that relying on rules developed by external authorities denies patients their right to litigate their case.[39]

Few cases reject independent assessments of medical appropriateness based on how the assessment was performed or worded. Most of the decisions that have done so come from a recent flurry of cases involving ABMT. One court refused to honor an assessment of ABMT by the American Medical Association and the American College of Physicians.[40] The court was concerned that the report was five years old, that it did not clearly resolve the controversy, and that these sources had issued contradictory statements. More typical, though, is Leonhardt v. Holden Business Forms,[41] in which the third-party administrator for Holden Business forms "relied on information from the American Cancer Society, . . . , and the American Society of Clinical Oncology" in order to determine that the use of ABMT was experimental. The court rejected these sources of evidence, not because of how these external agencies conducted their assessments, but because the language of the academic reports and guidelines used different terminology to express their conclusions than the exact terms in the insurance contract (e.g., *investigational* rather than *experimental*).

Equally revealing is the finding that the outcome of these cases did not differ dramatically depending on whether the insurance contract, statute, or regulation used general coverage language such as *medically necessary* or *experimental*, or instead specifically excluded the treatment in question. Insurers won somewhat more often when exclusions were specific (52% vs. 43%), but not enough to be statistically significant (p = 0.412). This is surprising since courts so frequently fault insurers for not making their coverage exclusions more explicit. When insurers attempt to correct this defect, they are criticized for making the exclusion too narrow or technical. A leading example is the attempt to deny coverage for autologous bone marrow transplant (ABMT) to treat breast cancer. Specific exclusions to this effect have been held not to apply to newer cases that use a modified technique known as *peripheral stem cell rescue,* because the specific exclusion failed to anticipate and specify this newer approach.[42]

The one finding that mostly strongly suggests that courts are sensitive to evidence of the effectiveness of treatment comes from coding cases (mostly involving retrospective review) for whether the treatment in question appeared to have its intended effect in the particular case. Patients for whom the treatment actually worked were twice as likely to prevail. This difference was statistically significant in one multiple regression model (p = 0.02) and close to significant in a second model (p = 0.06). This finding is troubling for the health services research community because it suggests, in contrast with the prior findings, that courts are more influenced by what they see in the individual medical case before them than by more rigorously conducted studies measuring effects in a large number of cases.

Procedural Factors

These findings suggest that changes in the *substantive* wording of coverage terminology and in the source of appropriateness evidence are not likely to greatly effect the way that health insurance coverage disputes are decided in court. We have hypothesized in earlier work that *procedural* changes in the mechanisms for making coverage determinations and resolving coverage disputes are likely to have greater impact.[43] Accordingly, we and others have suggested alternatives to judicial resolution of individual coverage disputes and have articulated the practical and normative reasons for taking these decision-making processes out of the courts.[44] Specific proposals include grievance committees staffed by other patients and doctors in the same insurance plan (as is common in HMOs), or more formal modes of arbitration similar to those sponsored by the American Arbitration Association and used by HMOs to resolve malpractice disputes.

These proposals have been widely influential. Over half the states have adopted requirements that HMOs and other insurers provide an appeal mechanism whereby members can obtain independent, external review of coverage denials expeditiously.[45] Similar requirements apply to Medicare HMOs,[46] and are a major component of managed care *patient protection* legislation being debated in Congress.[47]

Independent, external review still allows some judicial oversight, albeit limited to ensuring that basic due process protections are afforded and that decisions are minimally rational and supported by credible evidence. This diminishes the authority of the courts by restricting their scrutiny to something akin to an *arbitrary and capricious* standard of judicial review, under which the judge must honor the prior decision even if she disagrees with it, so long as the decision has some rational basis in the existing record.[48] These are concepts taken from administrative law governing government agencies.

Another critical advantage of administrative review is relative speed and economy. Few patients can afford the costs and time entailed in litigating coverage denials. Grievance and appeal mechanisms at the plan level can and should be structured to provide assistance to patients in presenting and arguing their cases without great expense or delay.[49]

A number of our empirical findings shed light on how these innovations are likely to affect judicial resolution of coverage disputes. Most intriguing is the finding that insurers are much more likely to prevail in federal appeals court than in all others (61% vs. 37% in bivariate analysis; three times more likely in multiple regression analysis). One might speculate that this is because federal courts resolve Medicare disputes and those that arise under ERISA,[50] but multiple regression analysis revealed that the federal appeals effect is independent of these other two factors.[51] One possible reason for insurers' greater success in federal appeals courts is simply that insurers were appellees in 66% of the federal appeals cases but in only 45% of the state appeals cases. This alone could account for the federal appeals effect since, all other things being equal, appeals courts are more likely to affirm than to reverse a trial court, on account of the deference that is given to fact-findings and procedural rulings. We do not know why patients make up more of the appellants in federal court.

Another possible reason for different results in different courts is that appeals courts may be less swayed by sympathy for the plight of seriously ill patients. Unlike trial courts, they do not see the patient in person because they do not receive live testimony. To see if this speculation is plausible, we measured the effect of a number of possible sympathy factors across all the courts. In general, we found that *sympathy factors* had less effect on outcome than might have been expected. Factors such as the patient's age, condition, and gender did not consistently have a statistically significant effect on the outcome. Indeed, we found the apparent anomaly that patients who are likely to die prevail significantly less often that those with some chance of death (51% vs. 79%; p = 0.004).

Another possibility is that federal appeals courts apply a more lenient standard of review. However, we coded the cases specifically for the declared or apparent standard of review and found virtually no difference in the outcome (55% vs. 59% patient wins) when courts employed arbitrary and capricious rather than de novo review.

We also explored variations in contractual and statutory language that affect the authority and process for making coverage determinations. Most striking is the finding that insurers do better in court when the governing language gives them discretion to determine medical appropriateness and declares their decisions to be binding. This is intended to counter the historical tendency to defer to the treating physician. In such cases, insurers prevailed much more often than when they were not explicitly given discretion (67% vs. 20%; p = 0.000). This is because language of this nature reverses the presumption that usually applies in insurance cases that ambiguities are to be construed in favor of the patient. Insurer discretion to interpret coverage language in effect means that ambiguities are construed in favor of the insurer.[52]

Another area of relevant inquiry is the amount and quality of procedural protection that insurers give patients before a coverage denial is challenged in court. We did not extensively code for these procedural protections. However, we made a few noteworthy observations. We failed to find that providing patients with a grievance procedure, arbitration, or a formal hearing made a statistically significant difference in who wins in court, even though there were 49 such cases found. (However, we were unable to control for any possible selection effect that formal procedings might have on patients' decisions about which cases to pursue in court.) We also found nearly identical case outcomes when insurer review was conducted retrospectively as when it was prospective or concurrent to treatment. Nevertheless, one indication that courts may be impressed with ample procedural protections is insurers' high success rate in disputes arising from health insurance for federal government employees. In such cases, which follow an elaborate set of administrative procedures, courts found in favor of insurers much more often (69%) than under other types of public (30%) or private (46%) insurance.

It appears, then, that alterations in the procedural aspects of making coverage decisions and the forum for resolving disputes are likely to have greater impact on courts than are the more substantive changes described earlier. What remains to be seen is whether the resulting legal protections are sufficient to safeguard consumers' interests and to strike appropriate balances between costs and benefits.

Consumer Protection

A number of our findings bear on consumer protection issues.[53] The first finding of interest is simply how few cases we located. Over a period of 34 years, we found only 203 relevant, published decisions from all federal and state jurisdictions, encompassing both public and private health insurance. Partly, this was due to our criteria for relevance. Several hundred insurance coverage disputes cases were excluded because they did not involve a question of medical appropriateness or they turned on purely jurisdictional issues. Nevertheless, the relative paucity of cases suggests that a great many coverage disputes do not go through litigation and that the vast bulk of coverage decisions are never challenged. Our study looks only at the tip of an iceberg; we were unable to gain any knowledge of what occurs below the visible surface of reported decisions.

We can speculate about reasons that coverage denials do not result in reported judicial decisions. A good number of these decisions may be resolved amicably at the plan level. Decisions that are litigated may be settled before trial, or a trial decision may not be appealed, which in the state courts almost always results in no reported decision. It is also likely, however, that patients do not pursue coverage disputes into court because of the time and expense involved.[54] This is suggested by our finding that the median cost of treatment in reported decisions (unadjusted for inflation) is between $10,000 and $50,000, and the mean cost is between approximately $50,000 and $100,000.[55] It is also suggested by the finding that cases took about two-and-a-half years on average to reach final decision. One-quarter of the cases took four years or more, and 15% took five years or more.

On the other hand, we found a dramatic increase in the number of cases being litigated to a reported decision in recent years: 5 in the 1960s, 36 in the 1970s, 71 in the 1980s, and 90 from 1990 to June 1994. Partly, this increase is an artifact of how judicial decisions are reported in federal versus state courts. The 1980s and 1990s saw a marked shift from state to federal courts as a consequence of ERISA preemption,[56] and in federal courts trial decisions are reported much more often than in state courts. But this jurisdictional shift does not appear to fully account for the recent dramatic increase in the number of reported cases. The increase began about ten years after ERISA was enacted and has produced more appellate decisions than previously existed in state appeals courts. Thus, our impression is that health insurance litigation is on the rise. The most obvious explanation is that, with the shift to prospective review and the focus on expensive treatment in life-threatening situations, the stakes are now much higher than before.

An equally dramatic finding is the near absence of decisions arising from capitated settings. We attempted in several ways to identify cases that involve HMO insurance, but could locate only six of them. Several explanations are possible. First, it is not always possible to tell from the reported decision the precise structure of the insurance. Second, there is a time lag of several years between treatment denial and ultimate judicial decision, so our sample reflects mostly cases from the 1980s, when managed care was less prevalent.

A third explanation for the low number of reported opinions involving HMOs raises concerns, however, about consumer protection. Capitated payment settings such as HMOs may be less likely to produce coverage disputes, even though they may be more likely to deny treatment, because treating physicians play a larger role in making coverage decisions. Traditional indemnity insurance requires a third-party medical director with the insurance company to overrule the treating physician's recommendation. HMOs and other forms of managed care, in contrast, use professional and financial incentives to motivate physicians not to make unnecessarily costly treatment recommendations in the first place, and informed consent law presently does not require disclosure of these nontreatment decisions.[57] An absence of patient knowledge that potentially beneficial care is being foregone could easily account for the paucity of coverage disputes arising from managed-care settings. Yet, HMOs are the settings that provide the most procedural protections once a dispute is identified.[58] The paucity of HMO litigation could also reflect consumer satisfaction with these plan-level protections.

When disputes do reach the courts, the history of dispute resolution to date suggests that courts are fairly sympathetic to patients' perspectives. Patients won 57% of the reported decisions we studied, and courts have resisted contractual innovations intended to improve insurers' chance of success. The alternative dispute resolution proposals are likely to lessen the number and scope of conflicts between insurers and individuals. However, conflict will still arise, and the life and death stakes for some patients will ensure that they will use every avenue to obtain coverage, including the courts.

Conclusion

Whether courts properly resolve conflicts over health insurance coverage depends on one's point of view. The conflict in public policy is not simply between the economic interests of insurers and the medical interests of patients. The conflict might be more accurately stated as within ourselves. We are each of two minds on mixed questions of costs and benefits. When we purchase insurance, we want to economize; when we are sick and have insurance, we do not. Insurers tend to enforce the first perspective, while courts tend to enforce the second. There is no conclusive way to resolve this conflict in personal values that are held at two distinct points in time. Because legal conflicts mirror social conflicts, insurance coverage disputes will not abate until we resolve among ourselves the proper role of cost and effectiveness considerations at the point of treatment decision making.

Notes

1. For example, including abortion or family planning in a benefits package has been the subject of intense public policy debate within the federal and state legislatures for years.
2. Space does not permit us to explore the issues involving financial limitations. Briefly, these include the establishment of rules for copayments and deductibles, or maximum expenditure levels per year or over a lifetime. In recent years, financial limitations also include methods for paying providers such as capitation, DRGs, RBRVS, and discounted fee schedules. Insurers that are willing to pay rates that few, if any, providers are willing to accept are using payment policy as a form of coverage limitation.
3. H.R. 3600, S. 1757, *Congressional Record* 139, S16788, November 20, 1993.
4. A prime example is the enactment and very quick subsequent repeal of the Medicare Catastrophic Coverage Act of 1988. Although its coverage benefits were widely popular at the time of enactment, it proved hugely unpopular with wealthier seniors who were required to bear the brunt of the costs.
5. G. Borzo, 1993. Bare-bones Insurance off to Slow Start. *Am. Med. News* 15 February; 3.
6. C. Havighurst, 1990. Practice Guidelines for Medical Care: The Policy Rationale. *Saint Louis U. L. J.* 34:777, 796–97; D. Hadorn, 1992. Necessary Care Guidelines. In: *Basic Benefits and Clinical Guidelines*, Hadorn D. ed. Boulder, CO: Westview Press.
7. The following summary is adapted from Mark A. Hall and Gerard F. Anderson, Health Insurers' Assessment of Medical Necessity, 140 *U. Pa. L. Rev.* 1637 (1992).
8. Detailed citations and discussion of these cases can be found in Hall and Anderson, supra note 6.
9. See generally W.K. Mariner, Patients' rights after health reform: Who decides what is medically necessary? *Health Law and Ethics* 1994; 84(9): 1515–1520; Linda A. Bergthold, Medical Necessity: Do We Need It?, 14(4) *Health Aff.* 180 (Winter 1995).
10. John L. Colley M.D., in Medical Necessity: Proceedings of a Symposium on Policy Issues. Implementation Challenges and Tough Choice, April 28, 1995, Washington DC, p. 9.
11. E.g., John E. Wennberg et al., Are Hospital Services Rationed in New Haven or Over-Utilised in Boston?, *Lancet*, May 23, 1987, at 1185.
12. Theses regulations are discussed, among other places, in *Dallis v. Aetna Life Ins. Co.*, 768 F.2d 1303 (11th Cir. 1985) and *Shumake v. Travelers Ins. Co.*, 383 N.W.2d 259 (Mich. App. 1985).
13. Id.
14. Earl P. Steinberg, Sean Tunis, & David Shapiro, Insurance Coverage for Experimental Technologies, 14(4) *Health Aff.* 143 (Winter 1995); Nancy M. P. King, Experimental Treatment Oxymoron or Aspiration?, 25(4) *Hastings Center Rep.* 6 (July 1995); Angela Holder, Funding Innovative Medical Treatment, 57 Albany L. Rev. 795 (1994); Claudia A. Steiner, Neil R. Powe, Gerard F. Anderson, and Abhik Das, Technology Coverage Decisions by Health Care Plans and Considerations by Medical Directors, 35 *Med. Care* 472–489 (1997).
15. 562 N.Y.S.2d 908 (Supr. Ct. 1990).

16. Brook, R. 1991. Health, Health Insurance, and the Uninsured. *JAMA* 265:2998–3002; D. Hadorn, 1992. Necessary Care Guidelines. In: *Basic Benefits and Clinical Guidelines*, Hadorn D, ed. Boulder, CO: Westview Press. See also D.M. Eddy, 1991. What Care is "Essential"? What Services are "Basic"? *JAMA* 265:782–88.

17. Kalb, P. 1989. Controlling Health Care Costs by Controlling Technology: A Private Contractual Approach. *Yale L. J.* 99:1109.

18. David Eddy, Benefit Language: Criteria that will Improve Quality While Reducing Costs, *28 JAMA* 650 (1996).

19. C.C. Havighurst, Health care choices: Private contracts as instruments of health reform. Washington, D.C.: *American Enterprise* Institute, 1995.

20. G., Anderson, M., Hall, and E. Steinberg, 1993. Medical Technology Assessment and Practice Guidelines: Their Day in Court. *Am. J. Public Health* 83:1635–39.

21. I. M. Ellman, and M. A. Hall, 1994. Redefining the Terms of Health Insurance to Accommodate Varying Consumer Risk Preferences. *Am. J. Law & Med.*, (1994).

22. Sara Rosenbaum and David Frankford, Who Should Determine When Health Care is Medically Necessary, 340 *N. Engl. J. Med.* 229 (1999).

23. Mark A. Hall, Teresa R. Smith, Michele Naughten and Andrea Ebbers, Judicial Protection of Managed Care Consumers: An Empirical Study of Insurance Coverage Disputes, 24 *Seton Hall L. Rev.* 101 (1996); Gerard F. Anderson, Mark A. Hall, and Teresa R. Smith, When Courts Review Medical Appropriateness, 36 *Med. Care* 1295 (1998). For extensive commentary on this study, see William Sage, Judicial Opinions Involving Health Insurance Coverage: Trompe L'Oeil or Window on the World?, 31 *Ind. L.* 49 (1998), and other articles in the same symposium issue.

24. T.F. Carney, Content analysis: A Technique for Systematic Inference from Communications (1989). For instance, content analysis has been used to analyze written texts, human behavior, speech patterns, and other widely varying phenomena. This research technique imposes an objective protocol that helps to minimize the personal subjectivity that otherwise would plague the analysis of qualitative observations. It is thus based on epistemological assumptions that are dramatically different than those that usually guide the analysis of legal decisions.

25. Cases were assigned to one reader each, and coding reliability was assessed at periodic intervals by having approximately 15% of the cases recoded by the other two readers.

26. Where a decision was not definitive, for instance, where it called for the case to be sent back to the trial court for additional findings, coders were asked to classify the decision as primarily favoring one party or the other, or as indeterminate. Only the determinate results were classified as coverage upheld (patient wins) or coverage denied (insurer wins).

27. Virtually all of these decisions (122) occurred since 1980, and 60% (75) occurred in the first half of the 1990s.

28. Where the insurer relied on more than one, the case was categorized first according to the highest in the following priority of assessment sources: private sector, public sector, and internal insurer.

29. This notation refers to the statistical probability that this observed difference could be the result of chance alone. When this probability falls to 0.05 or below, it is likely to occur because of chance less than one out of 20 times. This is a conventional standard for statistical significance.

30. *Wilson v The Travelers Insurance* Co., 605 P2d 1327 (Okla. 1980).

31. *American Society of Cataract and Refractive Surgery v. Sullivan,* 772 F.Supp. 666 (D.C. 1991).

32. I.V. *Services of America, Inc. v. Trustees of American Consulting Engineers Council Ins.* Trust Fund, 136 F.3d 114 (2d Cir. 1998).
33. *Waldrip v. Connecticut National Life Insurance Co.*, 573 So.2d 1172 (5th Cir. 1991); *Hyde v. Humana Insurance Co.*, 598 So.2d 876 (Ala. 1992).
34. *Meusberger v. Palmer*, 900 F.2d 1280 (8th Cir. 1990).
35. *Heasley v. Belden & Blake Corp.*, 2 F.3d 1249 (3d Cir. 1993); *Didomenico v. Employers Cooperative Industry Trust*, 676 F.Supp. 903 (N.D. Ind. 1987).
36. *Lowery v. Healthchicago*, 1994 U.S. Dist. LEXIS 6380 (N.D. Ill. 1994); *Grethe v. Trustmark Insurance Co.*, 1995 WL 222161 (N.D. Ill. 1995); *Bechtold v. Physicians Health Plan of Northern Indiana*, 19 F.3d 322 (7th Cir. 1993).
37. *Barnett v. Barnett*, 32 F.3d 413 (9th Cir. 1994).
38. *Uhrich v. Caterpillar*, 1993 U.S.Dist. LEXIS 16420 (N.D. Ill. 1993).
39. *Friedrich v. Secretary of Health and Human Services*, 894 F.2d 829 (6th Cir. 1990).
40. *White v. Caterpillar*, 765 F.Supp. 1418 (W.D. Mo. 1991).
41. *Leonhardt v Bradford National Life Insurance Co.*, 828 F. Supp. 657 (Minn 1993).
42. E.g., *Mattive v. Healthsource of Savannah*, 893 F.Supp. 1559 (S.D. Ga. 1995); *Frendis v. Blue Cross Blue Shield of Michigan*, 873 F. Supp. 1153 (N.D. Ill. 1995).
43. Mark A. Hall and Gerard F. Anderson, Health Insurers' Assessment of Medical Necessity, 140 *U. Pa. L. Rev.* 1637 (1992).
44. Id.; G.F. Anderson, The Courts and Health Policy: Strengths and Limitations, *Health Aff.*, Winter 1992, 95–110; David S. Hsia, Benefits Determination under Health Care Reform, 15 *J. Leg. Med.* 533 (1994); WK. Mariner, Patients' rights after health reform: Who decides what is medically necessary? *Am. J. Public Health* 1994; 84(9): 1515–1520; Mark R. Fondacaro, Toward a Synthesis of Law and Social Science: Due Process and Procedural Justice in the Context of National Health Care Reform, 72 *Denver U. L. Rev.* 304 (1995); Symposium, 47 *Admin. L. Rev.* 373 (1995).
45. Karen Pollitz, Geraldine Dallek, and Nicole Tapay, External Review of Health Plan Decisions: An Overview of Key Program Features in the States and Medicare (November 1998); Tracy E. Miller, Center Stage on the Patient Protection Agenda: Grievance and Appeal Rights, 26 *J. L. Med. Ethics* 89–99 (1998).
46. Jennifer E. Gladieux, Medicare + Choice Appeal Procedures: Reconciling Due Process Rights and Cost Containment, 25 *Am. J. Law & Med.* 61–116 (1999).
47. See, for instance, the Patient Protection Act of 1999, H.R. 448, 106th Cong.
48. Mark A. Hall and Gerard F. Anderson, Health Insurers' Assessment of Medical Necessity, 140 *U. Pa. L. Rev.* 1637 (1992); Mark R. Fondacaro, Toward a Synthesis of Law and Social Science: Due Process and Procedural Justice in the Context of National Health Care Reform, 72 *Denver U. L. Rev.* 304 (1995).
49. Gordon Bonnyman and Michele Johnson, Unseen Peril: Inadequate Enrollee Grievance Protections in Public Managed Care Programs, 65 *Tenn. L. Rev.* 359 (1998); Rand E. Rosenblatt, Equality, Entitlement, and National Health Care Reform: The Challenge of Managed Competition and Managed Care, 60 *Brooklyn L. Rev.* 105 (1994); Margaret G. Farrell, The Need for a Process Theory: Formulating Health Policy Through Adjudication, 8 *J. L. & Health* 201 (1993–94).
50. As most readers are well aware, ERISA is the federal statute that primarily governs employee pension plans, but also covers other employee benefits such as health insurance. One of its effects is to require employees who challenge health benefits determinations to bring these suits in federal court. Under ERISA, which is based on trust law, courts give much greater deference to the insurer's decision than under state contract law if the insurance contract gives the insurer discretion to interpret the contract's terms. *Firestone Tire & Rubber Co. v. Bruch*, 489 U.S. 101 (1989).

51. Indeed, much to our surprise, a large apparent effect from ERISA versus other sources of law, which showed up in bivariate analysis, completely disappeared in multivariate analysis. This suggests that the apparent effect of ERISA is mostly explained by other legal and contract factors that were controlled for in the regression analysis but not in the bivariate analyses.

52. *Winters v. Costco Wholesale Corp.*, 49 F.3d 550 (9th Cir. 1995). See generally Michael Rappaport, The Ambiguity Rule and Insurance Law: Why Insurance Contracts Should not be Construed Against the Drafter, 30 *Ga. L. Rev.* 171 (1995).

53. This portion of the chapter is based in large part on excerpts from Mark A. Hall, Teresa R. Smith, Michele Naughten, and Andrea Ebbers, Judicial Protection of Managed Care Consumers, 26 *Seton Hall L. Rev.* 1055 (1996). For additional discussion of these issues, see other articles in the same issue of that journal, as well as the sources cited in note 49 supra.

54. See Margaret Gilhooley, Broken Back: A Patient's Reflections on the Process of Medical Necessity Determinations, 40 *Vill. L. Rev.* 153 (1995) (patient's first-hand account of difficulties in challenging medical necessity denial).

55. Precise figures are not available because cases were coded within specified ranges. The costs would be higher if they were all converted to current dollars.

56. See note 50 supra.

57. Mark A. Hall, Informed Consent to Rationing Decisions, 71 *Milbank Q.* 645–67 (1993).

58. Note, Securing Access to Care in Health Maintenance Organizations: Toward a Unified Model of Grievance and Appeal Procedures, 94 *Colum. L. Rev.* 1674 (1994).

5

FINANCIAL INCENTIVES AS A COST-CONTROL MECHANISM IN MANAGED CARE

Thomas Rice

One of the principal ways in which managed-care plans have attempted to control costs is through the use of financial incentives aimed at affecting physicians' behavior. Although widespread, the practice is highly controversial. This chapter discusses the purpose of such incentives, indicates the types and their prevalence, summarizes previous research on their effects, examines how patients and doctors view physicians' financial incentives, and discusses two key policy issues—disclosure of financial incentives and the regulation of these incentives.

Purpose of financial incentives

To understand why managed-care plans [which throughout this chapter are defined as health maintenance organizations (HMO) or point-of-service (POS) plans, but exclude less-restrictive arrangements such as preferred-provider organizations] employ financial incentives in paying physicians, one must understand the financial incentives faced by the plans themselves. Different payers such as employers, Medicare, and Medicaid, may use different methods in determining how—and how much—they pay health plans, these payers nearly always share one key characteristic: they pay the managed-care plan a fixed amount of money per patient per time period, regardless of how much is ultimately spent on treating the patient. The term usually used to convey this concept is *capitation*, although this should not be confused with the capitation of physicians, which is discussed below. The fact that managed-care plans are capitated means that it is essential for them to control their costs.

Health plans, of course, do not directly determine what services will be provided; doctors do. Plans naturally want physicians to use resources sparingly, both to keep premiums at a competitive level and to maintain profits. To achieve this, plans can use non-financial methods, which may include physician education (e.g., disseminating practice guidelines) and feedback (perhaps, comparisons to peers in service utilization). Group and staff model HMOs can also seek to develop a *corporate culture*, in effect trying to establish a group ethic that results in peer pressure to conform through parsimonious provision of care. This does not work well in the independent practice association (IPA) and in network-model HMOs, however, since physicians are usually members of numerous health plans and practice in their own private offices.

The problem with these methods is that physicians can simply ignore them. Financial incentives are different in that they are designed to put physicians in the same mind-set as the HMO: to make them *want* to provide or to recommend fewer services.

Thus, the major purpose of financial incentives is to make physicians think not only about the patient's well-being, but also about the cost of services—which, of course, is why they are so controversial. But there are secondary purposes as well. Financial incentives can be used by plans in an attempt to *fine tune* physician-practice patterns. For example, because (as will be described below) capitation encourages physicians to stint on care, some HMOs using this payment method sometimes also pay bonuses to physicians who achieve good quality or high patient-satisfaction ratings. Similarly, putting physicians on salary may encourage slothfulness, so HMOs that pay salaries often tie them to productivity. And plans relying on fee-for-service may withhold a percentage of payments if physicians do too much.

Types and prevalence of financial incentives

There are three ways in which physicians can be paid: fee-for-service, capitation, and salary. Each provides its own set of strong financial incentives. In addition, within each there are a number of secondary incentives that can be employed— most of which involve either bonuses or withholds. These methods are briefly described below, together with their prevalence.

Under fee-for-service systems, physicians are paid an additional amount for each service they provide. It is sometimes claimed that this automatically motivates them to increase the volume of services, but the incentive is actually somewhat more complicated. There is an incentive to increase volume only if the payment for providing the services exceeds the physician's cost, including his or her time. This may seem a trivial caveat; it is not. One of the reasons many physicians do not participate in Medicaid is that their costs exceed the program's often paltry payment rate.[1] With this caveat in mind, however, most analysts agree that fee-for-service payment provides a stronger incentive for physicians to provide more services than do other payment methods.

The incentives of fee-for-service with regard to the quantity of services provided are fairly clear, however the same cannot be said about the anticipated effect on the quality of care provided. Quality is encouraged in that physicians do not have an incentive to withhold services. But they may provide too many services under fee-for-service; this not only wastes resources, but could actually cause harm to the patient. Estimates are not available on the proportion of services provided that are actually harmful, but estimates of the portion of services that are not medically necessary range as high as 30%.[2]

In this regard, perhaps the most eloquent criticism of fee-for-service medicine is attributable not to Alain Enthoven, Paul Ellwood, or another pioneer in managed care, but rather to playwright George Bernard Shaw, who, in 1911, wrote:

That any sane nation, being observed that you could provide for the supply of bread by giving bakers a pecuniary interest in baking for you, should go on to give a surgeon a pecuniary interest in cutting off your leg, is enough to make one despair of political humanity.[3]

Capitation provides incentives that are diametrically opposed to those of fee-for-service. Under a full capitation system, physicians receive a fixed amount of money for providing services to a patient for a particular period of time—sometimes including the cost associated with referrals to hospitals or specialists, as well as the ordering of tests. This distinction in incentives can be illustrated through the analogy of a check. Under fee-for-service, physicians essentially are given a blank check; they can fill it in for a higher amount by providing more services. Under capitation, the check is already filled in when they receive it; working more does not raise income but does preclude engaging in other activities. Viewed this way, the difference in incentives could not be more stark.

It is sometimes claimed that this results in an economic incentive to provide as little care as possible per patient, and to maximize the number of patients under the physician's care, but again it turns out that the incentives are somewhat more complicated. It is true that underproviding services will lead to more money for the physician in the short-run but it may be a counterproductive strategy over time. This is because patients are likely to gravitate away from physicians who, they believe, are not giving them the attention they deserve. In addition, to the extent that preventive services can keep future utilization down, capitation can provide physicians with an incentive to recommend to patients necessary preventive services.

The third major way of paying physicians is through an annual salary. This is a fixed sum of money not per patient, but for all patients treated (and all other job responsibilities) over a specified time period. In managed-care settings, the use of salary tends to be confined to group and staff model HMOs, where the physician works exclusively for one organization. But using salaries is unwieldy when a physician is a member of more than one managed care plan, as is typically the case in IPA/network model HMOs.[4] In these circumstances, it is not clear how a particular physician's salary can be divided up among several competing health plans in which the doctor participates.

Some view salary as a desirable remuneration method because it appears more neutral than fee-for-service or capitation: it would seem to encourage neither over- nor under-provision of services. The main potential problem concerns productivity: when one receives the same amount of money irrespective of what one accomplishes, there may be less financial incentive to achieve.

The tension between the health plan's incentive to control costs and the physician's incentive to both derive sufficient revenues from the practice of medicine and to provide good quality care to patients has resulted in the development of more specific financial incentives that can be used in conjunction with the three primary methods just discussed. Some of these include:[5]

- Withholding a percentage of the physician's revenue each year, and not returning it if the physician hospitalizes or refers patients to specialists more than is considered appropriate. Such withholds may be based on an individual physician's performance or the performance of the physician group as a whole.
- Subjecting the physician to financial risks over and above the withhold amounts by further deductions from compensation for going beyond prescribed limits.
- Awarding bonuses if there is a surplus in hospitalization funds or referral funds; again, such bonuses may be based on an individual physician's performance or the performance of the physician group as a whole.
- Putting the physician at financial risk for tests and other procedures that they order over and above set limits.
- Adjusting payment based on any or all of the following: utilization- or cost-measures; patient complaints or grievances; quality measures; consumer satisfaction surveys; productivity; or enrollee turnover rates.

Some of the most recent and comprehensive evidence available on the prevalence of different financial incentives comes from a 1999 national survey conducted by Mathematica Policy Research, Inc. for the Medicare Payment Advisory Commission.[6] The survey consisted of a stratified random sample of HMOs in 20 of the largest 60 market areas in the United States, areas comprising 86% of total HMO enrollment in the country. A total of 116 HMOs were surveyed. Considering the results, two caveats should be kept in mind. First, HMO respondents were asked how physicians were paid—but in many cases HMOs don't pay physicians directly, but rather pay medical groups, which in turn pay the physicians. Thus, HMOs might not know how the medical groups with whom they contract pay their physicians. Secondly, since different groups pay physicians in different ways, respondents were asked to choose the *predominant payment method*, but that may mask the true amount of heterogeneity in payment.

With this in mind, Table 5–1 shows how primary care physicians are paid in their commercial—as opposed to Medicare and Medicaid—contracts, nationally and by region. Table 5–2 provides the same information for how specialists are paid.

Capitation is by far the most common method used in paying primary care physicians (Table 5–1), with an estimated share of 61% of total HMO payments. Fee-for-service is second with 25%, and salary third with 14%. Withholds and bonuses are used about half the time in capitation and about one-third of the time in fee-for-service but are rarely used in salary arrangements. In addition, the results differ a great deal by geographic area. California, for example, is far more likely to use salary, mainly due to the presence of Kaiser Permanente, a large group model HMO. Fee-for-service arrangements are almost unheard of in California, but make up half the southern markets and about one quarter of the markets in other regions.

In contrast, except in California, fee-for-service is the most common method of paying specialists (Table 5–2). This method accounts for 75% of the market nationally, and over 90% in much of the country. Capitation of specialists accounts

TABLE 5–1. How Health Plans Pay Primary-Care Physicians

	ALL PLANS	CALIFORNIA MARKETS	MIDWEST MARKETS	NORTHEAST/ MID- ATLANTIC MARKETS	SOUTHEAST/ SOUTH CENTRAL MARKETS
Predominant payment method for primary-care physicians					
Fee-for-service (total)	24.7%	1.2%	23.2%	29.6%	50.9%
Without withholds or bonuses	15.1%	1.2%	2.3%	10.5%	50.9%
With withholds or bonuses	9.7	0.0	20.9	19.1	0.0
Capitation (total)	61.2%	59.5%	74.3%	69.2%	41.0%
Without withholds or bonuses	29.2%	30.7%	36.5%	31.6%	17.8%
With withholds or bonuses	32.0	28.8	37.8	37.6	23.2
Salary (total)	14.1%	39.4%	2.5%	1.2%	8.0%
Without withholds or bonuses	13.3%	39.4%	0.0%	0.0%	8.0%
With withholds or bonuses	0.8	0.0	2.5	1.2	0.0

Source: Medicare Payment Advisory Commission, "Health Plans' Selection and Payment of Health Care Providers, 1999," Washington DC: Medical Payment Advisory Commission, May 2000, Table B.4.

TABLE 5–2. How Health Plans Pay Specialists

	ALL PLANS	CALIFORNIA MARKETS	MIDWEST MARKETS	NORTHEAST/ MID- ATLANTIC MARKETS	SOUTHEAST/ SOUTH CENTRAL MARKETS
Predominant payment method for specialists:					
Fee-for-service (total)	75.3%	35.9%	100.0%	94.7%	80.2%
Without withholding or bonuses	52.2%	23.8%	57.2%	73.0%	56.6%
With withholding or bonuses	23.1	12.1	42.8	21.6	23.6
Capitation (total)	13.3%	25.1%	0.0%	5.3%	19.8%
Without withholding or bonuses	7.1%	12.0%	0.0%	4.1%	10.7%
With withholding or bonuses	6.2	13.1	0.0%	1.2	9.0
Salary (total)	11.4%	39.0%	0.0%	0.0%	0.0%
Without withholding or bonuses	11.4%	39.0%	0.0%	0.0%	0.0%
With withholding or bonuses	0.0	0.0	0.0	0.0	0.0

Source: Medicare Payment Advisory Commission, "Health Plans' Selection and Payment of Health Care Providers, 1999," Washington DC: Medical Payment Advisory Commission, May 2000, Table B.5.

for 13%, and salary, 11%. As before, salary is far more common in California than elsewhere. The presence of withholds and bonuses are comparable to those reported for primary—care physicians.

Strong financial methods for controlling costs in managed care are far more prevalent in the payment of primary care physicians. Only 15% were paid on a fee-for-service without any bonuses or withholds, compared to 52% of specialists.

Other findings showed that when physicians are paid on a capitation basis, payment always includes primary care office visits and usually—over 80% of the time—other services provided in their offices as well as inpatient visits. About half of the time, it also includes ancillary care provided by others, and referrals for specialist care. Finally, the study examined the types of performance measures used by health plans to adjust payments to primary care physicians; it found that quality measures were used most often (68%), followed by consumer surveys (48%), utilization and cost measures (46%), patient complaints (42%), and enrollee turnover rates (23%). On average, between 6% and 10% of compensation was affected by physician performance as defined by these measures.[7]

There is limited evidence that the prevalence of physician capitation may have peaked. A recent study by Robinson and Casalino looked at changes in physician compensation arrangements six health plans operated by a single insurer.[8] It found a reduction in the range of services included in capitation contracts.

It is too early to know whether this finding can be generalized to apply to other HMOs, but it would not be surprising if the authors' findings are indicative of a change at large, for several reasons. First, more physician practices find themselves in financial stress because of reliance on the capitation payment, so they may be seeking to negotiate other methods of compensation with health plans. Secondly, as consumers flex their muscles in the courtroom, health plans and physician group practices may find themselves more vulnerable to malpractice liability if their participating physicians are paid in a manner that appears to provide an incentive to stint on necessary services. Finally, a retreat from capitation payment is consistent with the so-called managed-care backlash. Many consumers object to the financial incentives inherent in capitation, so both health plans and physician group practices face pressure to use other payment methods.

Evidence on the impact of financial incentives

There has been a great deal of research on overall differences between HMOs and fee-for-service medicine, but surprisingly little on how they affect physician behavior. Five such studies—none of which deals with the quality of medical care—are noted below.

A study by Hillman and colleagues used data relating to the year 1987 to examine the impact of various physician compensation methods used in HMOs on service utilization.[9] Compared to those in fee-for-service, salaried physicians had 13% lower hospitalization rates, and capitated doctors eight percent lower. Two incentives—placing individual physicians at financial risk when they refer a large number of patients to specialists, and making physicians assume a financial risk above and beyond the amount of the withhold[10]—reduced the number of visits by about 10%.

A study by Stearns and colleagues examined state employees enrolled in an HMO in Dane County, Wisconsin.[11] In 1983, this IPA paid its primary care physicians on a fee-for-service basis. The following year, it altered its payment of primary care physicians to a capitated amount, with risk-sharing for hospital and specialist services. It was found that primary care visits increased 18% in the second year, while referrals to specialists outside the group declined by 45%. Hospital admissions fell by 16%, and length of stay by 12%.

Another study, by Ogden and colleagues, examined physicians from Rockford, Illinois who contracted with an IPA.[12] In 1987, they were paid on a fee-for-service basis, with a 15% withhold. In 1988, payment was on a capitation basis for primary care doctors, with shared risk for specialist services, and a bonus if hospitalization rates were held below a threshold level. The authors found that specialist costs increased by two percent in 1988, after increasing 12% in previous years. The cost of hospital outpatient services declined by seven percent after increasing 12% in previous years. Hospital utilization was largely unaffected by the change in payment for primary-care services.

In contrast, a more recent study by Conrad and colleagues examined the impact of primary care physician compensation method on Washington state physicians from a variety of practice settings, and found that individual physician incentives did not matter.[13] The study distinguished between whether a physician's medical group was at financial risk for utilization costs (almost all were) and whether these groups put their physicians at financial risk. It found no impact of giving financial incentives to individual primary care physicians, and their patients' inpatient and outpatient utilization and costs.

Finally, a study from Denmark, reported on by Mooney, provides an international example on physician incentives.[14] In October 1987, general practitioners (GPs) in Copenhagen changed from a fully-capitated payment basis to one that was based partly on capitation and partly on fee-for-service, so as to conform with physicians in the rest of the country. This new system enabled GPs to make extra money for consultations and prescriptions, as well as certain procedures and tests. There was a substantial increase in provision of services that provided extra fees and a large decrease in referrals to specialists and hospitals. From this, it was concluded that, "[t]here clearly is considerable discretion on the part of GPs in how they act, and remuneration systems can push them to go one way or another in how they treat their patients and whether they treat them themselves or refer them on in the system."[15]

It is indeed unfortunate that there is a dearth of literature on how individual physicians' financial incentives directly affect the quality of care. A number of studies that have looked at this indirectly, however, by assessing the overall impact of HMOs vs. fee-for-service medicine. These have been reviewed by Miller and Luft.[16] Their overall conclusion is that nearly equal numbers of studies indicate that HMOs provide better and worse clinical quality. One interpretation of this result is that there is much more variation in quality *among* plan types (e.g., between one HMO and another, or one fee-for-service provider or another) than *between* plan types (i.e., HMO vs. fee-for-service). Or, as stated by Miller and Luft, "The results show something that is simple, obvious, and yet sometimes underemphasized: HMOs produce better, the same, or worse quality of care, depending on the particular organization and particular disease."[17] The authors do express some concern, however, about those with chronic illnesses; three of five studies that examined these individuals found worse outcomes in HMOs than in fee-for-service plans.

Patients' and doctors' views on physicians' financial incentives

Financial incentives have been applied to physicians largely as a way to control utilization. Whether they remain tenable depends not only on how successful they have been in this regard, but also on the reactions they engender in doctors and patients alike.

We report on two studies that examine the attitudes of physicians about financial incentives. In the first, Grumbach and colleagues surveyed over 750 California physicians in 1996 who participated in managed care arrangements.[18] They found that those who believed that they faced an incentive to limit referrals were

2.5 times more likely than others to feel that the care they provided was compromised. Physicians who said that their compensation was based in part on productivity as measured by the number of patients they saw per day were 2.1 times more likely to believe that it compromised the quality of care they provided. Regarding satisfaction, those with incentives based on the number of patients seen per day were only 0.4 times as likely to be very satisfied with their practices, while those who faced quality-of-care and/or patient satisfaction incentives were 1.8 times more likely to be satisfied with their practices.

A study by Hadley and colleagues reported on a survey of over 1,500 physicians nationally.[19] The survey was conducted in 1997, so the prevalence of financial incentives was lower than reported earlier, with 15% of physicians reporting a "moderate or strong" incentive to reduce services. The authors found that:

Compared to physicians with a neutral incentive, physicians with an incentive to reduce services were from 1.5 to 3.5 times more likely to be very dissatisfied with their practices and were 0.2 to 0.5 times as likely to report that their expectations regarding professional autonomy and ability to practice good-quality medicine were met. They were also 0.2 to 0.6 times as likely to report having the freedom to care for patients the way they would like along several specific measures of practice style: sufficient time with patients, ability to hospitalize, ability to order tests and procedures, and ability to make referrals.[20]

It seems clear that physicians do not care for financial incentives that, on their view, limit their ability to act on the behalf of their patients. One study examines whether patients, too, share this view. Gallagher and colleagues report findings from a 1998 survey of 1,050 patients in parts of the country that have significant managed care penetration.[21] Patients were queried about two hypothetical financial incentives directed at their physician, one involving a 10% bonus for controlling costs, and another a similarly-sized bonus aimed jointly as cost-control and quality-enhancement.

Over 70% said that the cost-control bonus was a "bad idea" and almost as many said it would make them trust their physician less. In contrast, views on bonuses jointly aimed at costs and quality were more mixed (actually, slightly more thought this was a "good idea" than a "bad idea"), although more thought it would reduce, rather than use their trust in their physician. The results are consistent with those from a 1997 survey, reported on by Kao and colleagues, in which fee-for-service patients had a higher level of trust (94%) in their physicians to "put their health and well-being above keeping down the health plan's costs" than did those whose physicians were capitated (83%), salaried (77%), or were in managed fee-for-service (85%).[22]

Policy issues

This section examines two policy avenues for addressing concerns about financial incentives to physicians in managed care: disclosure of financial incentives and regulatory constraints on incentives.

Disclosure of Financial Incentives

Disclosure is one of the milder forms of economic regulation. In the case of financial incentives, disclosure implies that consumers be given information, or have the right to request information, about the financial incentives that health plans or medical groups provide physicians.

In 1998, 28 states required some form of disclosure of physician financial incentives,[23] although the nature of this disclosure varied a great deal. Most laws and regulations are directed at health plans, requiring them to explain their physician-compensation methods in written materials distributed to enrollees. In addition, the federal government requires plans participating in Medicare or Medicaid to disclose such incentives when requested by an enrollee.[24]

Although this might, at first glance, seem uncontroversial, it is not. Opponents have asserted that disclosure of financial incentives could impair the doctor–patient relationship. The argument goes that if patients knew that their doctors could benefit by using services more sparingly, they would no longer believe that they were receiving the appropriate amount of medical care—even if they were.

Another, perhaps more pragmatic, argument against disclosure is that it may be unfeasible. Health plans have multiple and complicated financial arrangements with medical groups and doctors that are not easily summarized and which, without proper context, would confuse rather than enlighten the patient. Furthermore, health plans may not even know the financial incentives faced by physicians, the latter often being paid directly by their medical group. Curiously, physicians probably are also often ignorant about the financial incentives they face, particularly when they are paid in different ways by different health plans.[25]

Despite these arguments, patients say that they want this information. In a study noted above, by Gallagher and colleagues, respondents were asked about two hypothetical physician-incentive schemes, one in which their physician would be given a 10% cost-control bonus, and another in which a 10% bonus was based on a combination of cost-control and quality of care.[26] The authors found that 91% of sample members believed that such bonuses should be disclosed to patients. Over 80% believed that they should be told without having to ask, in part because most also felt that they would find it awkward to discuss the issue with their physician. Finally, 85% said that they would choose a plan that did not offer such bonuses over those that did. One interesting point made by the authors is that the size of the bonus considered—10%—is rather small by today's standards.

Hall and colleagues have proposed a reasonable way in which to operationalize disclosure requirements, attempting to balance the consumer right-to-know and the difficulty in making these intricate financial arrangements understandable.[27] Their "layered approach" has three parts:

First, prior to enrollment, potential subscribers can be told simply whether plans use physician incentives in any fashion to contain costs . . . and subscribers can receive more detailed information if they request it. Second, following enrollment, managed care members can be given fairly detailed descriptions of the various physician incentive arrangements used in the network. . . . Third, when a patient signs up with or identifies a specific physician, either the plan or the physician group can inform the patient in writing of the incentive arrangements directed to and within the particular group.

This may not solve some of the more vexing problems of exactly what information to present and in what form (e.g., amounts of bonuses or withholds when certain thresholds are exceeded), but it does offer a starting point for implementation.

Regulation of Financial Incentives

The problem with simply disclosing financing is that it may not be sufficient to terminate practices that have the strongest potential to harm patients. As noted above, financial incentives can be very complicated; it is not surprising that patients have difficulty understanding them even when presented with the information. In one survey, Kao and colleagues found that only one-third of patients could identify their physician's primary payment method.[28] Similarly, in a study based on focus groups, Miller and Horowitz concluded that "many patients do not know their physicians' incentives and have no context for the information".[29]

The main example of regulation of physician incentives is from the Health Care Financing Administration (HCFA), and applies to Medicaid and Medicare managed care plans. HCFA's path-breaking regulations in this area went into effect in 1997. As described by Gallagher and colleagues, the regulations are designed to "prohibit financial incentives that are 'an inducement to reduce or limit covered medically necessary services furnished to an individual enrollee' ".[30]

Under the regulations, health plans must disclose to HCFA arrangements in which 25% of potential physician payments are subject to financial risk. Plans that put physicians at this level of risk are required to conduct and report the results of enrollee-satisfaction surveys, and must also ensure that physicians and physician groups have stop–loss coverage for at least 90% of risk exceeding 25%. Any of this information can be requested by program enrollees.

One problem with the regulations reported on by the authors is that they apply only to referral services, which "ignores incentives to control services within the plan or physician group." Another is that plans "need only disclose 'summary' information about incentives" rather than specific information about incentives affecting a person's own physician.

Whether and to what extent to restrict financial incentives aimed at physicians is a difficult question. On the one hand, financial incentives are perhaps the major tool that managed care plans use in their attempt to control health care costs. On the other, severe restrictions can result in harm to patients, who, even if they had access to detailed information on incentives, might not be able to process it.

Conclusions

Financial incentives in managed care are a concern, but they must be considered in the context of the U.S. health care system. There is not, nor has there ever been, an overall health care budget in the United States. Costs are therefore open-ended. The historic use of fee-for-service payment resulted in rapid cost inflation that had to be reined in. Managed care provided an answer, and physician financial incentives have been an integral part of managed care.

In many ways, this is an unfortunate state of events. Financial incentives that restrict the use of care are unpopular with doctors and patients alike and set up an environment that is not conducive to trust. As Marc Rodwin wrote:

Society makes a statement about the role of physicians when it provides incentives for them to help government or health care organizations reduce their costs. This is especially so if there are no equivalent financial incentives for physicians to improve quality of care. By using financial incentives to change the clinical practice of physicians, society calls forth self–interested behavior. In asking physicians to consider their own interest in deciding how to act, we alter the attitude we want physicians ideally to have. For if physicians act intuitively to promote their patients' interests, we will worry less that they will behave inappropriately. But if their motivation is primarily self–interest, we will want their behavior to be monitored more carefully.[31]

I believe that Rodwin is right when he says that physicians' practice behavior must be monitored more carefully. Despite the inherent difficulties, we owe it to patients to have both health plans and physician groups disclose the financial incentives to which they subject physicians. Whether we as a society actually regulate these incentives directly, or rely on the courts to do so, their existence should be made as visible as possible so that we understand the structure upon which our health care system operates. Only then is it possible to intelligently consider the advantages and disadvantages of alternative methods of reforming health care financing and delivery in the United States.

Acknowledgments

I would like to thank Sarah Galbraith for compiling much of the literature upon which this chapter is based.

Notes

1. Janet B. Mitchell, Physician participation in Medicaid Revisited, 29 *Med. Care* 645 (1991).
2. Lucian Leape, Unnecessary surgery, 24 *Health Serv.* Res. 351 (1989).
3. Bernard Shaw, Preface on Doctors from the Doctor's Dilemma, in *Bernard Shaw: Complete Plays with Prefaces* 1 (Dodd, Mead & Co. 1963).
4. Group and staff model HMOs are similar. A patient "goes" to an HMO, which usually has a physician staff that works exclusively for that organization. In a staff model HMO, the HMO employs physicians, whereas in a group model, the HMO contracts

with a medical group that is constituted by the physicians who practice at that HMO. IPAs (independent practice associations) and network model HMOs are sometimes called "HMOs without walls." Patients go to physicians or physician groups that see patients who are members of different HMOs, as well as those who are in preferred provider organizations or fee-for-service. In IPA model, the HMO contracts with a group that organizes physicians, whereas in a network model, the HMO contracts with two or more such organizations.

5. Alan L. Hillman, Mark V. Pauly, and Joseph J. Kerstein, How do financial incentives affect physicians' clinical decision and the financial performance of Health Maintenance Organizations, 321 New England J. Med. 86 (1989); Marsha R. Gold, Robery Hurley, & Timothy Lake, et. al, A national survey of the arrangements managed-care plans make with physicians, 333 N. Eng. J. Med. 1678 (1995).

6. Mathematica Policy Research, Inc., *Health Plans' Selection and Payment of Health Care Providers* for the Medicare Payment Advisory Commission (2000).

7. Id.

8. James C. Robinson and Lawrence P. Casalino, Reevaluation of capitation contracting in New York and California, *Health Aff.* (2001), available *at* www. healthaffairs.org.

9. Hillman, *supra* note 4.

10. Under a "withhold," the health plan holds back a percentage of the physician's payment and keeps some of this money if the physician does not meet productivity targets such as limiting referrals or hospitalizations. Suppose that the withhold is 10%. Some plans put their physicians at an even higher financial risk. For example, if the physician misses the target by 15%, the plan not only would retain the 10% withhold, but would charge the physician an additional five percent.

11. Sally C. Stearns, Barbara L. Wolfe, and David A. King, Physician responses to fee-for-service and capitation payment, 29 *Inquiry* 416 (1992).

12. D. Ogden, R. Carlson and G. Bernstein, The effect of primary care incentives, Proceedings of the 1990 Group Health Institute, *Group Health Association of America* (1990).

13. Douglas A. Conrad, Charles Maynard, and Allen Cheadle, et al., Primary care compensation method in medical groups: does it influence the use and cost of health services for enrollees in managed care organizations? 279 *JAMA* 853 (1998).

14. Gavin Mooney, *Key Issues in Health Economics* (New York: Harvester Wheatsheaf, 1994).

15. Id. at 127.

16. Robert H. Miller and Harold S. Luft, Does managed care lead to better or worse quality of care?, 16 *Health Aff.* 7 (1997).

17. Id. at 14.

18. Kevin Grumbach, Dennis Osmond, Karen Vranizan, et al., Primary care physicians' experience of financial incentives in managed-care systems 339 *N. Eng. J. Med.* 1516 (1998).

19. Jack Hadley, Jean M. Mitchell, and Danlel P. Sulmasy, et al., Perceived financial incentives, HMO market penetration, and physicians' practice styles and satisfaction, 34 *Health Serv. Res.* 307 (1999).

20. Id. at 307.

21. Thomas Gallagher, Robert F. St. Peter, Margaret Chesney, et al., Patients' attitudes toward cost control bonuses for managed care physicians, 20 *Health Aff.* 186 (2001).

22. Audiey Kao, Diane C. Green, Alan M. Zaslavsky, et al., The relationship between metho of physician payment and patient trust, 280 *JAMA*. 1708 (1998).

23. Tracy E. Miller and Carol R. Horowitz, Disclosing doctors' incentives: will consumers understand and value the information?, 19 *Health Aff.* 149 (2000).
24. Tracy E. Miller and William M. Sage, Disclosing physician financial incentives, 281 *JAMA.* 1424 (1999).
25. Id.
26. Gallagher, *supra* note 20.
27. Mark A. Hall, Kristen E. Kidd, and Elizabeth Dugan, Disclosure of physician incentives: do practices satisfy purposes?, 19 *Health Aff.* 156 (2000).
28. Kao, supra note 21.
29. Miller and Horowitz, supra note 152.
30. Thomas H. Gallagher, Ann Alpers and Bernard Lo, Health Care Financing Administration's new regulations for financial incentives in Medicaid and Medicare managed care: one step forward? 105 *Am. J. Med.* 409 (1998).
31. Marc Rodwin, *Medicine Money and Morals: Physicians' Conflicts of Interest* 153 (Oxford Univ. Press 1993).

6

MEDICAL ANTITRUST REFORM:
ARROW, COASE, AND THE
CHANGING STRUCTURE OF THE FIRM

Peter J. Hammer

The collapse of national health care reform has refocused attention on private markets as the primary force shaping the medical industry. The past two decades have witnessed a blizzard of entrepreneurial activity, marking fundamental changes in the way health care is financed and delivered. Physicians are forming new and larger groups. Hospitals are buying physician practices. Insurance companies are creating managed care networks that provide medical services. At the same time, an increasing number of health care providers are marketing their services on a prepaid basis in direct competition with traditional insurance companies. While it is sometimes difficult to move beyond the flood of various organizational acronyms, it is useful to make an economic distinction between integration and consolidation in medical markets.[1] The dominant theme is integration: the creation of health plans that combine in a single entity (bound either by common ownership or contractual relations) the components of physician services, hospital services, and medical insurance. But also increasingly important is horizontal consolidation: collaborative arrangements within component parts, such as a merger between two hospitals, the formation of a new or larger physician group, or the combination of managed care plans and insurance companies.[2]

Integration reflects a fundamental reorganization of the *firms* providing health care services and financing. Increasingly, the function of selling medical insurance is being combined *in-house* with the function of delivering medical services.[3]

This organization of the firm contrasts with the historically dominant structure in which physicians, hospitals and insurers constituted a triumvirate of separate and distinct entities—each pursuing independent economic objectives and each relating to the other through a series of separate market–based transactions. The significance of this transformation cannot be overstated. Economic structure largely dictates economic behavior. Integration fundamentally alters the decision rule governing when medical services will be provided and when they will be denied. The old decision rule, which was spawned by fee–for–service systems of compensation (contractual relations between independent providers and insurers) and passive third-party payor supervision (relaxed contractual monitoring of the actions of independent economic actors), essentially provided medical care whenever there was a positive expected benefit to the patient. The integrated provider, however, internalizes the economic costs of additional treatment and is not likely to provide care when the expected marginal costs exceed the expected marginal benefits. The difference between these decision rules is profound. Whereas the old rule was systematically biased in favor of overproviding care, the new rule underlying many forms of managed care raises the specter that care may be systematically underprovided.

Health care disputes frequently spill over from the economic to the political arena and back again. Proposed reforms of the nation's antitrust laws have triggered intense political battles. Over the years, physicians have sought reforms that would permit greater collective action against third-party payers, as well as rules making it easier to form physician networks. Similarly, hospitals would like rules governing mergers relaxed to permit greater collective decision making in the allocation of medical resources. These proposals directly challenge the prerogative of private markets and raise questions about when markets should be trusted to allocate health care resources and when they should be supplemented or displaced by other social institutions. Professors Arrow and Coase provide complementary perspectives as to how these questions might be answered. Kenneth Arrow envisions a range of nonmarket institutions filling the "optimality gaps" caused by medical market failures. Ronald Coase's theory of the firm provides a framework for understanding the transformation of the health care industry and for determining which interventions are likely to be helpful and which harmful in emerging medical markets.

This chapter examines these theories and proposes a set of evaluative criteria for assessing health care reforms, contending that appropriate nonmarket interventions should (1) be targeted at correcting recognized market failures; (2) result in a net increase in social welfare (static efficiency); and (3) not structurally interfere with the prospective development of efficient market operations (dynamic efficiency). Physician and hospital antitrust reforms are then evaluated in light of these criteria. The case for reforms giving physicians the right to collectively bargain or to form networks in the absence of substantial integration is largely unpersuasive. Antitrust rules should be defined in terms of structural economic considerations that are likely to facilitate more rational behavior in the health care sector. Coase's theory of the firm suggests that some level of actual integration should be required before physicians are entitled to more lenient antitrust treatment. Permitting physician combinations or collective bargaining without integration or risk sharing will not yield the same economic benefits and will hinder future market development.

Hospital reforms raise a different set of questions. The central issue is whether greater cooperation among hospitals is needed to counteract pressures driving non-price competition. While such claims possessed a plausible economic foundation in preintegrated health care markets, they are unpersuasive by contemporary standards. Integrated firms directly internalize the costs of underutilized capital and equipment and are likely to make appropriate investment decisions. Moreover, to the extent that excess hospital capacity does exist in many markets, such capacity can play an important role in ensuring that future health care markets are maximally competitive. Physical capacity facilitates the creation of additional integrated health plans and creates incentives for active price competition. Rather than justifying exceptions to antitrust laws, emerging medical markets call for vigilant antitrust enforcement. Competition between integrated health plans not only facilitates lower prices, it also checks the most significant danger associated with integration: the potential underprovision of care. Whether such competitive forces will be sufficient, or whether additional remedies are called for, particularly in markets too small to engender effective competition, remains an important policy question. This last issue is taken up in the conclusion as a postscript on health care reform.

Health care markets, market failures, and Coase's theory of the firm: a framework for evaluating health care reforms

Market Failures and Arrow's Optimality Gap: The Role of Social Institutions

Health care markets fail to correspond with many of the assumptions made about the behavior of buyers and sellers in textbook models of competition. Acknowledging the complexity of the issues, however, does not mean that health care problems are intractable, or that economic analysis cannot generate substantial insight. Private health care decisions, whether it is the purchase of insurance or the acquisition of medical services, are essentially economic decisions that can be understood in economic terms. That being said, it is necessary to acknowledge that these decisions take place within the context of substantial market failures. Imperfect information lies at the heart of these problems. Patients lack information about such fundamental issues as their need for, the marginal benefits of, and the relative quality of competing medical services. Physicians, on the other hand, are both sources of medical knowledge and providers of medical services. A result of this informational asymmetry is the formation of an awkward agency relationship between the consumers and the sellers of medical services. The prevalence of health care insurance and the shifting of incentives to behave in a price-sensitive manner from consumers and to frequently distant third party payers constitute additional complicating factors.

Market failures have direct implications for economic analysis and the appropiateness of antitrust reform. According to the first theorem of welfare economics, general competitive equilibria are Pareto-efficient, meaning that there exists no other allocation of resources that will make all participants better off.[4] Under such circumstances, there is generally no role for government regulation, and the proper focus of antitrust law is to safeguard the conditions necessary for effective competition. One implication of the market failures endemic in the health care sector is that any resulting market equilibrium is likely to deviate, perhaps substantially, from the socially optimal allocation of resources. Under such circumstances, it is at least conceivable that some external intervention could result in an outcome that would be Pareto-superior.[5]

In private settings, suboptimal resource allocations will trigger bargaining and additional transactions until the mutual gains of trade are exhausted.[6] Kenneth Arrow postulates a social analogue to this phenomenon: "when the market fails to achieve an optimal state, society will, to some extent at least, recognize the gap, and nonmarket social institutions will arise attempting to bridge it."[7] Arrow attributed many of the distinctive social institutions characteristic of traditional health care markets to society's efforts to bridge the "optimality gap."

[T]he special structural characteristics of the medical-care market are largely attempts to overcome the lack of optimality due to the nonmarketability of the bearing of suitable risks and the imperfect marketability of information. These compensatory institutional changes, with some reenforcement from usual profit motives, largely explain the observed noncompetitive behavior of the medical-care market.[8]

Arrow's apparently uncritical acceptance of the welfare-enhancing nature of health care's distinctive characteristics has been criticized by such commentators as Mark Pauly and Paul Starr. According to Pauly, "the problem is that such arrangements do not *necessarily* improve matters; we have no assurance that these characteristics really are attempts by politicians and medical trade associations to do what the welfare economists would suggest."[9] Starr makes a similar argument:

Arrow looks at the structure of the medical market as a rational adaption to certain inherent characteristics of medical care . . . There is the presumption that what is real is rational, or, as the economists say "optimal" . . . The result is not so much to explain as to explain away the particular institutional structure medical care has assumed in the United States.[10]

Certainly, the optimality gap is likely to invite private opportunistic behavior as well. Arrow's critics are appropriately skeptical of the welfare-enhancing attributes of traditional nonmarket institutions, and rightfully call for a more sophisticated analysis of special interest legislation. Nevertheless, Arrow's insight that social institutions and peculiar nonmarket deviations from competitive norms *can serve* corrective economic functions in markets dominated by market failures should not be overlooked. The presumption that "what is real is rational" has pragmatic force. While it is doubtful that traditional health care structures yielded Pareto-optimal results, it is equally doubtful that such institutions could have endured and become so entrenched if they had no welfare-enhancing attributes, or if there existed a plainly more efficient way of organizing the market.

Meaningful economic discussion, therefore, must recognize that social institutions may have significant economic content, not only as static constraints upon individual decision making, but because these institutions may themselves be the endogenous product of the very constellation of economic forces and market failures that they seek to regulate and control. As such, these institutions may possess economic information that can help explain how health care markets function (or fail to function). In Arrow's words, "institutional organization and the observable mores of the medical profession" should be included as "data to be used in assessing the competitiveness of the medical care market."[11] Unfortunately, the invitation to engage in a richer economic/institutional analysis of health care relations has gone largely unheeded by academic economists. [12] At a minimum, an understanding of the possible economic functions played by traditional institutions is helpful in identifying the problems that will be caused by their abandonment through integration. Integration, after all, is simply a different response to the same market failures that spawned traditional structures. Consequently, the equilibrium of the new market, one dominated by integrated firms, will likely result in its own optimality gap, and potentially a new array of corrective nonmarket institutions.

Traditional Markets, Integration, and Coase's Theory of the Firm

Coase's 1937 article, *The Nature of the Firm,* raises the basic question of why some economic decisions take place in the form of arms length market transactions, while other economic decisions are made internally by firms in the absence of a functioning market or an active price mechanism.[13] Traditional health care markets have many distinctive characteristics, including the important role of nonprofit status, state licensing requirements, and the pervasive self-regulatory activities of health care professionals. Underlying all of these features, however, is a distinctive structure of the market itself with its fragmented and economically segregated provision of (*1*) medical insurance, (*2*) physician services (human capital) and (*3*) hospital services (physical capital).[14] This fractured structure necessitates a series of market exchanges between consumers, as separate purchasers of medical insurance and medical services, and a triumvirate of insurers, hospitals and physicians, all independent and distinct economic actors.

The complementary nature of physician and hospital services makes it even more remarkable that these services are not jointly provided.[15] Factors that increase the demand for hospital services will also increase the demand for certain physician services and vice versa. Independent decision making by physicians and hospitals will not internalize these effects. Given this complementarity, Physician Hospital Organizations (PHOs) that integrated hospital and physician services could theoretically produce lower prices and higher levels of output simply by internalizing these externalities, independent of its ability to attain greater efficiencies.[16] There is no a priori reason why hospitals could not hire physicians as employees or, alternatively, why physicians could not own the hospital facilities at which they work. Few other industries so completely separate the human and physical capital associated with the provision of services. Lawyers, for example, form partnerships and own the physical assets of the firm. Automobile mechanics own their own tools and garage, or work as employees of the entity that controls the physical resources. Similarly, there is no a priori reason why the provision of medical services and the purchase of medical insurance take place in two separate market transactions. Segregating these functions substantially alters the economic incentives governing both the provision of medical care and the acquisition of technology. Moreover, segregating the functions of insurance and the delivery of medical services introduces substantial transaction costs associated with contracting, monitoring and utilization review. Again, either integrated health care providers could price their services in the form of an insurance commodity or, alternatively, insurance companies could integrate forward and arrange the intra-firm provision of medical services for their insureds.

Typically, high market-based transaction costs produce incentives to perform economic functions internally. From a Coasian perspective, therefore, one might expect more tightly integrated health care providers to represent the dominant firm structure. The strength of contemporary incentives driving integration are undeniable. While these incentives have triggered substantial restructuring in health care markets, often reducing the previous kaleidoscope of market exchanges into a more limited number of transactions between *health plans* and their subscribers, no dominant structure for the provision of managed care has yet emerged.[17] Indeed, in addition to highly heterogeneous patterns of managed care development, one observes chaotic conduct more akin to herding behavior than the rational evolution of Coasian firms. Regardless of the absence of a dominant set of managed care contracting practices, it is clear that the changes that have taken place to date have fundamentally altered both the nature of the economic entities providing medical services and the very nature of the product being sold.

Understanding Our Past

If contemporary incentives for integration are so strong, how can one explain the *anomalous* structure of traditional health care markets? In other words, why are traditional markets structured in a manner that is apparently *irrational* from a

Coasian perspective? As discussed earlier, the answer can be phrased largely in terms of imperfect information and agency problems. Patients must rely upon the expertise and advice of the sellers of medical services. In turn, physicians assume an agency relationship with their patients. The physician–patient agency relationship is not perfect, but various methods of structuring health care markets can make the agency relationship more or less imperfect. While physicians in private practice can abuse the agency relationship with respect to the services they directly control, the fractured structure of traditional markets afforded physicians some degree of institutional independence. This independence created a space for doctors to act as credible agents at least with respect to other suppliers of medical services.[18] More importantly, the structural independence of physicians from third-party payers, combined with a fee-for-service system of compensation, aligned the physician's private economic incentives with those of the patient. Under this system, health care professionals maximized revenue by providing rather than denying care, consciously biasing the expected direction of agency abuse. As a result, traditional structures, for all their shortcomings in terms of economic efficiency, were fairly well-designed for meeting patient needs, to the point of overtreating those individuals who could access the system.

Unfortunately, a medical system biased in favor of overproviding care imposes its own costs. Given the efficiencies that might be gained through integration, one would expect active exploration of alternative systems for delivering and financing health care. Wide-scale experimentation, however, failed to materialize until fairly recently.[19] Early experimentation was discouraged by laws that helped to entrench traditional health care structures, with physicians at the center. Laws prohibiting the corporate practice of medicine, for example, constrained the ability of insurance companies to integrate forward and directly arrange for the provision of medical services.[20] Moreover, a move from fee-for-service compensation to capitation or other systems of prepayment necessarily entails the creation of closed panels of providers and the ability to engage in selective contracting. Historically, such practices were inconsistent with many state insurance regulations.[21]

Just as one cannot unquestioningly accept the optimality of Arrow's non-market institutions, the mere existence of laws inhibiting the creation of alternative market responses, is an insufficient explanation for the longevity of traditional structures. Expected efficiency gains should motivate efforts to change prevailing laws, although the necessity of such changes can increase the costs associated with creating alternative systems. Nor is it sufficient to contend that traditional structures were maintained solely because they were in the interests of powerful groups such as physicians and hospitals. The self-interest of any particular constituency is unlikely to dominate an entire system over time unless the network of arrangements is broadly *acceptable* to other constituencies, with acceptability defined in terms of the benefits that could be collectively obtained within the next-best set of possible arrangements.[22]

Herein lies the problem. The relevant comparison is not between existing arrangements and some ideal state, but between existing arrangements and other feasible (even if imperfect) alternatives. Comparing sets of next-best arrangements is a difficult task. One is likely to find an entire range of second-best equilibria, each associated with distinct sets of Arrow's corrective institutions. These equilibria and associated institutions may be radically different from each other. The numerous and varied visions of reform in the Clinton-era national health care debate illustrate the point—serious reform proposals ranged from single-payer systems to various forms of managed competition, with the specter of direct government administration or completely decentralized medical savings accounts lurking in the background. Within this environment, policy choices are likely to be of a discrete rather than a continuous nature, with competing options representing sharply different sets of strengths and weaknesses. The reality of discrete policy choices means that the political option of compromise is not necessarily available.[23] Two discrete policy options cannot simply be melded together into a workable system in an effort to split the difference. From this perspective, the committee-style decision making of the Clinton Health Care Task Force may have been exactly the wrong approach to meaningful health care reform.

When confronting such uncertainty, it is often desirable to encourage experimentation to generate information and test the viability of competing systems. From this perspective, the legal damper placed on policy innovation (by corporate practice laws and state insurance regulations), coupled with the ability of physicians to anticompetitive frustrate the development of alternative systems of health care delivery and financing,[24] contributed greatly to the entrenchment of traditional structures. These measures suppressed the creation of information concerning alternative policy options. The lack of experimentation increased the uncertainty and risk associated with health care reform and probably raised the switching point at which old systems would be abandoned and new ones adopted.

This discussion need not imply that traditional structures were irrational at their inception. An economic market in which consumers are imperfectly informed about essential aspects of the transaction and must rely upon sellers as agents is subject to two types of abuses. If sellers are compensated on a fee-for-service basis, one would anticipate a competitive equilibrium characterized by the systematic overconsumption of medical resources. Alternatively, if buyers prepay sellers for services, one would expect a market equilibrium characterized by the systematic underprovision of care. Traditional structures can be defended as rational if the social costs of overproviding care were relatively more acceptable than the social costs associated with underproviding care. This may well have been the case when the practice of medicine was less capital-intensive. The costs associated with a passively supervised fee-for-service system, however, can only be expected to increase over time. The increase is compounded by the fact that the same factors encouraging the overprovision of care also create strong incentives for the research, development and acquisition of new medical technology. At some point, the costs of the traditional arrangements will no longer be acceptable to many constituents, and new structures will be actively explored. Employers, who during the 1940s, 1950s, and 1960s increasingly offered health care benefits as part of their wage packages, were the first to feel the pinch and respond. Large employers and employer groups led the call for increased utilization review, selective contracting and express negotiations with providers over the price and terms of treatment.

The New Optimality Gap and Criteria for Assessing Health Care Reform

Integration has been the most actively pursued response to the failings of traditional market structures. In many parts of the country, integrated managed care networks have displaced traditional entities as the dominant firm structure. As discussed earlier, integration changes economic behavior. Integrated firms will generally not provide care beyond the point where the marginal costs of treatment exceed the expected marginal benefits. Furthermore, by bringing each constituent function in-house (insurance, hospital facilities, and physician expertise), integrated firms internalize the costs associated with underutilized capacity and equipment, thereby creating more rational incentives for capital investment. Consequently, integration counteracts the most serious problem associated with traditional markets—the systematic overconsumption of resources.

Integration, however, is not a panacea. It largely involves trading in one set of problems for another, as policy makers choose amongst another set of second-best alternatives. Integration fails to resolve or even address certain market failures, such as informational asymmetries. The provider–patient agency relationship still exists and, as with all agency relationships, is still subject to abuse. If anything, integration exacerbates the problem. Within an integrated firm, individual physicians lack the structural independence that once may have enhanced their ability to act as credible agents. Moreover, within an integrated firm, the provider's economic incentives are adverse to the patients'. Simplistically, revenues are maximized (for at least the short term) by reducing the amount of care provided and resources expended. Whereas the agency relationship under traditional structures was abused by providing too much care (because it was in the agent's self-interest), abuse in integrated structures will be manifested by providing too little care (because it is in the agent's self-interest).

Given that integration will not fully address the market failures characteristic of the health care sector, it is inevitable that the equilibrium obtained in integrated markets will also be Pareto-inefficient, creating its own optimality gap. If Arrow is correct, one would expect to see new social institutions and nonmarket mechanisms arise in an effort to bridge the gap. If Starr and Pauly are correct, not every proposed nonmarket intervention will be in the public interest. Consequently, it is necessary to distinguish those nonmarket interventions that are likely to be wel-

122 THE PRIVATIZATION OF HEALTH CARE REFORM

fare-enhancing from those that will have the primary effect of furthering the private interests of particular groups.

The critical question is whether a proposed intervention will help bridge the optimality gap and result in a superior distribution of social resources.[25] Such interventions should be able to satisfy three criteria.[26] First, the intervention should be directly responsive to one of the underlying market failures triggering the optimality gap; this factor screens reforms that have a plausible economic foundation from those that do not. Second, the intervention should result in an increase in social welfare as compared with the unmodified market equilibrium. This factor separates the public from the purely private interest of reform advocates, and ensures that any change will be efficiency enhancing, at least from a short-term, static perspective. Finally, nonmarket institutions should not unnecessarily hinder the efficient structure, operation and evolution of competitive markets. This last requirement seeks to ensure that changes will be dynamically efficient and seeks to avoid short-term gains that may harm the long term structural performance of the market. As a corollary to these principles, a justification for one of Arrow's institutions should not be predicated upon a rationale that the market itself is capable of recognizing and rewarding. Proposals for medical antitrust reform can be evaluated in light of these criteria. The initiatives of physicians and hospitals will be considered in turn.

Physician proposals for medical antitrust reform

Physicians have sought various reforms of federal antitrust laws that either would exempt doctors from the per se rule against price fixing, permitting forms of collective physician bargaining or, alternatively, reforms that would expand the types of physician networks examined under the rule of reason standard. Before evaluating these proposals, it is helpful to briefly examine the antitrust standards currently governing physician conduct.

Summary of the Antitrust Laws

Federal antitrust law embraces competition as the preferred means of allocating social resources[27] and assumes that markets are capable of guaranteeing appropriate levels of quality and safety, not only for physical commodities, but also for professional services.[28] The law condemns as per se illegal horizontal agreements that are believed to always, or almost always, interfere with the operation of markets and produce anticompetitive effects.[29] Traditional categories of per se illegal agreements include price fixing, territorial allocations, boycotts, and tying arrangements. Agreements that fall outside the categories of per se illegality are evaluated under the *rule of reason* standard, meaning that courts assess the reasonableness of the alleged restraint on a case-by-case basis in light of the conduct's anticipated anticompetitive and potential procompetitive effects.[30] Restraints, even those affecting price, may be permitted under the rule of reason so long as the agreements are ancillary to a legitimate purpose and are sufficiently narrow in scope.[31] The conduct of economically integrated firms is frequently treated differently from similar actions undertaken by independent economic actors. Sufficiently integrated undertakings (such as a bona fide joint venture) are analyzed under the rule of reason. Ancillary aspects of such agreements will be judged in light of their competitive effects. Integration into a single corporate entity or partnership can entirely shield conduct from Section 1 scrutiny. Under the *Copperweld* doctrine, actions taken by different components of the same corporate entity do not constitute *agreements*, and therefore fall outside the scope of section 1 of the Sherman Act.[32]

It is helpful to illustrate these principles in the health care context. An agreement between independent physicians who are horizontal competitors would implicate Section 1's prohibition against restraints of trade. If the agreement pertained solely to the price physicians would charge insurance companies for their services, then the agreement would be *per se* illegal. The Supreme Court clearly established this rule in *Arizona v. Maricopa County Medical Society.*[33] If, instead, the agreement formed a new physician group in which the doctors combined practices then, depending upon the level and type of integration, the agreement would be assessed under the rule of reason. If the legal entity formed by the agreement was a new corporation (or partnership), then no Sherman Act Section 1 issues would be raised by the entity's subsequent pricing practices. As a matter of comparison, agreements between third party payers and individual physicians forming a managed care network would typically be subject to rule of reason analysis, given the nonhorizontal nature of the relationship (integration as opposed to consolidation).

The challenge, as a matter of law and policy, is to identify the characteristics that should distinguish those agreements that are considered per se illegal from those agreements that are examined under the rule of reason. In 1994 and 1996, the Department of Justice and the Federal Trade Commission jointly issued health care enforcement policy statements to provide guidance in this area.[34] The *1994 Statements* and the *1996 Statements*, however, drew the line separating the *per se* rule and the rule of reason in distinctly different places. According to the *1994 Statements*, rule of reason analysis will be applied to physician networks if the network either engages in substantial risk sharing or offers a new product.[35] No example of what constitutes a new product was provided. The *1994 Statements* did, however, elaborate on the risk-sharing requirement. A network shares substantial financial risk:

(1) when the venture agrees to provide services to a health benefits plan at a "capitated" rate; or *(2)* when the venture creates significant financial incentives for its members as a group to achieve specified cost-containment goals, such as withholding from all members a substantial amount of the compensation due them, with distribution of that amount to the members only if the cost-containment goals are met.[36]

By implication, if physicians enter into price-related agreements that do not meet the above standards, the enforcement agencies would consider such agreements to be per se illegal.

The *1996 Statements* built upon this framework, but made two important changes. First, the *1996 Statements* expanded the types of arrangements that constitute the sharing of substantial financial risk.[37] Second, and more importantly, under the *1996 Statements*, a physician network can qualify for rule of reason analysis even if there is no risk sharing, so long as there is substantial clinical integration and the network "creates significant efficiencies."[38] The *1996 Statements* define integration in the absence of financial risk sharing as follows:

> Such integration can be evidenced by the network implementing an active and ongoing program to evaluate and modify practice patterns by the network's physician participants and create a high degree of interdependence and cooperation among the physicians to control costs and ensure quality. This program may include: (*1*) establishing mechanisms to monitor and control utilization of health care services that are designed to control costs and assure quality of care; (*2*) selectively choosing network physicians who are likely to further these efficiencies; and (*3*) the significant investment of capital, both monetary and human, in the necessary infrastructure and capacity to realize the claimed efficiencies.[39]

If the network is "sufficiently integrated," network pricing will avoid the per se rule so long as the agreements with respect to price are reasonably necessary to obtaining the increased efficiency benefits.[40] This formulation is simply an application of the standard ancillary restraints test to physician networks. The ultimate significance of the 1996 provision, therefore, will depend upon the type of pricing agreements the enforcement agencies factually deem to be "reasonably necessary" for cost control and utilization review.

Physician Calls For Antitrust Reform Along Maricopa's Contested Border

Throughout the 1990s, health care providers sought federal antitrust reform as one of their primary legislative objectives. Physicians pursued a number of options, ranging from blanket exceptions from antitrust scrutiny, to the right to collectively negotiate with insurance companies, to more relaxed standards governing physician network formation. For example, H.R. 3486, a bill introduced during the national health care debate, would have created a *safe harbor* for physician networks of any type, so long as the network did not exceed 25% of the relevant market defined on a specialty-by-specialty basis.[41] The 1995 House bill reforming the Medicare system would have legislated that the rule of reason antitrust standard, rather than the standard of per se illegality, be applied to the conduct of *provider service networks* contracting for Medicare services.[42] Similarly, the *Antitrust Health Care Advancement Act of 1997*, championed by Representative Henry Hyde, would have legislated that entities qualifying as *health care provider networks* be evaluated under rule of reason analysis.[43]

Alternatively, physicians have advocated broadening the categories of integration and risk sharing to include forms of physician equity investment. Under such a standard, a physician network would be evaluated under the rule of reason so long as participating doctors had a sufficient amount of capital invested in the common venture.[44] Other measures championed by former Representative Thomas Campbell would have effectively displace the antitrust laws altogether. H.R. 3770, a bill introduced in 1996, would have granted complete antitrust immunity for physicians negotiating with third-party payers on wages, rates of payment and hours of work.[45] Similar proposals were introduced in 1998 and 1999. H.R. 4277 and H.R. 1304 would have applied the same antitrust exemption afforded unionized workers to the collective actions of independent health care providers.[46] H.R. 1304 actually passed the House of Representations in June 2000, but the measure was not brought to a vote in the Senate.

Ambiguities inherent in federal antitrust law necessarily complicate discussions about the need for legislative reform.[47] Despite the aura of certainty created by labeling conduct per se illegal, the actual boundary separating per se illegal conduct from conduct that will be evaluated under the rule of reason and now conduct examined under "quick look" rule of reason analysis is frequently unclear.[48] Efforts to delineate the standard governing physician networks must begin with the Supreme Court's decision in *Maricopa*.[49] After *Maricopa*, it is uncontroversial that Section 1 of the Sherman Act applies to agreements between physicians and that certain types of physician pricing agreements are per se illegal. The exact reach of the Court's holding, however, is debated. This controversy is heightened when one acknowledges that *Maricopa's* per se rule must be read against the backdrop of 20 years of Supreme Court precedent generally expanding the scope of rule of reason analysis.

The enforcement agencies' *1994 Statements* conservatively interpret *Maricopa* as holding that physician price-related agreements are per se illegal unless the arrangement produces a new product or involves the sharing of substantial financial risk, the later being defined in terms of capitation and fee-withholding. The exemptions for new products and for networks sharing financial risk come directly from the Supreme Court's efforts to distinguish *Maricopa* from its earlier holding in *Broadcast Music v. Columbia Broadcasting Systems*.[50] The Court suggested that rule of reason analysis would be appropriate if the physicians were able to market a *new product* (not in competition with their individually provided services), formed a *single firm* (an application of the principles underlying the subsequently announced *Copperweld* doctrine), or offered their services for a *flat fee* (capitation).[51] The Court rejected the physicians' claim that purported efficiencies, standing alone, justified the joint setting of prices,[52] and the Court was careful to distinguish the agreement it approved in *Broadcast Music* from a *joint sales* agency.[53]

The enforcement agencies' *1996 Statements* take a more expansive view of

Maricopa, contending that price-related agreements in conjunction with substantial clinical integration will be subject to rule of reason analysis (in the absence of the sharing of financial risk), so long as the price-related agreements are reasonably necessary for obtaining the alleged efficiency gains.[54] Clark Havighurst also advocates a more expansive view of *Maricopa*. He argues that physician networks should be viewed as joint sales agreements that lower the transaction costs of physician–payer contracting and hence justify rule of reason analysis.[55] Havighurst's characterization of physician networks as joint sales agreements differs importantly from the substantial clinical integration standard adopted in the *1996 Statements*. Clinical integration produces economic efficiencies that are only tangentially related to network price agreements. Havighurst, on the other hand, focuses directly on the efficiency attributes of joint pricing agreements—the reduced costs of negotiating and drafting a single contract.

In evaluating these many reform proposals, it is useful to distinguish between physician agreements that constitute classic examples of horizontal price fixing (uncontroversially governed by the per se rule); physician agreements that satisfy the enforcement agencies' *1994 Statements* requirement of substantial risk sharing (uncontroversially governed by the rule of reason); and physician agreements falling short of the enforcement agencies' 1994 standards for sharing financial risk and yet not reminiscent of classically prohibited per se illegal conduct. This last category lies in a doctrinally indeterminate zone, where courts interpreting *Maricopa* may or may not apply the rule of reason standard and where the enforcement agencies' own line has shifted over time. The most extreme physician antitrust reforms would legalize forms of collective bargaining falling within the first category—behavior that would incontrovertibly be considered per se illegal. Other reforms would focus on behavior in the third category—seeking to extend the scope of the rule of reason to include physician networks predicated on shared equity investment, the *1996 Statements'* substantial clinical integration requirement, or Havighurst's joint sales arrangements. The merits of these proposals will be considered in turn.

Collective Physician Bargaining—Assessing the Wisdom of the Per Se Rule

The original Clinton administration health care reform proposal would have granted physicians limited authority to collectively negotiate over fees with newly-created state or regional health care purchasing cooperatives.[56] The demise of national health care reform did not temper physician desires to engage in collective bargaining; it simply shifted the target of negotiations to private insurance companies. H.R. 3770 would have granted blanket antitrust immunity to physicians engaging in collective negotiations with health service plans regarding wages, rates of pay, hours of work and other terms and conditions of contract, so long as the health care service plan had a *presumption of market power.*[57] H.R. 4277 and H.R. 1304, the Campbell bills, would have gone even further and immunized collective physician conduct even in the absence of alleged countervailing market power. These bills proposed extending groups of independent health care professionals the same antitrust immunity that the law extends to labor unions.[58]

Legislative action in this area is required because *Maricopa's* per se rule would clearly outlaw collective bargaining by independent health care professionals. While the per se rule is firmly established as a matter of antitrust doctrine, these legislative proposals force us to ask whether the law's prohibition against physician price fixing is defensible as a matter of health care policy. To answer this question it is helpful to recall the evaluative criteria developed earlier and ask (*1*) whether collective bargaining is responsive to an identifiable market failure; (*2*) whether a collectively-bargained-for equilibrium would result in an increase in the social welfare (static efficiency); and (*3*) whether collective bargaining would disrupt the structure and efficient operation of health care markets (dynamic efficiency).

To qualify as one of Arrow's optimality–gap-filling, nonmarket institutions, a reform must be responsive to an underlying market failure. The most significant market failures in the health care industry involve agency problems and imperfect information. While physicians frequently cloak proposed antitrust reforms in a rhetoric of patient rights, there is no immediate or logical connection between concerns over patient care and the right of physicians to fix prices. Collective bargaining does not facilitate the ability of physicians to act as credible agents for their patients, and community levels of physician compensation are unrelated to the underlying problem of informational asymmetries. Market failures may justify some types of external intervention, but the right to fix prices is not one of them. Information market failures may call for measures protecting open communications between physicians and their patients about treatment options. Agency failures may justify the imposition of fiduciary duties on health care providers and managed care companies. The physician–patient agency relationship, however, is atomistic in nature and safeguards for the relationship, if necessary at all, should entail carefully designed individual protections rather than warrants for collective action.

In an effort to justify collective bargaining, physicians complain that individually negotiated fees result in insufficient levels of physician compensation. Two conflicting claims are often put forward to explain why. The first concerns the possible exercise of market power by third party payers. The other concerns a possible oversupply of physicians. Neither explanation justifies a change in the antitrust laws to relax the per se prohibition against price fixing. If third party payers possess monopsony power capable of forcing subcompetitive rates of compensation, the appropriate solution is to apply the antitrust laws directly against the source of third party payor market power, not to sanction collective bargaining in the form of an antitrust exemption.[59] Similarly, if low levels of compensation are caused by an oversupply of physicians in particular markets, collective bargaining is not the answer. Lower rates of compensation serve the necessary economic function of encouraging physicians to move to markets where there is a relatively greater need for their services. Permitting physicians to collectively bargain in such circumstances would simply perpetuate existing market dislocations and prevent what would ultimately be a more desirable allocation of social resources. More particularly, this is precisely the type of misallocation that competitive markets are well-equipped to handle. This argument applies to the appropriate allocation of physician resources across specialties and subspecialties, as well as the allocation of physician services geographically.

Collective physician bargaining fails the second criterion as well—collective bargaining is likely to decrease (not increase) social welfare.[60] At its most benign, it would systematically increase the price that third party payers (and ultimately patients) would pay for physician services. Higher prices would further increase health care costs and further limit patient access to the health care system. The absolute degree of the price increase would depend upon how effective physicians were in presenting a united front to third party payers and the nature of the sanctions physicians would be able to impose upon doctors who chose to defect from the collective agreement and offer their services at a lower price. On a distributional level, collective bargaining would shift a greater portion of whatever economic rents are available in health care markets to the respective physician constituencies. Doctors would gain, while the hospitals, third party payers and patients would lose.

Finally, collective physician bargaining runs the risk of undermining the dynamic efficiency of the market, violating the third criterion. Cooperative action between otherwise independent physicians could be used to block the creation of new integrated health plans. Physicians who favored traditional health care market structures with the fee-for-service system of compensation, the segregation of insurance, physician, and hospital services, and the pivotal role of physicians as the patient's point-of-entry into the system would be given a powerful tool. Boycotts of alternative systems of delivery have long been used to prevent and forestall change in the health care system.[61] To the extent that integration reflects a Coasian transformation of the firm and a more rational method of arranging health care transactions as intra-firm decisions rather than separate market-driven exchanges, these efficiencies would be lost. In short, calls to abandon the per se rule against price fixing and to permit collective physician bargaining should be rejected.

Risk Sharing Requirements for Physician Networks—Defining the Scope of the Rule of Reason

More subtle questions are raised by physician proposals to permit the formation of physician networks in the absence of substantial risk sharing. Under the enforcement agencies' *1994 Statements*, physicians were free to form provider networks so long as the network marketed its services as a prepaid insurance product (capitation) or engaged in structured fee-withholding arrangements.[62] Efforts to eliminate or substantially weaken these requirements should be closely scrutinized. Economic form often dictates economic behavior. Integrated providers have incentives to directly compare the costs and benefits of treatment decisions.[63] Integration can also reduce transaction costs, such as the need for third party monitoring and post-treatment utilization review. Finally, depending upon the anticipated length of the plan/patient relationship, the integrated health plan will have economic incentives to make investments that decrease the expected long-term costs of an enrollee's medical care. Other proposed triggers for rule of reason analysis will not necessarily have the same beneficial economic effects.

Capitation is not the only form of risk sharing recognized by the *1994 Statements*. A fee-for-service physician network will also be evaluated under the rule of reason if the network engages in structured fee-withholding.[64] Physicians contend that the same objectives could be achieved through equity investment and advocate joint capital investment as an equivalent rule of reason trigger.[65] Fee-withholding, however, embodies more than just the efficiencies associated with cost-minimizing network operation. Fee-for-service systems of compensation are systematically biased in favor of overproviding care (prescribing treatment beyond the point where the marginal benefits of additional care equal the marginal costs). Capitated reimbursement is one means of counteracting these incentives. A different solution involves the imposition of external constraints that establish limits on a physician's ability to abuse the patient-provider agency relationship. Fee-withholding constitutes just such a device. The cost-containment objectives represent pre-committed limits on the charges that the network will make. To be credible, of course, the system must be properly structured. If the amount withheld is too small, profits earned by over-providing care may be large enough to justify forfeiting the withheld portion.

Replacing fee-withholding arrangements with joint equity investment will not achieve the same objectives. Physicians argue that equity investments give each physician a stake in the network and commit each physician to the financial success of the venture.[66] The problem, however, is not with ensuring the physicians' commitment to the profitability of the venture, but rather with pre-determining how it is that the network will maximize its profits. Under a capitated system, networks make profits by strictly controlling costs and limiting expenses. Under a system of fee-withholding, the value of the withheld fee serves as a countervailing incentive for traditional fee-for-service networks, under which profits are maximized by meeting cost containment objectives, i.e., limiting aggregate levels of care. Physician networks anchored in equity investment have no such countervailing incentives. These networks can be expected to maximize profits both by using whatever market power they possess to charge higher prices *and* by practicing medicine by traditional standards, which are intrinsically biased in favor of over providing care.

The *1996 Statements* implicitly recognize the limitations of simple equity investment and reject joint capital contributions as an independent trigger for rule of reason analysis. The *1996 Statements* will permit rule of reason analysis (in the absence of financial risk sharing) only if the network (*1*) establishes mechanisms to monitor and control utilization to control costs and to assure quality, (*2*) selectively chooses network physicians who are likely to further efficiency objectives, *and* (*3*) engages in significant investment in the physical and human capital infrastructure needed to realize the claimed efficiencies.[67] Ironically, none of these actions raise serious antitrust issues by themselves. Physicians could easily enter into limited agreements to jointly invest in utilization, monitoring and management systems, and such joint actions would be evaluated under the rule of reason. Under the *1996 Statements*, however, a physician network engaging in the above actions can then proceed to jointly fix prices, to the extent that such price agreements are deemed *reasonably necessary to the venture's achievement of efficiencies.*[68]

The treatment of price agreements in the context of substantial clinical integration is a straight forward example of ancillary restraints analysis.[69] The weakness of the *1996 Statements* is not its characterization of the legal standard, but rather its implied assertion of fact. The factual nexus between the ability to engage in utilization review and the need to collectively negotiate with third party payers over the price of physician services is highly suspect. In the *1996 Statements'* only example of a legitimate physician network joint venture based on substantial clinical integration, the purported need to fix prices is asserted as a conclusion without explanation.[70] The ultimate scope of the clinical integration exception will depend upon the rigor with which the enforcement agencies demand that price-related agreements, in fact, be reasonably necessary for achieving alleged efficiencies. Rigorous enforcement of the *reasonably necessary* requirement would render the exception a narrow one. A relaxed standard, on the other hand, would permit physician networks to bootstrap price fixing agreements onto largely unrelated efforts to engage in monitoring and utilization review.

Early experience with the *1996 Statements* suggests that the actual sharing of financial risk is still the favored approach. The physician networks receiving favorable responses from the enforcement agencies under the Business Review Procedure typically involve express forms of risk sharing.[71] Moreover, the enforcement agencies have continued to condemn as per se illegal physician price setting arrangements in the absence of meaningful integration.[72] The FTC has also ruled that joint investment in physical capital, standing alone, does not constitute substantial clinical integration because the subsequent joint setting of prices was not reasonably necessary to sustain the initial investment.[73] Unfortunately, however, there is still no clear understanding of exactly what constitutes substantial clinical integration.[74]

Clark Havighurst similarly advocates extending rule of reason analysis to encompass physician price setting, but he bases his argument on efficiencies that are directly attributable to joint negotiations and contracting.[75] Even in the absence of substantial clinical integration, physician networks can reduce the transaction costs associated with separate and independent negotiations between physicians and third party payers. Havighurst contends that these transaction cost savings alone provide a sufficiently strong procompetitive justification to warrant application of the rule of reason. I disagree. The economies associated with reduced bargaining costs should not be treated in the same manner as the economies associated with capitation and fee-withholding. Meaningfully integrating the financing and delivery of medical services affects the basic manner in which medicine is practiced, introducing an express comparison between the costs and benefits of additional treatment. Transaction-cost-reducing networks, on the other hand, will not practice medicine any differently. At the same time, physician networks that serve only a transactional function pose serious anticompetitive risks, both from the direct exercise of market power and from indirect forms of spillover collusion. While effective application of the rule of reason might reduce some of these threats, the application of the rule of reason standard is not costless. At a minimum, the added antitrust enforcement costs would have to be balanced against any alleged contracting efficiencies.

Havighurst's strongest contention in support of a more liberal application of the rule of reason is his caution against prejudging the market.[76] An antitrust standard predicating rule of reason analysis upon capitation, global fees and fee-withholding will have the effect of encouraging these types of networks and discouraging other forms of physician collaboration. Ideally, private parties should be able to make unconstrained choices regarding the structure of their business agreements. Taken to an extreme, however, this argument proves too much. The entire purpose of antitrust law is to permit some forms of agreements and to prohibit others, based on the realization that the profits derived from successfully obtaining and exercising market power can motivate business agreements just as powerfully as the drive for legitimate economic opportunities. Almost every antitrust doctrine has the effect of constraining some forms of private conduct and prejudging the market. Under *Copperweld*, for example, intrafirm conspiracies are not subject to Section 1's prohibition against restraints of trade. Such a rule undoubtedly encourages integration in some instances where it might not otherwise occur.

At the same time, it is easy to exaggerate the degree to which integration requirements prejudge the market. The higher transaction costs associated with individual bargaining act more like a tax than a prohibition. Third-party payers are still free to form arrangements with a network of independent physicians through separate negotiations, and physicians are also free to operate within the confines of a messenger model Preferred Provider Organization (PPO). In a messenger model, the PPO acts as a literal messenger, carrying price quotes between third-party payers and individual physicians without disclosing the bargaining position of individual members to physicians as a group.[77] The relatively higher costs associated with this type of negotiation mean that fewer such networks will be formed, not that such networks will be unavailable to market participants if there is sufficient market demand.[78]

Economic arguments in favor of relaxing antitrust standards to permit network formation by physicians who are equity stakeholders, or who engage in substantial clinical integration without financial risk sharing, or on the basis of the reduced transaction costs of joint bargaining should be rejected. In the absence of economic structures inducing more rational decision making with respect to how medical resources are consumed, the per se prohibition against price fixing is warranted. By the same token, while capitation, global fees and structured fee-withholding constitute defensible forms of risk sharing, they do not exhaust the type of structural arrangements that can engender more rational intra-firm decision making with respect to the provision of health care. From a policy perspective, courts and the enforcement agencies should continue to be sensitive to other organizational forms and firm structures that meet the risk sharing criteria.

Physician Barriers to Entry

Physicians claim that they face distinct disadvantages in the battle to form integrated health plans. They maintain that antitrust requirements forcing doctors to price their services on a capitated basis discourage network formation because physicians lack the knowledge and experience necessary to price medical services as an insurance product.[79] They claim too, that they have more difficulty accessing capital markets. Finally, given that the physician component of the integrated health plan involves the largest number of actors, physicians claim that they face greater collective action problems in network formation than do hospitals and insurance companies. Doctors contend that these problems mean that most health plans today and in the foreseeable future will be dominated by hospitals and third party payers. Physicians further assert that policy makers should be concerned about their comparative disadvantage in network formation because physician-dominated networks are superior to payor-dominated networks,[80] and that physicians are able to practice managed care medicine in a more cost-effective manner.[81] Allegedly, these claims entitle physicians to special assistance in eliminating or reducing the barriers to physician entry into the market for integrated health plans.

Physician claims to practice managed care medicine in a more cost effective manner are self-defeating in terms of justifying special antitrust treatment. If physician claims are true, then physician-dominated plans should enjoy relatively greater success in the market. Active physician control and involvement may indeed be a significant factor in predicting network performance, and this difference may correspond to the provision of better medical services. Similarly, physician control may serve as an effective signaling device and a foundation for greater patient trust, much the same way that nonprofit status may have functioned in the past. If physician claims are true, however, these attributes will be rewarded in the market and give physician-dominated plans a comparative economic advantage.[82]

Physician claims of facing unique barriers that prevent them from even entering the market deserve more serious attention. It is true that most physicians lack the knowledge and experience to price a capitated insurance product. It is equally true that most insurance executives lack the knowledge, experience and state certification required to practice medicine. This fact, however, has not stopped insurance companies from establishing integrated health plans. Third party payers hire or contract with physicians to treat patients. Similarly, if physicians want to form integrated health plans, the solution is not to price the capitated product themselves, but rather to hire or contract for the insurance expertise. Just as there is a market for physician services, there is a market for actuaries and management personnel who can price health plans. Similarly, access to capital markets, particularly if physicians are correct in their contention that they can provide managed care in a more effective manner, should not stand as a prohibitive obstacle to physician-sponsored network formation. Finally, physician collective action presents no significant antitrust obstacles once physicians cross the hurdle of sufficient integration. Physicians in an integrated network can act collectively and their conduct will be evaluated under the rule of reason—the same legal standard applied to similarly situated hospitals and third party payers.

The sheer number of physicians involved in a managed care network is an unavoidable fact of life. The problem, however, is not unique to physician-sponsored networks. While it is a collective action problem from the perspective of physicians forming a network, it can be reciprocally characterized as a problem of contract monitoring for hospitals or third-party payers arranging the physician component of a managed-care plan. The theory of the firm teaches that there are many possible solutions to these types of problems. The solutions that will ultimately prevail in the market will be those that minimize the relative transaction costs and maximize the value of network performance. These are questions and problems that markets are well-suited to address.

Hospital proposals for medical antitrust reform

The Desirability of Hospital Competition and a Preliminary Assessment of Reform Proposals

Antitrust principles constrain the conduct of hospitals as well as that of physicians.[83] Hospitals have advocated antitrust reform that would permit increased consolidation and greater collective authority in planning the provision of medical services.[84] In essence, hospitals maintain that increased concentration or the express sanctioning of cooperative agreements is necessary to compensate for the inability of competitive market forces to efficiently allocate social resources. "The AHA believes that increased collaboration will allow local communities to establish programs designed to prevent or reduce excess capacity and unnecessary duplication of services, equipment, and facilities."[85] The ethic is one of cooperation in lieu of competition. According to the hospitals, competition creates incentives to over invest in capacity and equipment. Cooperation is necessary to counteract the effects of unfettered economic rivalry.

It is true that many hospital markets have substantial amounts of what might be termed *excess* capacity and that occupancy rates as low as 50% are not unusual. Historically, the pervasiveness of private insurance, fee-for-service systems of reimbursement, the price insensitivity of purchasing health care consumers, and government subsidies all helped to contribute to the over bedding of America. These perverse incentives were exacerbated by the irrational structure of the firm and the fractured economic relations between third party payers, hospitals and physicians. The role of physicians as patient-brokers gave hospitals incentives to engage in intense competition for physicians as a surrogate means of stimulating inpatient demand.[86] Most of this competitive energy was diverted along nonprice dimensions in the form of physician amenities, additional capacity, and new technology and equipment.

Earlier, this chapter developed a set of evaluative criteria to assess proposed antitrust reforms. An application of these standards to hospital proposals reveals that hospital calls for greater horizontal cooperation are actually third-best, rather than second-best solutions. Hospital reforms are not aimed at remedying market failures, such as imperfect or asymmetric information. Rather, they are aimed at reducing the detrimental side effects of traditional non-market responses to these underlying market failures. In essence, hospital proposals are designed to remedy the inefficiencies associated with the peculiar, non-Coasian structure of traditional health care markets and the corresponding tendency of these structures towards the over consumption of medical resources. The real problem is not with competition per se, but with competition between improperly organized firms. Competition between newly integrated entities, however, is unlikely to produce the same inefficient results. Consequently, the emergence of integrated health plans eliminates much of the underlying economic justifications for hospital antitrust reform.

Rejecting antitrust reforms in integrated health care markets, however, does not constitute a complete response to the problems raised by reform proponents. Hospital markets are predominately local in nature. While the case against greater physician cooperation was largely invariant to market structure—physician proposals are no more persuasive in concentrated markets than they are in competitive markets—hospital proposals require a tiered analysis that distinguishes between integrated markets, markets where integration is possible, and markets that are unlikely to ever cross the threshold of substantial integration. As just stated, antitrust reforms are unpersuasive in integrated markets. In smaller markets, however, there may be little or no chance of inducing substantial levels of integration, or of achieving effective competition between integrated health plans. While the welfare effects of hospital consolidation in these markets are ambiguous, a plausible argument can be made that hospital market power may curb pressures for non-price competition and may improve social welfare. Consequently, it is appropriate to discuss the desirability of reforming antitrust law in this setting.

In markets that have not yet experienced substantial integration, but which are capable of being integrated, the antitrust prescription is essentially the same as that for integrated markets. The dominant concern here is dynamic efficiency. Antitrust policy should be directed at maintaining the conditions necessary for effective competition between integrated health plans. Antitrust standards should be strictly enforced in these markets, even in the face of significant levels of excess capacity and calls for increased cooperation. Competition in these markets is likely to produce desirable results and the levels of physical capacity that are retained in these preintegrated markets will determine the degree of price competition that will ultimately emerge. This suggestion runs contrary to the prevailing wisdom, which tends to view retiring capacity from hospital markets as an unambiguous efficiency gain. The common wisdom, however, fails to appreciate the strategic incentive that health care providers have to establish capacity constraints as a means of restricting price competition. The full competitive virtues of existing hospital capacity must be recognized and expressly balanced against whatever efficiency gains might be obtained from its elimination.

Firm Structure and the Incentives to Acquire Capital and Technology

In evaluating hospital arguments for antitrust reform, one needs to understand the degree to which historic incentives to invest in hospital capacity and technology were influenced by the structure of hospitals, physicians and insurance companies as separate and independent economic firms. Ordinarily, a firm will invest in new capacity if it believes that the discounted revenues generated from being able to serve a greater number of customers will exceed the cost of the investment. Similarly, a firm will invest in a new technology if it believes that the cost savings from a superior method of production or the increased revenue derived from increased demand for the new service will exceed the cost of the investment.

There are many ways in which the fractured organization of traditional markets altered these basic calculations. A fee-for-service system of reimbursement, coupled with passive third party payor supervision, eliminated much of the economic penalty associated with underutilized capacity and technology. Rather than engaging in marginal cost pricing, hospitals traditionally charged a set mark-up over the average total cost of the service, passing the costs of underutilization on to third party payers in the form of higher charges. This behavior was not substantially different from that of a public utility. The third party payers that ultimately paid for the technology had little or no input into initial investment decisions. Furthermore, given that insurance companies reviewed hospital charges on the basis of a *reasonable and customary community standard*, there was no penalty when other hospitals in the same market invested in the same underutilized equipment. If another hospital acquired the same device, decreasing per-hospital rates of utilization, each hospital could submit a comparably higher *community* charge reflecting the equally underutilized nature of their respective services.

The fractured nature of the firm created additional incentives for acquiring new technology and services. In markets where patients implicitly selected a hospital through their choice of physician, hospitals could increase demand by cultivating physician loyalty and affiliation—forms of non-price competition. Given that physicians were independent economic actors who did not internalize the costs associated with underutilized hospital equipment, physicians had incentives to demand levels of capacity and technology that exceeded what they would rationally choose for themselves. For example, they might demand built-in excess hospital capacity if such capacity facilitated the physician's ability to access the facility by better accommodating the physician's scheduling needs.

These economic incentives are substantially altered once the disparate functions of insurance, physical capital and human capital are integrated into a single economic firm.[87] The integrated entity internalizes the costs associated with underutilized capacity. Moreover, in assessing the need for new technology, the firm will consider only the increased revenue that can be generated by the device in terms of increased utilization or reduced costs. Similarly, integration eliminates incentives to engage in nonprice competition for physicians. Competition for physician loyalty and affiliation can take place directly in terms of compensation, bonuses and salary. Finally, if firms are properly structured, the incentives of physician as stakeholders of the firm to demand new capacity and technology will be aligned with the needs of the organization.

The Superficial Case for Antitrust Reform

The irrational structure of the firm encourages overconsumption of health care resources. Competition between these fractured entities exacerbates these effects. Historically, hospital competition has manifested itself in higher levels of capital acquisition and nonprice competition in competitive markets than in markets that were relatively less competitive. These activities come at a substantial price. The consensus of empirical research employing data from traditionally structured markets finds a consistently positive and statistically significant relationship between indicia of competition and measures of hospital costs.[88] All other things being equal, the more hospitals there are, the higher the expenses associated with providing hospital care. Simplistically, if hospital expenses are *higher* in competitive markets than in concentrated markets, and one believes that hospital expenses in general are too high, then one possible means of reducing health care expenses is to encourage greater hospital consolidation, or to permit arrangements in competitive markets that mimic the types of resource allocations observed in economically concentrated hospital markets. Instead of integration, hospital consolidation and provider cooperation are advocated as solutions to the problem of increasing medical costs.

Determining whether this is an appropriate antitrust policy requires a careful examination of the welfare effects of nonprice competition. For hospital reform proposals to be persuasive, proponents must be able to demonstrate that the lower level of nonprice competition observed in concentrated markets represents a superior distribution of resources. In terms of the second criterion outlined earlier, consolidation must produce a net increase in social welfare—static efficiency. This proposition has yet to be demonstrated with any level of economic rigor. While many commentators are quick to condemn non-price competition as wasteful duplication, these amenities have some positive value to consumers. To assess the impact of consolidation on total welfare, one must acknowledge the loss to consumers and balance it against any potential increase in hospital surplus (profits) associated with curtailing nonprice investments. If the gain to hospitals more than offsets the loss to consumers, then the reduction in non-price competition would result in a net increase in social welfare.[89]

Ironically, even if increased hospital concentration resulted in an improved allocation of resources, there is no guarantee that the resulting outcome would be *optimal* from an economic perspective. The resource distribution characteristic of concentrated hospital markets could represent either an overinvestment in nonprice attributes (if the underlying market failures are sufficiently strong), or an underinvestment in nonprice attributes (if the monopoly or oligopoly outcome overcompensates for the underlying market failures). This is one of the difficulties inherent in relying upon second-best (or in this case potentially third-best) remedies to the problem of market failures. A Pareto-superior outcome, when compared with a suboptimal starting point, only represents a defensible move in the right direction, not necessarily the appropriate ending point.

The Coasian restructuring of the firm, on the other hand, is a more direct and theoretically more defensible response to the problem of nonprice competition. Integration internalizes the costs and benefits of the investment decision into a single economic decision maker. This will produce fundamentally different incentives and behavior. The incentives to overinvest in resources that characterized traditional health care markets are substantially muted, if not eliminated. Moreover, there is greater reason to be confident that informed consumer choices between the variety of price/non-price packages likely to be offered by integrated health plans will more closely reflect the amount consumers are willing to pay for nonprice attributes, at least to the extent that differences in premiums reflect actual differences in the costs of services.[90]

If integration and consolidation were complementary strategies relating to the problem of overinvestment, hospital antitrust reforms might still be warranted, regardless of the simultaneous transformation of health care markets through integration. The two strategies, however, are not complementary. Greater cooperation between hospitals, just as collective physician bargaining, could be used to forestall or to block integration. Moreover, increases in hospital concentration will constrain the total number of integrated health plans that can operate in any given market. Competition between integrated plans is necessary both to engender lower prices, and to protect patients from the specter of integrated plans underproviding care. Increased provider cooperation will dull the market penalty for denying care and could introduce the possibility of collusive underinvestment strategies among providers. Consequently, integration increases rather than decreases the need for vigilant antitrust enforcement efforts to enforce prohibitions against horizontal concentration and the accumulation of market power.

Designing Future Markets—The Competitive Virtues of Excess Capacity

Decisions made today regarding physical capacity will influence the extent to which the competitive promise of integration will be realized. Efforts to facilitate horizontal cooperation and eliminate excess capacity can substantially undermine the development of competitive markets and the stimulation of future price competition. Even if hospital consolidation produced a short-term increase in social welfare (static efficiency), in those markets capable of making the transition to complete integration, long-term competitive concerns militate in favor of strict antitrust enforcement (dynamic efficiency). Physical capacity represents the most serious constraint upon the total number of health plans. The addition of new capacity is discrete, expensive, and can take place only with a relatively long lag period. These barriers are substantially higher than the barriers associated with the entry of physicians or third party payers, which have substantial inter-market mobility.

Physical capacity, including potential excess capacity, can have substantial procompetitive virtues. Aggregate market capacity plays a significant role in determining the strength of incentives to engage in price competition. Moreover, it is important to remember that the level of capacity present in any market is, in part, determined by the decisions of market participants themselves. Not surprisingly, if given the option, market participants will often choose to be capacity constrained—enter the market with less productive capacity than they would be capable of both producing and selling. By reducing the amount of market capacity, private actors know that they can credibly precommit to strategies that yield higher market prices and higher profits.

Understanding the dynamics of this process provides the tools with which to assess proposals to reduce hospital capacity in the name of reducing medical costs. Some basic models of industrial organization help illustrate the role that market capacity plays in encouraging active price competition, as well as the countervailing incentives that individual competitors have to be capacity constrained. The Bertrand model of price competition shows how market capacity can yield low prices, even when there are relatively few producers in the market.[91] In the Bertrand model, competitors independently submit price bids. The lowest bidder wins, and is obligated to supply the entire market demand triggered by the successful bid. If more than one bidder submits the same low bid, the winners equally divide the market demand. In the resulting Bertrand equilibrium, each competitor submits a bid equal to their marginal costs and equally divides market demand at that price. *So long as each firm has sufficient individual capacity to supply the entire market,* as few as two firms can generate a competitive equilibrium characterized by marginal cost pricing.[92]

The Cournot model, in contrast, illustrates how unilaterally imposed capacity constraints can permit supracompetitive pricing. In the Cournot model, firms compete in terms of output rather than price. Each firm independently selects a level of output, assuming that its decision will not influence the decisions of other firms. Prices are determined by the aggregate output of the market. In a Cournot equilibrium, firms rationally choose to be capacity constrained, with the ultimate severity of the constraint determined by the total number of firms in the market.[93] The fewer the number of firms in the industry, the lower the level of industry output, and the higher the market price and equilibrium producer profits. The Cournot model illustrates how the number of firms in the market affects how closely the market can approximate the competitive outcome. Generally speaking, the fewer the number of firms, the less competitive the outcome.

The strategic nature of a firm's incentive to manipulate levels of capacity can be illustrated by a two-stage game in which firms first independently select their physical capacities and then, knowing the capacity choices made by other firms in the first stage, engage in Bertrand price competition. The resulting equilibrium of this two-stage game is not the desirable equilibrium characteristic of the one-stage Bertrand game, where firms have the ability to produce unlimited quantities and prices reflect marginal costs. Rather, the equilibrium of the two stage game is exactly the same as that of the one-stage Cournot game.[94] Why? The answer is that firms intentionally choose to constrain their ability to produce, because imposing capacity constraints represent one of the few means available for establishing prices that are above marginal costs. The relative strength of the incentives to reduce or eliminate capacity is, in turn, determined by the number of firms in the market. The larger the number of firms, the more capacity will be on the market and the lower will be the market price. This two-stage model is important because it illustrates how active price competition *alone* will not guarantee a truly competitive outcome. Price competition must be coupled with sufficient levels of market capacity to achieve competitive results.[95]

If firms have rational, private incentives to be capacity constrained, how can one explain the pervasive excess capacity that characterizes most hospital markets? The answer is that the level of capacity that exists today is the result of an historic shift in the operative economic regime governing health care markets. Hospital markets are currently characterized by levels of physical capacity that hospitals would not knowingly select if they knew that they would have to engage in active price competition—selective contracting and bidding as opposed to fee-for-service reimbursement. By the same logic, hospitals have strong contemporary incentives to retire capacity from the market in an effort to impose new capacity constraints. Just as rational firms in the two-stage game would not choose to build the level of capacity that hospitals are currently saddled with, so hospitals saddled with that capacity today will rationally choose to eliminate as much of it as possible, so as to impose meaningful new capacity constraints as they enter an economic regime characterized by increased price competition.

As the beneficiaries of a shift in prevailing economic regimes, antitrust and health care policy makers have a unique opportunity. If nothing is done, physical capacity will be systematically retired from the market and a Cournot-type equilibrium characterized by newly imposed capacity constraints will assert itself. The social costs of such an equilibrium will consist of relatively higher prices than would otherwise exist and relatively more restricted patient access. The elimination of capacity will also limit the number of integrated health plans that are likely to be formed. The smaller the number of plans in a market, the less likely it is that competition between plans will effectively temper incentives to abuse the plan-patient agency relationship by underproviding care. Alternatively, antitrust laws could be employed and policies designed to take advantage of the competitive opportunities wrought by the additional capacity. A strong case can be made in favor of adopting policies that strive to retain the physical capacity that hospitals might otherwise want to retire from the market.

Balancing Competition, Capacity, and Efficiency

Emphasizing the often-neglected virtues of excess capacity does not mean that legitimate arguments for eliminating capacity cannot be made in some markets. Markets with substantial excess capacity are subject to criticism in terms of the potential sustainability of the resulting market equilibrium and in terms of the efficiency costs associated with underutilized productive resources. There is a necessary trade-off between the benefits derived from enhanced competition and the costs associated with decreased efficiency. Devising the appropriate balance involves weighing the benefits of increased competition against the potential loses in efficiency due to firms operating below the minimum efficient scale of production or due to the higher fixed costs associated with underutilized capacity. Health care markets are not the first markets in which such trade-offs have been made. In markets for military contracts, for example, the government frequently makes a conscious decision to preserve competition by cultivating multiple suppliers, even when fewer suppliers might be able to fulfill contract requirements. Increased competition is purchased at the price of decreased economic efficiency. The costs of preserving capacity in hospital markets are significantly less than the costs of systematically building in similar redundancy. The capacity already exists, although one must be sensitive to the opportunity costs associated with the continued deployment of those resources in the health care sector.

The costs and benefits of retaining hospital capacity can be assessed on a case-by-case basis. The inherent procompetitive virtues of physical capacity combined with the anticompetitive private incentives to impose capacity constraints justify a policy presumption favoring the retention of capacity on the market. Proponents of increasing economic concentration, however, should be allowed to make a contrary case. If the evidence indicates that the efficiency gains of eliminating capacity exceed the competitive benefits of retaining it, the capacity should be retired from the market. Some markets may simply not be capable of supporting more than one or two facilities. In these circumstances, it is unwise to force competition or preserve redundant capacity. Some level of market power either by a free-standing hospital or a single integrated health plan may be inevitable. If this is the case, then the appropriate policy response may be forms of regulation like those employed with natural monopolies and many public utilities. Similar problems are raised by hospitals that function substantially below the minimum efficient scale of operation. This problem can be addressed by the efficiency defense in merger cases. The *1994 Statements* carve out a safety zone for hospitals with less than 100 beds and less than 40% occupancy for the last three years.[96] Similarly, the *1994 Statements* suggest that the enforcement agencies will consider hospital efficiencies and projected cost savings in deciding whether to prosecute those mergers that fall outside the safety zone.

It is important that the special problems confronting small hospitals and small markets not obscure the larger picture. The Coasian reformation of modern health care markets renders obsolete the once plausible argument that increased economic concentration is necessary as a third-best solution to the pressures driving nonprice competition. Beyond the fact that current incentives are no longer biased in favor of acquiring additional capacity and technology, existing levels of capacity have the positive virtue of facilitating more active competition. In general, the greater the capacity in the market, the greater the level of competition and the lower the price of health care services.

Conclusion and a postscript on health care reform

Disputes over the structure of health care markets will continue in both economic and political arenas. Arrow's welfare analysis helps bridge these realms and provides a framework within traditional economic analysis to assess when private markets should be supplemented with nonmarket institutions. A careful examination of physician and hospital proposals to reform federal antitrust law, however, reveals that increased provider cooperation is largely undesirable in emerging health care markets. This conclusion follows from the realization that integration represents a Coasian transformation of the firms delivering health care services and financing. Newly integrated firms have very different economic incentives and should make substantially more rational decisions concerning when to provide medical care and when to aquire medical equipment. Furthermore, competition between integrated firms will not only produce lower prices, it should help counteract whatever incentives integrated health plans may have to underprovide care.

Recognizing that active antitrust enforcement will play an important role in emerging health care markets does not mean that other types of nonmarket interventions might not be appropriate. The market equilibrium characteristic of competition between integrated firms will likely suffer its own optimality gap, engendered by the same informational and agency market failures that have always plagued the medical industry. While efforts to systematically reform the health care system failed in 1993 and are unlikely to be revived soon, initiatives targeted at particular aspects of the system will continue. Some of these proposals attempt to control the type of integration that is taking place, others try to influence the behavior of integrated firms, still others represent a direct backlash against managed care providers. This backlash is motivated by a growing appreciation of the incentives managed care plans have to underprovide care and a realization that the current legal system may not be adequately developed to hold health plans accountable for their actions.[97]

Proposals designed to control the type of integration include *any-willing-provider* laws that restrict the ability of networks to exclude otherwise qualified physicians who want to participate in their health plans,[98] as well as initiatives that give physician-sponsored networks more favorable legal treatment than payor-sponsored networks, such as the exemptions from federal and state antitrust laws or exemptions from certain state insurance laws.[99] By far, however, the most vigorous efforts of late to influence health care markets through the political process are initiatives designed to regulate the conduct of integrated networks through various self-styled patient protection acts or patient's bill of rights.[100] Some of these provisions are designed to protect open communication between patients and health care providers, prohibiting so-called gag orders, while others attempt to regulate the substantive decision making of providers, legislating rules that establish the conditions under which it is appropriate to seek emergency treatment or set the number of days a plan must provide inpatient care after certain medical procedures and performed. Another common feature are provisions to provide greater legal accountability for integrated health plans, the most important of which would expose employer-sponsored ERISA plans to greater state tort liability.

The evaluative criteria developed in this chapter can be applied to these proposals as well. Within an Arrowinian framework, desirable legislative reform should have as its primary objective the remedy of identifiable market failures. Calls for the adoption of any-willing-provider laws and differential state insurance treatment of provider-sponsored networks generally fail this first criterion. Some provisions of the patient protection acts, however, are aimed at providing patients information, imposing disclosure requirements for health plans, preventing abuses of the plan-patient agency relationship and imposing fiduciary obligations on providers. These initiatives are responsive to medical market failures. Whether such reforms are ultimately desirable will depend upon whether they would result in a net increase in social welfare (static efficiency) and whether their implementation would unnecessarily interfere with the effective structure and operation of the market (dynamic efficiency). These are the types of concerns that the health care debate should be focused on. Regardless of whether these laws are enacted, strict antitrust enforcement and facilitating effective competition between health plans may be the first and best response to plan/provider agency failures in integrated markets.

Acknowledgments

I am grateful to Clark Havighurst and the other participants in the Georgetown University Law Center's Symposium on "The Privatization of Health Care Reform" for their comments and suggestions on an earlier draft of this chapter. I am also grateful for comments and suggestions from Steven Croley, Heidi Li Feldman, Richard Friedman, Peter Jacobson, Thomas Kauper, Kyle Logue, Theodore Sims, John R.C. Wheeler, and the participants in the University of Michigan Law School's Law & Economics Workshop. I wish to extend particular thanks to Gregg Bloche for his insightful comments, encouragement, and editorial assistance.

Notes

1. The terminology of integration and consolidation roughly tracks the antitrust distinction between vertical and horizontal relations, which in turn plays a significant role in determining the applicability of the *per se* rule and the *rule of reason. See* infra notes 27–31 and accompanying text. The *vertical* label, however, fails to capture the full nature of an integrated health plan. The joint provision of insurance and medical services is not *vertical* in the traditional sense of reflecting different stages of physical production, such as the mining of bauxite and the forging of aluminum ingot. Baxter & Kessler similarly criticize antitrust law's distinction between vertical and horizontal relations, advocating instead a distinction between arrangements that involve economic complements and substitutes. See William F. Baxter & Daniel P. Kessler, Toward a Consistent Theory of the Welfare Analysis of Agreements, 47 *Stan. L. Rev.* 615 (1995).

2. A complete distinction between integration and consolidation breaks down at the edges. In certain markets, effective integration may require a scope of geographic coverage of physician and hospital services that can only be accomplished through greater consolidation. Moreover, consolidation may be a stepping stone to integration. Integration may take place either in the form of agreements between constituent parts (a relationship between an existing insurance carrier and an existing physician

group) or through a process of internal expansion (a large physician group marketing its services as an insurance product). Further complicating the problem is the increasing level of consolidation between integrated entities such as mergers between HMOs or managed care plans.

3. An illustration of the fluidity of this process is instructive. The number and size of physician groups has increased dramatically. These groups may enter into contractual relationships with third-party payers forming the basis of a managed-care network, or independently market their services as an insurance product. Alternatively, physician groups may enter into relationships with hospitals, ranging from loose contractual affiliations to fully integrated Physician Hospital Organizations (PHOs). The same story can be retold from the perspective of hospitals and insurance companies, each entailing a possible combination of mergers, joint ventures, new contractual affiliations or efforts at internal expansion. In the end, depending upon the route taken, the physician may be a business partner, owner, independent contractor or salaried employee of a hospital or insurance company. See generally, James C. Robinson, *The Corporate Practice of Medicine: Competition and Innovation in Health Care* (1999). This fluid environment where ownership and contract are each viable competing forms of market organization naturally lends itself to a Coasian theory of the firm analysis. See infra notes 13–14 and accompanying text.

4. Arrow and Debreu were the first to demonstrate that a general competitive equilibrium will in fact exist (with the satisfaction of numerous restrictive assumptions). See K. J. Arrow and G. Debreu, Existence of an Equilibrium for a Competitive Economy, 20 *Economica* 265 (1954). For a definition and discussion of Pareto efficiency see David M. Keeps, *A Course in Microeconomic Theory* at 153–56 (1990) (hereinafter Keeps, Microeconomics); Hal R. Varian, *Intermediate Microeconomics: A Modern Approach* at 484–86 (1987) (hereinafter Varian, Intermediate); Hal R. Varian, *Microeconomic Analysis* at 5, 198, 203 (2d ed., 1984) (hereinafter Varian, Advanced). For discussions of general equilibrium theory and the first welfare theorem see Keeps, Microeconomic at 199–205; Varian, Intermediate at 493–96, 500–02; Varian, Advanced at 189–211.

5. Market failures can threaten both the allocative efficiency of a partial equilibrium and the Pareto optimality of a general equilibrium. Identifying the source of market failure is easier than devising appropriate corrective action. Corrective action frequently implicates *second-best* analysis. While second-best analysis in the context of a single market is problematic, its difficulties in the context of multiple markets may be overwhelming. See generally, R. G. Lipsey and Kevin Lancaster, The General Theory of Second Best, 24 *Rev. Econ. Stud.* 11 (1956); Richard S. Markovits, A Basic Structure for Microeconomic Policy Analysis in Our Worse-Than-Second-Best World: A Proposal and Related Critique of the Chicago Approach to the Study of Law and Economics, 1975 *Wis. L. Rev.* 950 (1975).

6. This insight can be formalized in the context of what economists call an Edgeworth box, in which private parties have incentives to bargain until they reach an agreement lying somewhere along their *contract curve*, representing a point where neither party can be made better off through additional trades. See Keeps, Microeconomics, supra note 4, at 152–56; Varian, Intermediate, supra note 5, at 481–86; Varian, Advanced, supra note 4, at 190–91. Edgeworth's classic analysis provided a substantial part of the motivation underlying the Coase Theorem. See Ronald H. Coase, Notes on the Problem of Social Cost, in *The Firm, The Market, and The Law* at 160 (1988).

7. Kenneth J. Arrow, Uncertainty and the Welfare Economics of Medical Care, 53 *Am.*

Econ. Rev. 941, 947 (1963) (hereinafter Arrow, Uncertainty and Medical Care). Arrow's landmark 1963 article has recently been the subject of a multi-disciplinary retrospective sponsored by the Robert Wood Johnson Foundation Health Policy Investigator Award Program. See Kenneth Arrow and the Changing Economics of Medical Care, 26 *J. Health Polit. Policy Law* 823 (2001) (Special Issue, Peter J. Hammer, Deborah Haas-Wilson, and William M. Sage, eds.). See also M. Gregg Bloche, Corporate Takeover of Teaching Hospitals, 65 S. *Cal. L. Rev.* 1035, 1096–1103 (1992) (discussing Arrow's analysis).

8. Arrow, Uncertainty and Medical Care, supra note 7 at 947.

9. Mark Pauly, Is Medical Care Any Different? in *Competition in the Health Care Sector: Past, Present and Future* at 29 (Waren Greenberg ed., 1978) (emphasis in original).

10. Paul Starr, *The Social Transformation of American Medicine* at 227 (1982). See also Clark C. Havighurst, Doctors and Hospitals: An Antitrust Perspective on Traditional Relationships, 1984 *Duke L. J.* 1071, 1085–86 (1984). For Professor Arrow's response to these criticisms, see Peter J. Hammer, Deborah Haas-Wilson, and William M. Sage, Kenneth Arrow and The Changing Economics of Health Care: "Why Arrow? Why Now?, 26 *J. Health Polit. Policy Law* 835, 843 (2001) ("Professor Arrow was refreshingly open-minded when discussing these criticisms. He acknowledges that his 1963 discussion of professional norms as an optimality-gap-filling mechanism was probably too functional and too formalistic. He also appreciates the need to incorporate special interest considerations into the analysis of nonmarket institutions. Nevertheless, he still believes that the existence of market failures and the presence of optimality gaps help explain where non-market institutions are likely to take root, and that such failures give these institutions political legitimacy in the first instance. This is a proposition he defends as an important *conjecture*. Obviously, he admits, there needs to be a fuller explanation of when norms exist, what they do, why some emerge while others do not, and the role of individual self-interest.").

11. Arrow Uncertainty and Medical Care, supra note 7, at 944.

12. But see Oliver E. Williamson, The New Institutional Economic: Taking Stock, Looking Ahead, 38 *J. Econ. Lit* 595 (2000).

13. Ronald H. Coase, The Nature of the Firm, 4 *ECONOMICA* 386 (1937). The firm is the most basic building block of a market economy. Coase's primary insight is that the boundary line separating the firm from the market is fluid. The ultimate location of the line, the organization of the firm relative to the market, however, has significant economic content. The internal makeup of the firm reflects a fundamental division between economic activities that are performed "internally" and those that are carried out by market transactions between distinct economic entities. An alternative way of formulating the distinction is in terms of decisions that are made in terms of hierarchical command (intra-firm decisions) and those that are guided by the price mechanism (inter-firm, market-based transactions). See generally Ronald H. Coase, The Firm, the Market and the Law (1988); Harold Demsetz, The Economics of the Business Firm, (1995); Michael Dietrich, Transaction Cost Economics and Beyond: Towards A New Economics of the Firm (1994); *The Economics Nature of the Firm: A Reader* (Louis Putterman and Randall S. Kroszner eds., 2d ed. 1996).

14. In reality, the operation of a hospital is a very labor-intensive activity. It is not uncommon for hospitals in some cities to be the community's largest single employer. Still, it is meaningful to focus upon the separation of the ownership and control of specialized physician expertise and the hospital's physical resources and, for simplicity, to phrase this distinction in terms of a division between physical and human capital.

15. Two products are complementary if the demand for one is positively correlated with the demand for the other, such as the demand for pencils and erasers. Since the demand for product A affects the demand for product B, the pricing decisions of producer A will affect the pricing decisions of producer B, and vice versa. This raises a classic externality problem. Lower prices for product A will increase the demand for product B, which will increase producer B's profits. If producers A and B are separate economic entities, however, these effects will not necessarily be internalized. Neither economic entity will have an incentive to independently incorporate the interrelated effects of their pricing decisions. Consequently, if firms have any discretion in setting prices, and decisions are made independently, prices for products A and B will be higher and output for each product will be lower than if a single economic entity were to jointly produce and price the two commodities. Common ownership can lead to lower prices and higher output than separate ownership. Of course, contractual arrangements short of common ownership may also provide a mechanism to internalize the externality. For a discussion of the possible role of contracts and other informal responses to this problem see Richard D. Friedman, Antitrust Analysis and Bilateral Monopoly, 1986 *Wis. L. Rev.* 873, 878–83 (1986).

16. The complementary nature of physician and hospital services may help explain some of the attributes of traditional physician–hospital relations. The fact that physicians typically used hospital facilities without charge may have reduced the detrimental effects of the lack of integration. If hospitals charged physicians for the use of facilities, it would increase physician costs and prices, which would negatively affect the hospital's own demand. One can postulate that many aspects of traditional physician–hospital relations that otherwise appear anomalous were in fact designed to approximate or attempt to approximate the behavior of a single economically integrated firm.

17. See generally James C. Robinson and Lawrence P. Casalino, Reevaluation of Capitation Contracting in New York and California, 20 *Health Aff.* 7 (July/August 2001); James C. Robinson, Physician Organization in California: Crisis and Opportunity, 20 *Health Aff.* 80 (July/August 2001); Gloria Bazzoli, Robert H. Miller, and Lawton R. Burns, Capitated Contracting Relationships in Health Care, 45 *J. Healthcare Manag.* 170 (2000); James C. Robinson and Larry P. Casalino, The Growth of Medical Groups Paid Through Capitation in California, 333 *N. Eng. J. Med.* 1684 (1995).

18. Alternatively, this fractured structure may simply have provided another avenue through which the agency relationship could be abused. The independence of physicians, combined with the physician's control over patient decision making historically encouraged nonprice competition by hospitals for physician loyalty and affiliation as the primary source of inpatient demand. For discussions of the institutional factors motivating nonprice competition within traditionally structured fee-for-service relations, see Paul L. Joskow, The Effects of Competition and Regulation on Hospital Bed Supply and the Reservation Quality of the Hospital, 11 *Bell J. Econ.* 421, 431–33 (1980); James C. Robinson and Harold S. Luft, Competition and the Cost of Medical Care, 1972–1982, 257 *JAMA* 3241, 3241–42 (1987); James C. Robinson and Harold S. Luft, The Impact of Hospital Market Structure on Patient Volume, Average Length of Stay, and Cost of Care, 4 J. *Health Econ.* 333, 334–35(1985); George W. Wilson and Joseph M. Jadlow, Competition, Profit Incentives, and Technical Efficiency in the Provision of Nuclear Medicine Services, 13 *Bell. J. Econ.* 472, 473 (1982). For an extensive discussion of the problems non-price competition raises for the assessment of hospital mergers see Peter J. Hammer, Ques-

tioning Traditional Antitrust Presumptions: Price and Non-Price Competition in Hospital Markets, 33 *Mich. J. L. Ref.* 727 (1999) (hereinafter Hammer, Questioning Traditional Antitrust Presumptions).

19. This is not to say that there were no efforts to design alternative structures. See Emily Friedman, Capitation, Integration, and Managed Care: Lessons from Early Experiments, 275 *JAMA* 957 (1996).

20. See generally John Wiorek, The Corporate Practice of Medicine Doctrine: An Outmoded Theory in Need of Modification, *8 J. Leg. Med.* 465 (1987); Jeffrey F. Chase-Lubitz, The Corporate Practice of Medicine Doctrine: An Anachronism in the Modern Health Care Industry, 40 *Vand. L. Rev.* 445 (1987); Alanson W. Willcox, Hospitals and the Corporate Practice of Medicine, 45 Cornell L. Q. 432 (1960); Horace R. Hansen, Laws Affecting Group Health Plans, 35 *Iowa L. Rev.* 209 (1950); Joseph Laufer, Ethical and Legal Restrictions on Contract and Corporate Practice of Medicine, 6 *Law. & Contemp. Probs.* 516 (1939).

21. The creation of a closed panel of physicians is a prerequisite for any form of meaningful integration. Traditionally, however, freedom of choice acts and anti-discrimination laws forced third party payers to compensate their insured's expenses regardless of where the insured received medical treatment. These laws severely restricted the ability of third party payers to form entities like Preferred Provider Organizations (PPOs), which are predicated on imposing some limits on where insureds receive care. For a discussion of these and other state laws inhibiting the ability of third party payers to bargain and engage in selective contracting, see Thomas L. Greaney, Competitive Reform in Health Care: The Vulnerable Revolution, 5 *Yale J. On Reg.* 179, 185–89 (1988).

22. I do not intend to minimize the difficulties associated with making political and economic changes, or to disallow the possibility that existing structures in health care (or other sectors) could be both entrenched and suboptimal. Collective action problems may be substantial, particularly where the expected benefits of change are dispersed over large, unorganized groups. Moreover, actions that are collectively rational may be irrational from an individual perspective. The contention here, rather, is that there are countervailing reasons to believe such problems in health care markets would be relatively more isolated in scope and less robust over time than history may suggest. Health care occupies a central role both for individuals and society. Entities such as large employers and lobbying groups for the elderly or for a variety of high-profile ailments, could help circumvent many collective action problems. Finally, old coalitions can fracture over time with individual, profit-motivated defections, as witnessed by the current division between physicians in managed care practices and those fighting to retain traditional fee-for-service systems of compensation.

23. See Peter J. Hammer, Arrow's Analysis of Social Institutions: Entering the Marketplace with Giving Hands? 26 *J. Health Polit. Policy & Law* 1081, 1090–91 (2001) (discussing how policy making in this setting often involves menus of "lumpy" or discontinuous choices).

24. FTC Commissioner Terry Calvani cataloged the many allegations that have been made against health care providers in their efforts to resist integration and the emergence of managed care. This list includes claims that hospitals conspired to boycott PPOs; that trade associations refused to deal with non-Blue Cross reimbursers such as HMOs except at prices higher than Blue Cross rates; that trade associations organized hospitals to refuse to accept contracts with managed care entities unless the contracts maintained levels of charges at rates equal to the providers' usual private rates; that

providers collectively refused to accept third party payor reimbursement as payment in full; and that providers have collectively resisted utilization review efforts. In the Matter of Hospital Corporation of America, 106 F.T.C. 361, 1985 FTC Lexis 15 at *280 n.32 (F.T.C. 1985) (citing cases), aff'd, 870 F.2d 1381 (7th Cir. 1986), cert. denied, 481 U.S. 1038 (1987).

25. This discussion takes the existing societal distribution of resources as given and asks whether those resources, as distributed, could be used differently to increase social welfare. Social welfare may also be improved by policies with a direct redistributional focus. Such policy analysis is beyond the scope of this chapter. Regardless of the initial distribution, it is reasonable to seek to ensure that social resources (however allocated) are put to their most productive use.

26. These criteria are developed in greater detail and applied in a variety of health care and non-health care settings in Peter J. Hammer, Antitrust Beyond Competition: Market Failures, Total Welfare, and the Challenge of Intramarket Second-Best Trade-offs, 98 *Mich. L. Rev.* 849 (2000).

27. Federal antitrust laws establish the basic ground rules governing the operation of private economic markets. Fundamentally, antitrust law strives to preserve the benefits that are engendered when economic conduct is motivated by independently rational and autonomous decision making. Section 1 of the Sherman Antitrust Act broadly prohibits "every contract combination . . . or conspiracy in restraint of trade." 15 U.S.C. § 1. Section 2 of the Sherman Antitrust Act prohibits monopolization and attempted monopolization. 15 U.S.C. § 2. While Section 1 is directed at agreements between separate and independent economic entities, Section 2 is directed at the unilateral conduct of firms possessing market power. Other relevant antitrust provisions include section 7 of the Clayton Act, which prohibits mergers and acquisitions where the effect "may be substantially to lessen competition, or to tend to create a monopoly," 15 U.S.C. § 18, and section 5 of the Federal Trade Commission Act, which prohibits "unfair methods of competition." 15 U.S.C. § 45. Both the Department of Justice (DOJ) and the Federal Trade Commission (FTC) (collectively the "enforcement agencies") have jurisdiction to enforce the antitrust laws.

28. See, e.g., *National Soc'y of Professional Eng'rs v. United States*, 435 U.S. 679, 695 (1978) (declaring the Society's ethical cannon prohibiting competitive bidding to be per se illegal); *Superior Court Trial Lawyers Ass'n v. F.T.C.*, 493 U.S.410 (1990) (declaring a strike by trial lawyers for higher publicly determined rates of compensation for representing indigent criminal defendants to be a per se illegal group boycott). Courts have readily incorporated these beliefs in evaluating restraints of trade in health care markets. See *Arizona v. Maricopa County Medical Society*, 457 U.S. 332 (1982) (declaring a schedule of fees established by the County Medical Society a per se illegal price fixing agreement); *F.T.C. v. Indiana Fed'n of Dentists*, 476 U.S. 447 (1986) (declaring the Federation's concerted practice of refusing to submit dental x-rays to third party payers for utilization review an unreasonable restraint of trade). For a critical assessment of the ability of contemporary antitrust doctrine to address problems of health care quality and nonprice competition see William M. Sage and Peter J. Hammer, Competing on Quality of Care: Developing a Competition Policy for Health Care Markets, 33 *Mich. J. L. Ref.* (1999); William M. Sage & Peter J. Hammer, A Copernican View of Health Care Antitrust, 65 *Law and Contemp. Probs.* (Special Issue, Is the Health Care Revolution Over?, Clark C. Havighurst, ed.) (forthcoming 2002).

29. Section 1 of the Sherman Act outlaws only those agreements that constitute unreasonable restraints of trade. The strictest level of antitrust scrutiny is reserved for anti-

competitive agreements between independent horizontal competitors (roughly the agreements previously characterized as reflecting consolidation in the industry). Traditionally, four categories of horizontal agreements have been classified as per se illegal: (1) price fixing; (2) territorial allocations; (3) group boycotts; and (4) tying arrangements. Today, a hard per se rule applies primarily to price fixing agreements and territorial allocations, although group boycotts and tying arrangements continue to raise serious antitrust concerns (particularly in health care markets). For a general discussion of per se rules, see Robert H. Bork, *The Antitrust Paradox: A Policy at War with Itself* at 18–19, 66–67, 267–70, 276–77 (1993); Lawrence Anthony Sullivan, *Handbook of the Law of Antitrust* 182–86, 192–97 (1977); Richard A. Poser, *Antitrust Law: An Economic Perspective* at 23–26 (1976).

30. Rule of reason analysis involves a case-by-case assessment in which courts examine the economic impact that the alleged restraint will have on competition. See *Continental T.V., Inc. v. GTE Sylvania, Inc.*, 433 U.S. 36, 49 (1977) ("Under this rule, the fact finder weighs all of the circumstances of a case in deciding whether a restrictive practice should be prohibited as imposing an unreasonable restraint on competition."); *Monsanto Co. v. Spray-Rite Services, Corp.*, 465 U.S. 752, 762 (1984) ("In *Sylvania* we emphasized that the legality of arguably anticompetitive conduct should be judged primarily by its 'market impact'."). See also Sullivan, supra note 24, at 186–89; Herbert Hovenkamp, Federal Antitrust Policy: The Law of Competition and its Practice 185 (1994).

31. The formulation of the ancillary restraints test is generally attributed to Judge (later President and Chief Justice) Taft. See *United States v. Addyston Pipe & Steel Co.*, 85 F. 271 (6th Cir. 1898), *aff'd*, 175 U.S. 211 (1899).

32. Different components of the same corporate entity are incapable of entering into an "agreement" in violation of section 1 of the Sherman Act. See *Copperweld Corp. v. Independence Tube Corp.*, 467 U.S. 752 (1984) (rejecting the doctrine of intraenterprise conspiracies). Actions by single economic actors are still subject to Section 2's prohibition against monopolization and attempted monopolization. Moreover, the initial decision to create the new corporate entity may itself be subject to antitrust scrutiny.

33. See *Maricopa, supra* note 28.

34. See Department of Justice and Federal Trade Commission Statements of Enforcement Policy and Analytical Principles Relating to Health Care and Antitrust, reprinted *in* 4 Trade Reg. Rep. (CCH) § 13,152 (hereinafter *1994 Statements*); Department of Justice and Federal Trade Commission Statements of Antitrust Enforcement Policy in Health Care, reprinted in 4 Trade Reg. Rep. (CCH) § 13,153 (hereinafter *1996 Statements*). The purpose of the Statements is "to provide education and instruction to the health care community in a time of tremendous change, and to resolve, as completely as possible, the problem of antitrust uncertainty." *1994 Statements* at 20,769. The enforcement agencies' statements, however, do not have the force of law and are not binding upon the courts. Nevertheless, the statements are significant because they indicate how the enforcement agencies will exercise their prosecutorial discretion.

35. *Statement of Department of Justice and Federal Trade Commission Enforcement Policy on Physician Network Joint Ventures, 1994 Statements*, supra note 34, at 20,788 ("Physician network joint ventures will be viewed under a rule of reason analysis and not viewed as per se illegal either if the physicians in the joint venture share substantial financial risk or if the combining of the physicians into a joint venture enables them to offer a new product producing substantial efficiencies.") (*Eighth Statement*).

36. *1994 Statements*, supra note 34, at 20,788.
37. *1996 Statements*, supra note 34, at 20,816 (defining payment systems based upon a pre-determined percentage of premium or revenue from the plan, global fees, and all-inclusive rates as legitimate forms of financial risk sharing, in addition to the capitation and fee-withholding systems recognized in the *1994 Statements*). This provision is largely uncontroversial. The *1994 Statements* never intended capitation and fee-withholding to be the only forms of risk sharing recognized by the enforcement agencies. *1994 Statements, supra* note 34, at 20,788 ("[T]he Agencies will consider other forms of economic integration that amount to the sharing of substantial risk; the enumeration of the two examples above is not meant to foreclose the possibility that substantial financial risk can be shared in other ways.").
38. 1996 Statements, supra note 34, at 20,816–17.
39. 1996 Statements, supra note 34, at 20,817.
40. 1996 Statements, supra note 34, at 20,817 ("To the extent that agreements on prices to be charged for the integrated provision of services are reasonably necessary to the ventures achievement of efficiencies, they will be evaluated under the rule of reason.").
41. Health Care Antitrust Improvements Act of 1993, H.R. 3486, 103d Cong., 1st Sess. § 3(1) (1993).
42. H.R. 2425, 104th Cong., 1st Sess., § 15021, Application of Antitrust Rule of Reason to Provider Services Networks (1995). Another provision of the same House bill would have exempted numerous other types of cooperative physician conduct from the reach of antitrust law. See H.R. 2425 § 15221, Exemption from Antitrust Laws for Certain Activities of Medical Self-Regulatory Entities. For an examination of this proposal see Peter J. Hammer, Price and Quality Competition in Health Care Markets: The Comparative Institutional Case Against an Antitrust Exemption for Medical Self Regulation, in *Achieving Quality in Managed Care: The Role of Law* at 123 (ed. John D. Blum) (ABA monograph) (1997) (hereinafter Hammer, *Price and Quality*).
43. *Antitrust Health Care Advancement Act of 1997*, H.R. 415, 105th Cong., 1st Sess. (1997).To qualify as a "health care provider network" a physician group must, among other things, include joint capital investment, institute a program to review the quality, efficiency, and appropriateness of treatment, establish a program to monitor and control utilization of health care, and establish a management program to coordinate the delivery of health care services. *See* H.R. 415 § 2(b)(5). There are substantial similarities between H.R. 415's definition of a "health care provider network" and the definition of substantial clinical integration contained in the *1996 Statements*, which will also trigger rule of reason analysis. *See 1996 Statements*, supra note 34, at 20,817.
44. Brian McCormick, Some New Antitrust Leeway; but AMA says Updated Federal Rules Still Too Narrow for Physicians, 37 *Am. Med. News* October 17, 1994 at 1 (responding to the enforcement agencies' *1994 Statements*).
45. *Health Care Professionals Coalition Act of 1996*, H.R. 3770, 104th Cong., 2d Sess. (1996) (a law to make the antitrust laws inapplicable to the negotiations of a coalition of health care professionals and a health care service plan).
46. *Quality Health-Care Coalition Act of 1998*, H.R. 4277, 105th Cong., 2d Sess. (1998) (a bill to ensure and foster continued patient safety and quality of care by making the antitrust laws apply to negotiations by groups of health care professionals and certain other associations that are engaged in negotiations with health maintenance organi-

zations and other health insurance insurers in the same manner as such laws apply to collective bargaining by labor organizations under the National Labor Relations Act); *Quality Health-Care Coalition Act of 1999*, H.R. 1304, 106th Cong., 1st Sess. (1999) (a bill to ensure and foster continued patient safety and quality of care by making the antitrust laws apply to negotiations between groups of health care professionals and health plans and health insurance issuers in the same manner as such laws apply to collective bargaining by labor organizations under the National Labor Relations Act.).

47. The medical antitrust debate has strong regulatory overtones. The enforcement agencies' standards in the health care field more closely resemble administrative rules than the recitation of case law. The regulatory overtones of contemporary antitrust standards contrast sharply with the more traditional law enforcement model of the Department of Justice. See Thomas E. Kauper, The Justice Department and the Antitrust Laws: Law Enforcer or Regulator? in *The Antitrust Impulse: An Economic, Historical and Legal Analysis* 435 (Theodore P. Kovaleff ed., 1994); Thomas L. Greaney, Regulating for Efficiency in Health Care Through the Antitrust Laws, 1995 *Utah L. Rev.* 465, 486–89 (1995).

48. In *Maricopa*, the Court condemned the physicians' maximum fee schedule as per se illegal price fixing, but proceeded to give fairly detailed rule-of-reason-type consideration to the physicians' proffered justifications. In *Nat'l Soc'y of Prof'l Eng'r v. United States*, 435 U.S. 679 (1978), *Nat'l Collegiate Athletic Ass'n y Bd of Regents*, 468 U.S. 85 (1984), and *F.T.C. v. Indiana Fed'n of Dentists*, 476 U.S. 447 (1986) the Court purportedly claimed to be employing rule of reason analysis, but proceeded to condemn the conduct in a summary fashion, without giving substantial consideration to the alleged justifications. These cases gave birth to what courts and commentators termed "quick look" rule of reason analysis. In *California Dental Ass'n v. F.T.C.*, 526 U.S. 756 (1999), the Court attempted to clarify the role of "quick look" analysis in antitrust law, but few would claim that these categories are substantially more clear in the wake of the Court's opinion.

49. *Maricopa*, supra note 28.

50. *Broadcast Music, Inc. v. Columbia Broadcasting Systems, Inc.*, 441 U.S. 1 (1979).

51. See *Maricopa*, supra note 28, 457 U.S. at 356–57.

52. Id. at 353–54.

53. Id. at 355 n. 31.

54. *1996 Statements*, supra note 34, at 20,817–18.

55. Havighurst presents an extensive critique of the enforcement agencies' *1994 Statements* governing physician network formation. *See* Clark C. Havighurst, Are the Antitrust Agencies Overregulating Physician Networks?, 8 *Loy. Consumer L. Rep.* 78 (1996) (hereinafter Havighurst, Overregulating).

56. *Health Security Act*, H.R. 3600, 103d Cong., 2d Sess. § 1322 (1993). Such proposals are not entirely different from the Canadian (or German) system where physicians collectively negotiate with the government at the Provincial level for the annual budget to be spent on health care services. See Daniel W. Srsic, Collective Bargaining by Physicians in the United States and Canada, 15 *Comp. Lab. L J.* 89, 94 (1993).

57. H.R. 3770, 104th Cong., 2d Sess., § 4 (1996). A presumption of market power is defined as a Herfindahl-Hirschman Index (HHI) level exceeding 2,000. Id. § 2(2). An HHI level of 2,000 corresponds to the presence of 5 or fewer equally sized health plans competing for physician services.

58. H.R. 4277, 105th Cong., 2d Sess., § 2(a) (1998) ("The members of any group of health care professionals . . . which is negotiating with a health insurance insurer . . .

shall, in connection with such negotiations, be entitled to the same treatment under the antitrust laws as that which is accorded to members of a bargaining unit recognized under the National Labor Relations Act."). H.R. 1304, 106th Cong., 1st Sess., § 3(a) (1999) ("Any health care professionals who are engaged in negotiating with a health plan regarding the terms of any contract under which the professionals provide care items or services for which benefits are provided under such a plan shall, in connection with such negotiations, be entitled to the same treatment under the antitrust laws as the treatment to which bargaining units which are recognized under the National Labor Relations Act are entitled in connection with collective bargaining."). A slightly amended version of H.R. 1304 passed the House in June 2000, but was not brought to a vote in the Senate. For a critical assessment of these proposal see Statement of Federal Trade Commission Presented by Robert Pitofsky, Chairman of the Federal Trade Commission, before the Committee on the Judiciary United States House of Representatives, 105th Cong., 2d Sess. (July 29, 1998).

59. If a single third party payer is exercising market power, then physicians can file a section two claim alleging the exercise of monopoly or monopsony power. While courts to date have not been very receptive to provider allegations of monopsony power, see *Kartell v. Blue Shield*, 749 F.2d 922 (1st Cir. 1984), cert. denied, 471 U.S. 1029 (1985); *Ball Memorial Hosp. v. Mutual Hosp. Ins., Inc.*, 784 F.2d 1325 (7th Cir. 1986), the correct antitrust prescription is to attack market power directly (where and if it exists), not to facilitate the creation of countervailing market power in the form of collective bargaining. If third party payers are colluding to artificially suppress physician fees, conduct that would itself be per se illegal, then physicians can file a section one antitrust claim against the offending parties. Obviously, the problem is more complicated if the payer in question is the federal government in its capacity of running programs such as Medicare and Medicaid. The solution, however, would still not be a right to collectively negotiate with private third party payers. The result of such a remedy would be an inefficient system of cross-subsidization, where physicians could exact supracompetitive prices from private payers in order to subsidize Medicare and Medicaid patients (assuming that the same physicians or health plans treated a sufficiently diverse patient mix to make such a scheme workable). The appropriate remedy to inadequate levels of government compensation lies in the political realm. Governments are not immune from economic reality. Paying non-competitive rates will decrease the number of physicians taking Medicare patients and decrease the quality of the Medicare physician pool. Either of these effects should result in political lobbying from patient constituents that could form the basis of a political solution.

60. If the third party payer market is reasonably competitive, then the exercise of physician market power would result in higher prices, decreased output and a reduction in social welfare. If third party payers possessed monopsony power, however, then it is theoretically possible that the exercise of countervailing market power by physicians could improve upon the suboptimum monopsony outcome, resulting in an increase in total welfare. By the same token, it is possible that the exercise of countervailing market power could make the monopsony outcome even worse, further decreasing social welfare. The burden should rest on the advocates of collective bargaining to demonstrate that countervailing market power would be welfare enhancing and, therefore, constitute an acceptable second best solution to alleged third party payer market power. To my knowledge, no persuasive case for this position has even been attempted.

61. See cases cited in Hospital Corporation of America, supra note 24, 1985 FTC Lexis 15 at *280 n.32.

62. See *1994 Statements, supra* note 34, at 20,788. The *1996 Statements* broaden the categories of acceptable risk sharing to include compensation calculated as a "pre-determined percentage of premium or revenue from the plan," global fees and all-inclusive rates. *1996 Statements*, supra note 34, at 20, 816. These changes are consistent with the *1994 Statements* financial risk sharing requirement.

63. This chapter employs an admittedly simplistic model of the incentive structure of integrated health plans, focusing on the first order effects of combining the payment and treatment function within the same economic entity. Integrated firms have strong incentives to compare the costs and benefits of treatment. As such, the integrated firm will generally not provide care when the costs exceed the expected benefits, even when the expected benefits of care are still positive. The actual behavior of integrated health plans will be influenced by a number of additional factors, such as the length of expected enrollment of plan participants, the demographics of the patient population, the ability to engage in risk selection or exclude coverage for pre-existing conditions, and the structure of the market (i.e., the degree of competition among health plans). For present purposes, however, the incentives to directly compare costs and benefits, as contrasted with the incentives of traditional health care structures, provide a sufficiently clear distinction for antitrust policy analysis.

64. While fee-withholding retains a fee-for-service system of compensation, the network participants establish an incentive structure under which a certain percentage of fees are withheld and subsequent bonuses paid once specified cost-containment objectives are achieved. *1994 Statements, supra* note 34, at 20,788. See also *1996 Statements*, supra note 34, at 20,816 (recognizing both fee-withholding, as well as systems of financial rewards and penalties based upon overall cost and utilization targets).

65. McCormick, supra note 44, at 1. ("Substantial investment in the network itself also puts the member doctors at financial risk, AMA lawyers said, and should be recognized as integrating the physicians enough to eliminate antitrust risk.")

66. Id. (' "It's classic capitalism at work,' he said, arguing that the promise of increasing the value of an initial investment is a strong inducement to run an efficient network.") (quoting Edward Hirshfeld, AMA Associate General Counsel).

67. *1996 Statements*, supra note 34, at 20,817.

68. *1996 Statements*, supra note 34, at 20,817.

69. If a restraint is ancillary to and reasonably necessary for a lawful objective, e.g., information systems and cost/utilization review, *and* the restraint is narrow in scope, then the restraint will be lawful under the rule of reason. See Addyston Pipe, supra note 31.

70. *1996 Statements, supra* note 34, at 20,820–21 ("The price agreement under these circumstances is subordinate to and reasonably necessary to achieve these objectives.").

71. See, e.g., Response Letter on Behalf of Vermont Physician's Clinic, 1997 WL 432402 (D.O.J.) (July 30, 1997) ("VPC's participating physicians will share 'substantial financial risk' as that term is described in the Statements of Antitrust Enforcement Policy in Health Care."); Staff Advisory Opinion on Behalf of New Jersey Pharmacists Association, 1997 WL 458499 (F.T.C.) (Aug. 12, 1997) ("This form of risk sharing among network members, based upon capitation, is sufficient to bring the joint fee setting arrangement outside the *per se* treatment and into the rule of reason."); Response Letter on Behalf of Joint Venture Proposed by First Priority Health, 1997 WL 688781

(D.O.J.) (Nov. 3, 1997) ("As proposed, FPHS is a bona fide joint venture in which all its participating owners, including all of the NEPPO physicians will share substantial financial risk as described in the Policy Statements."); Staff Advisory Opinion on Behalf of Phoenix Medical Network, 1998 WL 293759 (F.T.C.) (May 19, 1998) ("If Phoenix operates in the manner described, its members will share substantial financial risk through contracts with third-party payers to provide medically necessary services to certain of their enrollees for a percentage of the premiums collected"); Response Letter on Behalf of The Heritage Alliance ("THA") and Lackawanna Physicians Organization ("LPO"), 1998 WL 678339 (D.O.J.) (Sept. 15, 1998) ("In this case, the members of the Network propose to share substantial financial risk in providing Network services.").

72. See In re Mesa County Physicians Independent Practice Association, Docket No. 9284 (F.T.C.) (Feb. 19, 1998) (Agreement Containing Consent Order to Cease and Desist) ("Mesa IPA's members have not integrated their medical practices so as to create efficiencies sufficient to justify their collective contract negotiations.").

73. See In re Urological Stone Surgeons, Inc., File No. 931–0028 (F.T.C.) (1998) (Agreement Containing Consent Order to Cease and Desist) ("The Complaint charges that while the owners of USS and SCA have financially integrated by jointly investing in the purchase and operation of the two lithotripsy machines the Parkside operates, collective setting of the price for their lithotripsy professional services, or for other non-investor urologists using Parkside, is not reasonably necessary (or 'ancillary') to achieving any efficiencies that may be realized through their legitimate joint ownership and operation of the machines.").

74. The enforcement agencies have acknowledged the difficulties involved in precisely defining the meaning of substantial clinical integration. "In drafting the definition of clinically integrated arrangements, the Agencies sought to be flexible due to the wide range of providers who may participate, types of clinical integration possible, and efficiencies available. Consequently, the definition of a clinically integrated arrangement is by necessity less precise than that of a risk sharing arrangement." In re M.D. Physicians of Southwest Louisiana, Inc., File No. 941–0095 (F.T.C.) (1998) (Agreement Containing Consent Order to Cease and Desist).

75. See Havighurst, Overregulating, supra note 55, at 84–87.

76. See Havighurst, Overregulating, supra note 55, at 89–92.

77. For discussions of the messenger model PPO see Statement of Department of Justice and Federal Trade Commission Enforcement Policy on Providers' Collective Provision of Fee-Related Information to Purchasers of Health Care Services, 1994 Statements, supra note 34, at 20,782–84 (Fifth Statement); 1996 Statements, supra note 34, at 20,834–35; James C. Dechene, Preferred Provider Organization Structures and Agreements, 4 Ann. Health L. 35, 53–59 (1995).

78. To date, messenger model PPOs have been infrequently utilized. There is a tendency to blame higher costs for the infrequent use of the vehicle. An equally plausible explanation would focus on the ability of the messenger model to effectively prevent anticompetitive behavior such as physician collusion that might result in higher prices. If the messenger format effectively prevents physicians from exercising market power, then the expected benefits (profits) of network formation would be reduced and fewer such networks would be formed.

79. "Since physicians generally do not have the accounting sophistication necessary to organize capitation and fee-withholding arrangements, nor the necessary funds to make capitation successful, they cannot offer a PPO product that would be character-

ized as legal under current antitrust doctrine." Statement of Merle W. Delmer, M.D., American Medical Association, Before the Economic and Commercial Law Subcommittee, Committee on the Judiciary, United States House of Representatives, 103d Cong., 2d Sess. (June 15, 1994) (hereinafter *AMA Delmer Testimony*).

80. *Id.* ("Appropriate modification of the antitrust laws will enable physicians to reassert their traditional role as patient advocates, even in a health care arena dominated by managed care organizations. The market power of these organizations must be balanced by encouraging the formation of physician-directed health care networks. Physicians, with their knowledge and skill in clinical decision making, can provide the expertise necessary to enable managed care entities to deliver quality medical care in the most cost-effective manner.").

81. *Id.* ("It must be recognized that physician-sponsored networks can offer lower costs and higher value.").

82. Ultimately, the success of any integrated health plan will depend upon each plan's ability to provide cost-effective, quality care. No initiative will be successful without effective physician cooperation. Managed care involves difficult decisions regarding the type of care that should be provided and when care should be curtailed or denied. Physicians, as health care providers, may have privileged insight into how these decision can best be made. If this is true, then physician-dominated plans may have a long-term advantage, completely unrelated to the need for preferential antitrust treatment.

83. Hospital agreements pertaining solely to price, territory, or service menus would constitute per se illegal antitrust violations. Similarly, mergers between hospitals may violate Section 7 of the Clayton Act if they substantially lessen competition or tend to create a monopoly. The enforcement agencies treatment of hospital mergers is outlined in the *1994 Statements*. See Statements of Department of Justice and Federal Trade Commission Enforcement Policy on Mergers Among Hospitals, 1994 Statements, supra note 34, at 20,774–75 (*First Statement*). Finally, hospital joint ventures, such as those designed to share the cost of new equipment or clinical services, constitute "agreements" between horizontal competitors, which may constitute restraints of trade. See Statements of Department of Justice and Federal Trade Commission Enforcement Policy on Hospital Joint Ventures Involving High Technology or other Expensive Health Care Equipment, 1994 Statements, supra note 34, at 20,775–79 (Second Statement); Statement of Department of Justice and Federal Trade Commission Enforcement Policy on Hospital Joint Ventures Involving Specialized Clinical or Other Expensive Health Care Services, 1994 Statements, supra note 34, at 20,779–82 (Third Statement). The *1996 Statements* made no substantive changes in the evaluation of hospital conduct.

84. Frederic J. Entin, Tracey L. Fletcher and Jeffrey M. Teske, Hospital Collaboration: The Need For An Appropriate Antitrust Policy, 29 *Wake Forest L. Rev.* 107, 110 (1994) ("The antitrust laws, as currently enforced, are inappropriately inhibiting the rational restructuring of the health care system through collaborative efforts.").

85. *Id.* Some proposals have been introduced at the federal level to introduce greater levels of "planning" in the allocation of health care resources, particularly as it affects the needs of underserved segments of the community. See, e.g., *Essential Health Facilities Investment Act of 1997*, H.R. 735, 105th Cong., 1st Sess. (1997) (to establish a program of assistance for essential community providers of health care services, to establish a program to update and maintain the infrastructure requirements of safety net hospitals, and to require States to develop plans for the allocation and review of

expenditures for the capital-related costs of health care services). H.R. 735 would have immunized cooperative conduct taken pursuant to the act from federal and state antitrust laws.

86. See articles cited *supra* note 18.

87. As with the discussion of the integrated firm's incentives to provide incremental care, this discussion presents a simplified analysis that focuses primarily upon the effects of having the same decision maker consider the costs and benefits of the investment. Even with integration, market imperfections may continue to distort investment decisions. For example, in a world of imperfect information, new technology may serve reputational and signaling functions, acting as a proxy for product quality. If this is the case, then even firms in integrated markets will exhibit a tendency to over invest in medical technology. This tendency, however, will be less pronounced than similar tendencies in unintegrated markets. Furthermore, integration does little to alter distortions created by improperly formulated systems of administrative prices, or ill-founded Medicare or Medicaid policies.

88. For reviews of the empirical literature see Entin, et. al, supra note 84, at 153–67; Paul A. Pautler and Michael G. Vits, Hospital Market Structure, Hospital Competition and Consumer Welfare: What Can the Evidence tell Us? 10 *J. Contemp. Health L. & Poly* 117 (1994); Peter J. Hammer, *Mergers, Market Power and Competition: An Economic and Legal Evaluation of Hospital Mergers*, 1–33 (Dissertation, University of Michigan, Dept. of Economics) (1993). See also articles supra note 18.

89. These issues are explored in greater depth in Hammer, Questioning Traditional Antitrust Presumptions, supra note 18.

90. See Hammer, Price and Quality, supra note 42 at 133–34 ("[T]o the extent that market outcomes in managed care markets reflect actual choices of consumers between different price/quality combinations, the presumption that the level of quality provided by market forces is efficient (the basic assumption made by antitrust law) has a *prima facie* validity that it lacked in traditional healthcare markets.").

91. For discussions of Bertrand competition see Keeps, *Microeconomics*, supra note 4, at 330–35; Varian, *Intermediate*, supra note 4, at 461–62; Jean Tirole, *The Theory of Industrial Organization* at 209–11 (1988).

92. The Bertrand model is problematic given its restrictive and arguably unrealistic cost assumptions. The model assumes that there are constant returns to scale and that there are no fixed costs. Both of these assumptions are violated in medical markets. Hospitals have high fixed costs and, at least initially, there are significant increasing returns to scale in terms of hospital size. Furthermore, the model assumes that each competitor is capable of supplying the entire market demand, although this assumption can be relaxed as the number of firms increases beyond two. The basic lessons of the Bertrand model, however, that the relative strength of incentives to engage in price competition is affected by levels of productive capacity, and that physical capacity, to some extent, can substitute for the usual competitive assumption that there are a larger numbers of producers, are valid and are generalizable to health care markets.

93. In the Cournot equilibrium, price and profits are a function of the number of firms in the industry. Cournot prices will always be higher than marginal costs, with prices converging to marginal costs in the limit case of perfect competition, i.e., as the number of firms in the market approaches infinity. See Keeps, *Microeconomics*, supra note 4, at 326–28; Varian, *Intermediate*, supra note 5, at 447–58, *Tirole*, supra note 91, at 217–21; *Hovenkamp*, supra note 30, at 152–54.

94. See David M. Keeps and Jose A. Scheinkman, Quantity Precommittment and

Bertrand Competition Yield Cournot Outcome, *14 Bell J. Econ.* 326 (1983); William A. Brock and Jose A. Scheinkman, Price Setting Supergames with Capacity Constraints, 52 *Rev. Econ. Stud.* 371 (1985); *Tirole*, supra note 91, at 228–34.

95. This discussion has not considered the effect that new market entry can have on aggregate market capacity. Market entry serves as an important check on the efforts of individual firms to limit output. Market entry will occur so long as a new firm's expected profits exceed the costs of entry. If existing firms sufficiently restrict output and raise prices to the point where industry profits are high enough for a new firm to profitably enter the market, entry should occur. As a result of entry, market capacity will increase and prices and profits will fall. Consequently, while there is an internal market dynamic for existing firms to restrict output in an effort to raise prices, there is another dynamic stimulating entry, which ultimately limits the ability of firms to raise prices.

96. See Statement of the Department of Justice and Federal Trade Commission Enforcement Policy on Mergers Among Hospitals, *1994 Statements*, supra note 34, at 20,774.

97. See Peter J. Hammer, *Pegram v. Herdrich*: On Peritonitis, Preemption, and the Elusive Goal of Managed Care Accountability, 26 *J. Health Polit. Policy & Law* 767 (2001).

98. See, e.g., Recent Legislation: Health Care Law—HMO Regulation—Arkansas Require HMOs to Accept Any Provider Willing to Join Their Networks.—Patient Protection Act, 1995 Ark. Acts 505, amended by 1995 Ark. Acts 1193, 109 *Harv. L. Rev.* 2122 (1996). Some courts have held that federal ERISA legislation preempts these state laws. See *CIGNA Healthplan, Inc. v. Louisiana*, 82 F.3d 642 (5th Cir. 1996) (declaring Louisiana any willing provider statute invalid insofar as it related to ERISA-qualified benefit plans). For a general discussion of any willing provider laws see Karen A. Jordan, Managed Competition and Limited Choice of Providers: Countering Negative Perceptions Through a Responsibility to Select Quality Network Physicians 27 *Ariz. St. L.J.* 875, 915–20 (1995).

99. Health care providers that market their services as an insurance product, such as those that assume risk by accepting capitated payments, are potentially subject to state insurance regulation. To date, there has been little consistency in state approaches, see Risk-Bearing Network Regulations Described as "All Over the Board, 23 *Pension & Benefits Rep.* (BNA) No. 10 at 598 (March 4, 1996), although the National Association of Insurance Commissioners generally favors greater state regulation of provider-sponsored networks. See State Insurance Laws Should Apply to Risk-Bearing Networks, NAIC Says, 22 *Pension & Benefits Rep.* (BNA) No. 35 at 1953 (August 28 1995). Physicians generally oppose such regulatory efforts and have sought federal protection. The House version of the 1995 Medicare reform bill, for example, would have exempted physician-sponsored-networks contracting for Medicare services from state insurance regulations and established separate federal standards for such organizations. See H.R. 2425, 104th Cong., 1st Sess. § 1854 (1995). A similar provision was enacted into law in the Balanced Budget Act of 1997 which, among other things, established the Medicare+Choice Program. See 42 U.S.C. § 1395w-25 (1998). For a discussion of these provisions see James J. Unland, The Range of Provider/Insurer Configurations, 24 *J. Health Care Fin.* 1, 3–5 (Winter 1998).

100. See generally, Special Issue, The Managed Care Backlash, 24 *J. Health Polit. Policy & Law* 873 (1999).

7

WHY DO PUBLIC TEACHING
HOSPITALS PRIVATIZE?

Larry S. Gage

A growing crisis faces many urban public teaching hospitals today. It is influenced by many factors and often takes different forms in different communities. What is certain, however, is that public teaching hospitals face the same fiscal and competitive pressures that confront the entire hospital industry in America today, while also bearing the unique burdens that result from their safety–net mission and governmental status. A landmark study released in March, 2000 by the Institute of Medicine (IOM) summarized their situation:

> The funding and organization of the safety net have always been tenuous and subject to the changing tides of politics, available resources, and public policies. Despite their precarious and unstable infrastructure, these providers have proven to be resilient, resourceful, and adept at gaining support through the political process. Today, however, a more competitive health care marketplace and other forces of change are posing new and unprecedented challenges to the long-term sustainability of safety net systems and hold the potential of having a serious negative impact on populations that most depend on them for their care.[1]

The multiple missions of education, research and patient care for the uninsured and underinsured place many public teaching hospitals at great financial risk today. With cutbacks in the Medicaid and Medicare programs, these hospitals face an erosion in their traditional sources of funding. Recent changes in the competitive health marketplace, particularly the evolution of managed care, have added to the financial pressures on them.

158

In many cases, these pressures also include substantial constraints imposed by their governmental status. As a result, *privatization* or some other form of appro-priate restructuring—such as the creation of new, quasi-independent governmen-tal entities, merger, or contract management—is one way to improve viability and competitiveness. While privatization (or restructuring) will not by itself solve all of the fiscal and competitive problems facing public teaching hospitals, in many cases it has contributed significantly toward leveling the playing field for these es-sential providers.

Privatization is not always viewed as a way of strengthening the safety net, however. Sometimes, state or local politicians seek to privatize their public teaching hospital in order to shift to others the administrative or financial bur-den of its multiple missions. Indeed the word privatization itself is often a provocative one in the public sector in America, galvanizing employees and pa-tient advocates into strenuous and protracted opposition. Some of the most suc-cessful initiatives discussed in this chapter have avoided the term in favor of "restructuring" or "reorganization". And in some cases, these efforts have in-volved the creation of new, more flexible governmental entities rather than out-right privatization.

With these caveats in mind, many public teaching hospitals have made exten-sive and valuable use of such tools as restructuring and privatization in order to better compete and survive in this highly competitive health care market.

This chapter will:

- summarize the trends and pressures facing urban public teaching hospitals nationally;
- describe the many reasons such safety net providers consider privatization (or other forms of reorganization) a valuable tool and discuss the various forms pri-vatization can take; and
- provide specific examples of successful (and unsuccessful) public hospital pri-vatization efforts.

In so doing, I will draw upon my experience of 20 years as President of the Na-tional Association of Public Hospitals and Health Systems (NAPH). NAPH rep-resents over 100 of the nation's public and non-profit safety-net hospitals, com-prising the essential infrastructure of many of America's urban health systems. These hospitals provide over 80 percent of their services to Medicare, Medicaid, and low-income, uninsured, patients. They provide nearly one-quarter of all un-compensated hospital care in the U.S. while representing less than two percent of all hospitals. They also provide many preventive, primary, and costly tertiary care services to the entire community, not just to the poor and elderly. These services include top-level trauma centers, neonatal intensive care, emergency psychiatric programs, and crisis response units for both natural and man-made disasters.

Environmental factors affecting urban public teaching hospitals

The last decade has seen a dramatic transformation in the role of the hospital in our nation's health system, with a profound impact on every important element of that system. From the way we purchase and pay for health coverage to where and how we provide needed care, the metamorphosis has been swift and intense. New systems and networks spring to life overnight, mergers and acquisitions shrink the number of players, and traditional payment mechanisms turn upside down very quickly.

These trends have resulted in a number of general health system changes with implications for the financial viability of all hospitals. For example, purchasers—public and private—continue to form ever-larger coalitions to demand health-cost reductions. And despite some notable recent failures, in many parts of the country successful providers have responded by developing fully-integrated regionwide delivery systems. Ultimately, only the strongest systems will survive; the ability to control costs and generate strong patient satisfaction will be key.

While all hospitals are affected by these trends, public safety-net teaching hospitals have felt their impact disproportionately. The pressure for change is especially acute for those providers who rely most heavily on federal, state and local governmental funding to pay for a wide range of primary, acute and public health services. For such systems, market pressures are intensified by a variety of other factors: growth in the numbers of uninsured, reductions in Medicaid funding and in local support, greater competition for Medicaid patients, the need to provide public health and community–wide services, inadequate governance, the need to conduct the most sensitive business in meetings open to competitors, and other cumbersome political or bureaucratic obstacles.

As a result of these challenges, safety-net hospitals and systems face major threats to their future survival. The health of many millions of low-income patients and the viability of the health system for rich and poor alike in many metropolitan communities will be in danger if these threats are not adequately addressed.

In order to more fully understand why many public teaching hospitals would consider a step as radical privatization, it may be helpful to provide a more detailed overview of their current situation.

The characteristics of such hospitals typically include:

- a mission to treat anyone in need of care regardless of insurance status or ability to pay, leading to high volumes of inpatient and outpatient care to Medicare and Medicaid patients and to the poor and uninsured;
- an essential role in the provision of specialty services to entire communities (such services include trauma, burn and neonatal intensive care, and additional services too costly for other hospitals to provide);
- a responsibility to serve as major teaching hospitals for both undergraduate and graduate medical education, as well as in the training of nursing and ancillary medical personnel; and

- a considerably greater reliance on Medicare, Medicaid and state and local subsidies to support the various aspects of their mission, or, in the absence of some
  or all of these sources, the need to heighten market competitiveness to increase
  funding from non-governmental sources.

The situation of safety-net teaching hospitals can be further illustrated by reference to newly published 1999 data collected by NAPH in its annual Hospital
Characteristics Survey, augmented by data from the American Hospital Association's Annual Survey, the University HealthSystem Consortium, the Association
of American Medical Colleges and other sources.

The mission of NAPH members, and of other safety-net teaching hospitals, includes willingness, to the extent of their financial ability, to serve all individuals,
regardless of insurance status or ability to pay. While often a characteristic of
public hospital systems, this is by no means exclusively a public mission. In many
cases, it is undertaken voluntarily by public and private, nonprofit teaching hospitals alike.

This mission is reflected first and foremost in the tremendous volume of patient-care services provided to all patients in safety-net teaching hospitals. In
1999, NAPH members averaged over 15,000 inpatient admissions—more than
double the number for the average acute-care hospital in the nation—and almost
320,000 outpatient and emergency room visits annually, more than triple the national average for acute-care hospitals.

However, these numbers tell only part of the story. For most safety-net systems,
this volume reflects an even more significantly disproportionate provision of services to the elderly and the poor, especially by those hospitals that also serve as academic medical centers. In 1999, NAPH members provided, on average, 81% of
their services to Medicare, Medicaid and *self-pay* patients. Most self-pay patients
represent, in effect, the uninsured (who typically pay little or nothing for their
care). NAPH members provided, on average, 28% of their services (as measured
by gross charges) to self–pay patients in 1999. (Fig. 7–1).

Most self-pay patients end up as bad debt or charity care for NAPH member-
hospitals, and the costs of these patients must be covered from a variety of other
sources. Eighty-five NAPH members had over $4.6 billion in uncompensated care
costs in 1999, or an average of $58 million per hospital.

Like the underlying safety-net mission, the provision of substantial amounts of
uncompensated care is not limited to public teaching hospitals. In fact, private
nonprofit teaching hospitals also provide a substantial proportion of their services
to the uninsured and underinsured. The Association of American Medical Colleges has found that its 274 member hospitals (both public and private), constitut-
ing just 6% of the nation's hospital beds, provide 39% of all charity care.[2]

One major difference between public and private teaching hospitals is the way
in which they finance charity care. In 1999, NAPH members on average received
just 20% of their net revenues from Medicare and another 19% from commercial

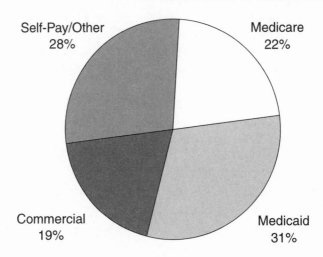

FIGURE 7-1 Gross revenues by payer source, National Association of Public Hospitals and Health Systems (NAPH) member hospitals, 1999.

insurance and managed-care plans. They received 39% of their revenues from Medicaid payments, 8% from self-pay patients, and 14% from direct state and local subsidies (Fig. 7–2). Private teaching hospitals, by contrast, receive little or no state and local subsidy, and must rely instead on obtaining a higher proportion of their revenues by serving Medicare and commercially–insured patients.

Public teaching hospitals nationally also face increased competitive pressures, including competition for privately-insured patients, and for selected Medicaid patients as well. In the area of obstetrics, for example, NAPH members have seen a dramatic reduction in the number of deliveries, as private providers increasingly seek to compete for the simpler, less-complicated Medicaid cases. In particular, between 1993 and 1999, NAPH members saw their Medicaid birth market share decrease by 28%, from 25% of all births in their markets in 1993 to 18% in 1999 (Fig. 7–3).

Perhaps the most significant pressure on public teaching hospitals stems from increasing numbers of uninsured. Even in the strong economy of the late 1990s, when the number of uninsured appeared to level off, many of the new jobs created were in small businesses or service industries which do not traditionally provide adequate insurance coverage.[3] More recently, the economic downturn of 2000–2001 led to increased unemployment and fears that the number of uninsured will again grow. In addition, in good times and bad, lower-income workers often refuse coverage even when it is offered if substantial cost-sharing is involved. Welfare and immigration reforms have led to reduced eligibility for Medicaid programs among some of the most vulnerable populations, and in most states even many of those eligible for Medicaid and other programs are simply never enrolled.

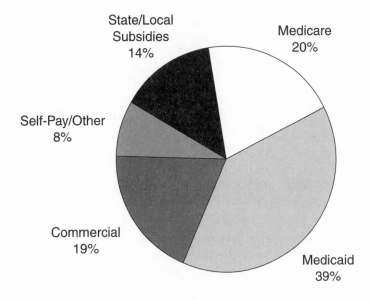

FIGURE 7–2 Net revenues by payer source, National Association of Public Hospitals and Health Systems (NAPH) member hospitals, 1999.

Increased reliance on managed care has also affected the ability of public teaching hospitals to provide rising levels of uncompensated care and fulfill their multiple missions. States have used managed care to contain costs in their Medicaid programs. While in rare instances, states have attempted to expand coverage to the uninsured with the savings, in most states the focus has been primarily on cost.[4] This focus on cost containment, and the intense competition for patients brought on by managed care, have further jeopardized important financing mechanisms for teaching programs, research and uncompensated care.[5,6]

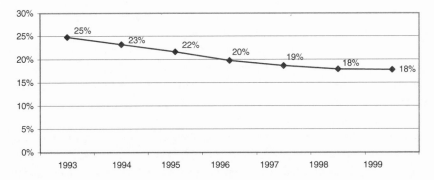

FIGURE 7–3 Medicaid births in National Association of Public Hospitals and Health Systems (NAPH) hospitals, 1993–1999.

Why public hospitals privatize

With traditional sources of revenues evaporating, and with the appearance of new competitors for many of the traditional safety net patients, public teaching hospitals in future will have to rely on aggressive reforms to keep pace and continue to finance their safety-net mission. Even if current funding sources can be protected and appropriate restraints placed on the cost-cutting behavior of managed-health plans, safety-net hospitals and health systems must recognize that they are part of an industry in which all hospitals are fighting for survival. Many will lose. If safety-net providers are to be among the winners, they must begin to take steps themselves to level the playing field and become better able to compete for all patients, not just the poor.

One approach to becoming more competitive is through reorganizing a public hospital's legal structure and governance. In the past decade or so, a substantial number of public hospitals have restructured their governance and legal organization through mergers, affiliations with private institutions, and conversions to more independent organizational forms such as private nonprofit corporations, authorities or public benefit corporations. It is important to note that not all these changes involve full privatization, but they all typically involve radical reorganization of the institution (and its services, operations, and personnel.). A recent survey of NAPH members indicated that less than one-third remain under direct ownership and operation of a city, county, or state university. The rest range over a wide spectrum of structures and relationships.

While it is by no means a panacea, privatization or restructuring can be an important tool to help level the playing field for public hospitals and health systems. Reorganization can take many forms—from the straightforward restructuring of a city or county agency to outright privatization through sale or lease to (or merger with) an existing private nonprofit or for-profit organization. In the most extreme cases, if all else has failed, public systems may be privatized through outright closure—in effect, leaving it to the private sector to fill the role of safety-net. Public hospital reorganizations are undertaken for a variety of reasons, with the reason often dictating the structure selected. For example, if the reason is primarily negative (taxpayer opposition to continued subsidies or fear of future increases in those subsidies), a public hospital's governmental owner is more likely to close it or sell to a completely independent third party who makes no commitment to maintaining a public mission. On the other hand, if the goal is more positive (a desire to improve efficiency and competitiveness in support of a safety-net mission) a state or local government is more likely to seek to create a new private or quasi-public structure, or seek out a merger of equals with a private organization.

Whether positive or negative, the reasons for privatization must also be sufficiently compelling that they outweigh the loss of benefits and protections that governmental status can afford a hospital or health system. For example, in some cases public status provides the protection of sovereign immunity or ensures easier access to capital through issuance of lower-cost tax-exempt "general obligation" governmental bonds. On the other hand, public status may subject the hospital to burdensome governmental constraints, such as onerous civil service requirements, complex procurement procedures, and sunshine laws that prevent effective strategic planning out-of-earshot of rival institutions. These constraints can lead to severe competitive disadvantages and ultimately may diminish the financial viability of a safety-net system and undermine its ability to carry out its mission without increased taxpayer subsidies. Careful balancing of these public benefits and constraints plays a critical role in decisions to restructure or privatize.

Powerful justifications exist for privatization when legal and administrative obstacles place the public hospital at a distinct disadvantage in relation to its private counterparts. While most governmental rules, regulations and constraints exist for valid reasons, the operation of an acute-care hospital is fundamentally different and often far more complex than most of the governmental functions for which such legal and administrative controls were created. Institutionally, a hospital is a set of intricate and interrelated programs, systems and functions operating in close proximity to one another. Its operation depends on advanced and rapidly changing technology, and both plant and equipment have a far shorter useful life than is typical in other agencies of government. Moreover, it employs a large number of workers, ranging from the unskilled laborer to highly-trained professionals, many of whom may be in short supply. No administrative and fiscal environment has seen more rapid change in recent years than the hospital sector.

Rules and procedures that are useful for the operation of a local sanitation department or library system often present problems of a higher order for acute-care hospitals. While not every public hospital will experience problems in all of these areas, the accumulated burdens of even a few of these obstacles can be crippling to a major public teaching hospital. Potential governmental or bureaucratic obstacles include:

Civil Service and Personnel

Complex civil service ordinances often impede hospitals from recruiting, promoting, or retraining qualified health care personnel, or to effectively discipline employees when required. Civil Service pay scales or job categories frequently cannot be adjusted quickly enough to respond to the local market, and health care professionals, frustrated with a lengthy and cumbersome application process, may choose to apply elsewhere.

Procurement

Many local government procurement constraints may be appropriate for typical government activities but are unsuitable for the hospital industry. Under most procurement statutes and ordinances, the hospital cannot independently purchase necessary medical equipment because invariably these large ticket items exceed certain thresholds. Delays in acquisition impede the efficiency of hospital operations and occasionally compromise patient care. In certain instances, procurement rules may actually raise costs by rewarding equipment-leasing at prices below certain thresholds rather than outright purchase. One justification cited by several state university teaching hospitals for adopting an alternative structure involves the ability to participate in major group purchasing organizations, such as the University HealthSystem Consortium, VHA or Premier Alliance.

Decision Making

Many public hospitals are subjected to added layers of strategic or operational decision making which often preclude a rapid response to critical issues. In a swiftly-evolving regulatory and competitive environment, public hospitals often lose out on important opportunities for want of quick, decisive action.

Budgetary Inflexibility

Close governmental oversight of public hospital budgets sometimes deprives hospitals of needed flexibility to deploy resources effectively and to respond to constantly changing needs. Furthermore, with the size of local subsidies often dependent upon the amount of the hospital deficit, the incentives to maximize revenue may be inadequate.

Capital Access

Many public hospitals have an outdated or deteriorating capital infrastructure. However, they are often unable to develop capital reserves or to allocate funds to longer-term projects. At the same time, cities and counties are often subject to limits on their total bond capacity, which would be depleted by the hospital's needs alone. In other cases, the hospital's legal structure or its fiscal relationship with local government may preclude access to various capital-financing options.

Strategic Planning

Confidential decision making is often critical for effective strategic planning in a competitive local health market. While open meeting and records requirements associated with a hospital's public status may be an important aspect of public accountability, in many cases they preclude confidential planning.

Recruiting

The political scrutiny and constraints on employee compensation that come with working for a governmental entity can make it extremely difficult for public hospitals to compete with the private sector for top management or medical staff.

Joint Ventures and Entrepreneurial Activity

Legal constraints often prevent public hospitals from entering into affiliations or joint venture arrangements that may otherwise appear necessary or beneficial. Success, or even survival, in today's market hinges on cost containment, patient satisfaction, demonstrated quality, and the ability to offer payers a fully integrated health system, or one or more of its critical components. In order to respond to the challenges of managed care and greater patient choice, today's public hospital must be able to recruit the highest quality physicians and other staff and participate in an integrated system with private partners that provide the best fit in terms of services, location, culture, and various other factors. However, for reasons ranging from statutory or constitutional restrictions on uses of public funds to a potential private partner's reluctance to deal with a public provider, public hospitals suffer from their inability from being unable to freely choose their business partners without first undertaking organizational changes.

Governing Body

Many public hospitals lack a separate governing board whose responsibilities are limited to the governance of the medical center; instead, this role may be filled by elected bodies or by appointed officials who are subject to competing demands for their time and attention. In order to develop strong leadership, the members of the governing body must be able to give the hospital main allegiance.

Sunshine Laws

Laws requiring public hospitals to hold all their meetings in public allow competitors to sit in and listen to their most sensitive strategic planning, marketing strategy, recruiting goals and other information, placing public hospitals at a serious disadvantage vis-à-vis their private competitors in the same market. Moreover, public hospitals lose opportunities to contract or to partner with private health care practices and providers because private entities do not want their records to be subject to these laws.

In today's highly competitive health care environment, any one of these obstacles may be enough to cost a public hospital the competitive advantage in its market. Ultimately, the desirability of reorganization or privatization will depend on the balance between the benefits of government status and the advantages conferred by the private sector's greater administrative and financial flexibility. In sum, the more onerous and inflexible the legal restriction imposed on a public facility, and the greater the restriction's adverse effects on competitiveness, the more important it is for the facility to achieve either exemption from, or substantial modification of, the restriction.

Each of the elements identified above requires careful attention in any privatization or restructuring. Often, the legal issues involved are complex, as are the interests and concerns of various stakeholders. Due to space limitations, I will illustrate this need to balance interests and obstacles by discussing the way in which Sunshine Laws have been addressed in privatization initiatives in various states.

Although many towns and cities in the United States have a long history of town meetings for conducting business, other state and local governing bodies were not required by statute to open their meetings to the public until the 1950s and 1960s. All 50 states and the District of Columbia have some form of open meetings or sunshine laws.[7] Created to give citizens access to the decision-making process, these laws differ widely in their applicability, procedural requirements, and opportunities for exemption or exceptions. In recognition of the need to balance the desirability of public accountability with other legitimate and competing interests, most legislatures have included some statutory exemptions allowing for closed meetings or protection of records in certain circumstances. Typical of these are exemptions for meetings where discussion of personnel matters, public security, or real estate transactions will take place. These exemptions have been crafted to ensure that public access does not mean that some other interest—confidentiality of personal information, safety of the public, or the ability to compete in the marketplace—is compromised or, indeed, sacrificed.[8]

In states without these exemptions for public hospitals, the ability to compete in an ever more competitive health care environment has been severely compromised. In fact, sunshine laws were identified as one of the primary motivations for the privatization of public hospitals in a recently released report prepared for the Henry J. Kaiser Family Foundation.[9] Brackenridge Hospital in Austin, Texas, before its privatization in 1995, is an example of an institution that experienced numerous problems due to the state's sunshine laws. For example, at one point the hospital was pursuing construction of a new facility in a rapidly-growing locale. However, because board meetings were required to be open, with no competitive-information exceptions, a competitor learned of these plans, acquired the same (or nearby) property, and built its own hospital, preempting Brackenridge's planned facility.

As a result of the importance of relief from conducting sensitive business in public, virtually every public hospital privatization in the country has included at least some exemptions or exceptions to the open meetings and open records laws. California, for example, has enacted legislation addressing requirements for public meetings when a state agency transfers to a private corporation more than $50 million in assets for the operation of a hospital.[10] Closed meetings are allowed for a variety of matters, including the acquisition, disposition, or lease of property; the terms and conditions of contracts for the provision of health care services; and trade secrets. In addition, California has exempted specific facilities from open meetings and document disclosure requirements.

Other states have also granted exemptions from their sunshine laws when creating new health entities. The statute creating the Hawaii Health Systems Corporation allows the corporation's board to meet in executive session to consider certain matters, and exempts from disclosure some categories of government records, including marketing strategies and strategic plans.[11] The District of Columbia's Act creating its new Health and Hospitals Public Benefit Corporation, exempted the PBC from the DC Freedom of Information Act for records pertaining to "information which may be of competitive advantage."[12] Similarly, New York state legislation creating the Westchester County Health Care Corporation exempted certain trade secrets from disclosure, and allows the corporation to conduct executive sessions on matters likely to injure the corporation's competitive position if made public.[13] Each of these states has recognized the importance of giving its restructured health and hospital systems the ability to compete on an equal footing with private counterparts.

Organizational structures

A public hospital's goals in privatizing or otherwise reorganizing, and the particular obstacles faced in its current situation, will determine the final structure of any reorganized entity. The need to balance the value of some public accountability with the hospital's need to become more competitive has led to a wide variety of legal structures among urban public hospital systems in America. Models adopted by restructured or privatized public hospitals include:

Separate Board Within Governmental Entity

A hospital or public health board is created with authority to manage daily operations of the hospital. This entails a higher degree of autonomy than direct operation by state or local government but is often seen as inadequate to the tasks facing a safety-net health system today.

Hospital Taxing District

An independent instrumentality of the state government can be created, typically with taxing authority and defined geographic boundaries. A district is typically organized under generic, statewide legislation permitting cities or counties to create such entities for various purposes (although it may also be created by a specific state law). An election of voters within the geographic boundaries of the district is often required to establish the District, as well as to levy or increase taxes.

Hospital Authority

An authority is also a separate public entity independent of local government. While it typically does not enjoy taxing powers, it is governed by a separate board, often with the involvement of local government. A hospital authority may also be organized under generic, statewide hospital authority statutes, or created by special legislation.

Public Benefit Corporation

A distinctive public corporate entity may be created to provide specified benefits to state residents. While several states have enacted a body of law applicable to PBCs, this is generally a "designer option," with unique enabling legislation necessary to address the needs of the particular health system. In certain states (e.g. California), a PBC may be considered a private nonprofit corporation.

Nonprofit Corporation

Public hospitals may also be converted to private, nonprofit corporations. Such a corporation is typically tax-exempt under federal and state law, and acquires the hospital from its governmental owner by sale or lease. Being private, such entities often also enter into contractual agreements with the local government to provide safety-net health services.

Management Contract

Public hospitals may sometimes be privatized or restructured through management by an existing health system or management company. The degree of ongoing involvement by the local government varies, as does the length of the management contract.

Public-Private Partnership

Public hospitals may also be transferred to or combined with an existing private health system. For the sake of the present discussion, this option is distinguished from outright privatization by a high level of ongoing involvement by and accountability to local government.

Transfer to Existing Private Health System

Finally, a public hospital may be fully privatized by sale or long-term lease to, or merger with, an existing nonprofit or for-profit hospital or health system. While such a system may undertake obligations to continue certain safety-net services, local government does not retain a significant role in governance or operations.

Variations exist within each individual category discussed above. And, of course, the permanent closure of some public hospitals has also occurred (in effect, a form of privatization that occurs when other efforts at reform have failed). The following table sets out a list identifying a wide range of public hospitals (most of which are also teaching hospitals) that have privatized or otherwise restructured in one or another of these categories.

Protecting the public interest

Privatization of a public hospital does not mean that public accountability (for example, for the assets transferred by a public entity to a private corporation) must be lost. A variety of mechanisms exist to ensure ongoing public scrutiny and accountability. Examples include:

Statutory

If legislation is adopted in connection with the hospital's conversion to private status, the legislation may provide for continued public accountability. One method is to include broader language—perhaps a statement of purposes—in the statute, while reserving specific obligations to a contract. Legislation creating the Denver Health and Hospital Authority, for example, used this approach to affirm the Authority's general mission. The statute sets out a four–part mission including "access to quality preventive, acute, and chronic health care for all the citizens of Denver regardless of ability to pay," and further requires that transfer of assets to the Authority be conditioned on a contract by which the Authority agrees to fulfill this mission. The contract, on the other hand, is expected to quantify the Authority's obligation as well as the city's responsibility to fund it. In the case of St. Paul-Ramsey Medical Center, state legislation included an unquantified requirement to provide care for indigent patients, as well as a commitment to provide "major or unique" services currently provided by the hospital (e.g., its trauma center and burn unit) for a five-year period, and thereafter, to the best of its ability.

Contractual

The lease or other contracts between the city and the new, nonprofit corporation may spell out duties and obligations relating to public accountability. For example, placing specific requirements in the lease documents or transfer documents, which require approval by both parties for future revision, may create an adequate bar to eliminating community obligations while permitting the flexibility to alter them as needed. Furthermore, in many cases, the mutual intent is that the

TABLE 7–1.   Examples of Privatized or Restructured Public Teaching Hospitals

Privatization or other restructuring of public hospitals can take a variety of forms, from reorganization within a governmental entity to creation of a new authority or public–benefit corporation; creation of a private nonprofit corporation; merger; or the sale or lease to an existing private organization. The model selected often depends on the precise nature of the governmental constraints and competitive challenges that confront the public hospital or health system in its own community.

I. Separate Board Within Governmental Entity

As an initial step toward privatization, a separate governmental hospital or public health board has authority to manage daily operations of hospital is sometimes created to oversee a city or county owned hospital; such a board typically has a higher degree of autonomy than direct operation by state or local government.

Erie County Medical Center (NY)
Hurley Medical Center (Flint, MI)
Maricopa Medical Center (AZ)
MetroHealth Medical Center (Cleveland, OH)
San Francisco Health Commission (CA)

II. Hospital Authority

Separate body corporate and politic existing independent of local government; separate board with governmental involvement.

Alameda County Hospital Authority
Cambridge Public Health Commission (MA)
Denver Health Medical Center (CO)
Louisiana Health Care Authority (managed by Louisiana State University)
Miami-Dade County Public Health Trust (FL)
Pima Health Care System Commission (Kino Community Hospital, Tucson, AZ)
University of Colorado Hospital (CO)

III. Public Benefit Corporation

Distinctive public corporate entity providing a public benefit to state residents

DC General Health and Hospitals Public Benefit Corporation (Washington, DC)
Hawaii Health Services Corporation, Inc. (HI)
Indianapolis Health & Hospitals Corp. (Wishard Memorial Hospital; managed by Univ. of Ind.)
New York City Health & Hospitals Corporation (NYC)
Virgin Islands Health Care Corporation
Westchester County Medical Center (NY)

IV. Nonprofit Corporation

Created pursuant to a state's non-profit corporation statute, sometimes in concert with an existing private non-profit entity; often maintains contractual agreement with the local government.

Boston Medical Center (MA)
Detroit Medical Center
Dimensions Health Corporation (Prince Georges Cty., MD)
DeKalb General Medical Center (GA)
Lakewood Hospital (OH)
Medical Center of Central Georgia (Macon, GA)
Medical Center of Columbus (GA)
Memorial Medical Center (NM)

IV. Nonprofit Corporation (continued)

Memorial Medical Center (Savannah, GA)

Northside Medical Center (Atlanta, GA)

North Oakland Medical Center (MI)

Phoebe Putney Medical Center (Albany, GA)

The Regional Medical Center at Memphis (TN)

St. Louis Regional Medical Center

Tampa General Healthcare (FL)

Truman Medical Center (Kansas City, MO)

University Hospital (Cincinnati, OH)

University Hospital, Louisville (managed by partnership of Jewish Hospital HealthCare Services and Alliant Health System)

University of California at San Francisco/Stanford Health Care

University of Florida—Shands Medical Center

University of Indiana Medical Center

University of Maryland Medical Center

University of West Virginia Medical Center

V. Sale, Lease, Management Contract

Transfer of public hospital to pre-existing healthcare entity(ies).

Bernalillo County Medical Center

(managed by University of New Mexico)

Milwaukee County Medical Center (sold to non-profit Froedtert Memorial Lutheran Hospital)

Harborview Medical Center (King County-owned hospital managed by University of Washington)

Northwest Texas Hospital (Amarillo, TX; sold to Universal Health Services, Inc.)

San Diego County, Orange County, and Davis County Medical Centers, CA (sold to University of California)

Brackenridge Hospital Austin, TX (city-owned hospital leased to SETON Healthcare Network of the Daughters of Charity)

St. Paul-Ramsey Medical Center (MN) (county hospital acquired by HealthPartners, Inc, a Health Maintenance Organization)

University Medical Center (Fresno, CA)

Wishard Memorial Hospital (owned by Indiana Health & Hospitals Corp; managed by The University of Indiana)

---

formerly public medical center will continue to provide indigent care and to maintain key services (e.g., trauma and burn care and certain perinatal specialties), while the local government will continue to fund them. This should be spelled out in a contract, which can also include responsibilities for public accountability.

Corporate organizational documents

Public purposes as well as accountability mechanisms can be incorporated into the corporation's articles of incorporation, bylaws, and similar documents. While these can, of course, be amended, the documents themselves can set a high threshold for amendment.

Corporate governance

The presence of current or former public appointees, officials, or representative on the board of the private corporation is often a key element of continued accountability. These directors provide the overlap between the public and the private medical center. So long as the public appointees do not have a voting majority on the Board, this presence should not mean that the corporation is deemed a public entity and thus subject to sunshine and other legal constraints. Furthermore, there may be a supermajority requirement for key issues, such as amendment of articles, dropping key service areas, and approving strategic plans. Or, a *class* vote system may be used to require support of public representatives for major moves.

Periodic reporting requirements and annual, independent audits

The local government can maintain supervision of the new corporation through a variety of reporting requirements. St. Paul-Ramsey Medical Center, for instance, must provide its annual financial statement to the county, as well as an annual report on improvements to county property. Other systems are required to report on a specific list of issues each year. Local government may retain authority over the approval of certain key acts, such as sale of facilities, approval of management contracts, or elimination of specified safety-net services. Finally, reversion of the facility and other assets to the government, upon dissolution of the corporation or the breach of certain critical statutory or contractual requirements, constitutes another common mode of accountability.

Requirements of maintaining tax-exempt status

Private, tax-exempt corporations are subject to various prerequisites for maintaining their exempt status. An application for federal tax-exempt status must be filed, and annual financial reporting is required to maintain tax-exempt status. If the corporation earns any income from activities unrelated to its exempt purposes, it must track, report, and pay taxes on that income. The corporation must be careful to avoid earning too much income unrelated to its exempt purposes; or it will forfeit its exempt status. The corporation must also avoid arrangements resulting in private inurement—the conferral of financial benefits on private individuals in excess of the market value of the goods or services these individuals provide.

These mechanisms, in various combinations, allow the local government and the public to maintain supervision over the new private corporate entity while enabling it to respond quickly in a fast-paced and competitive environment.

Case studies of privatized or restructured public teaching hospitals

The remaining section of this chapter will seek to illustrate the trends and issues outlined above by describing a number of recent efforts at the privatization of public teaching hospitals.

Boston Medical Center

Boston Medical Center was created in July 1996, as a result of the consolidation of the public Boston City Hospital and the private nonprofit Boston University Medical Center Hospital. Boston Medical Center (BMC) is a private, nonprofit corporation. As part its creation, a new quasi-independent governmental agency called the Boston Public Health Commission accepted the public health responsibilities of the former Boston Department of Health & Hospitals and owns the physical plant of the former Boston City Hospital, which it leases to BMC. The need to consolidate and streamline services due to increased competition for patients and the cost-cutting mandated by managed care were the principal motivations for both hospitals in considering this privatization and merger. Increased competition even extended to indigent patients because of Massachusetts' generous uncompensated care pool. Additionally, Boston City Hospital, as a department of Boston City government, did not operate as efficiently as did its private competitors due to public constraints on purchasing, personnel, budgeting, other decision making and long-term planning.

The process of creating BMC began in earnest in 1992 when a Mayor's Health Care Commission was established. It's mandate was to develop strategies to ensure Boston City Hospital's long-term ability to meet the needs of its patient population and to recommend the appropriate relationships among the Community Health Centers (CHCs), private teaching hospitals and DHH, and develop a health care delivery system model for Boston. This commission was funded in equal parts by the city and the Conference of Boston Teaching Hospitals. Among other things, the commission's 1994 report recommended a restructuring of Boston City Hospital, integration into it of the CHCs, and full integration of Boston City Hospital with Boston University Medical Center Hospital. To follow up on this report, mayor Thomas Menino appointed a new commission, the Mayor's Advisory Committee on Health Care. Its May 1995 report recommended the merger of the two facilities under the Public Health Commission/private corporation structure described above. The advisory committee included subcommittees on governance, finance and debt, operations, clinical services, facilities planning, community relations, labor relations, and public health.

In the Fall of 1995, the Massachusetts state legislature and the governor approved a home rule petition authorizing the merger or consolidation of the city hospital with a private, non-profit university hospital. The legislation also authorized creation of the Public Health Commission to assume the responsibilities of the Boston Department of Health & Hospitals. Mayor Menino announced agreement on key merger terms in April 1996 and released financial projections for Boston Medical Center, in the face of vehement opposition from the hospital's key unions. While conflicts among unions, management and city council delayed final authorization of the merger, City Council approval was granted in July 1997, and the merger was immediately effected.

The Boston Public Health Commission is a public instrumentality but is not subject to the supervision of any other department, commission, board, bureau, agency or officer of the city, except to the extent and in the manner provided by its enabling act. Boston Medical Center is a nonprofit corporation, exempt from most sunshine law requirements. It is required to prepare and file an annual report on its provision of health care services to the city and to hold annually at least one meeting that is open to the general public.

BCH's public purposes were protected by the statutory requirement that BMC (and any subsequent merger partners) provide accessible health care services to all, regardless of insurance status or ability to pay; to maintain a commitment to vulnerable populations; to maintain a full range of primary through tertiary care; to serve urban and suburban communities in a "culturally and linguistically competent manner;" to enhance its role as a major academic medical center; and to provide managed-care services to the community. The new corporation must prepare and file with the City an annual report on its provision of health care services.

By blending two neighboring facilities into one medical center, BMC created a strong urban health care network for the community. The new entity is governed by a 30-person Board of Trustees whose original membership includes 10 representatives each from BCH and BUMC, 4 representatives from community health centers (CHCs), and 6 members who serve by virtue of specific leadership positions at the Commission or BMC. BMC provides seamless delivery of services to individuals who previously sought care at both institutions. The merger also capitalized on the strengths of each institution by bringing the strengths of a university hospital together with the Northeast's only Level One Trauma Care facility.

The Regional Medical Center at Memphis

In 1981, the Shelby County Health Care Corporation (SCHCC) was formed as a private, nonprofit corporation to run the Regional Medical Center at Memphis (the Med), which had previously operated as a public hospital authority. Pursuant to a Shelby County Resolution and the Tennessee Hospital Authority Act, a resolution was passed turning over the Med's assets to the SCHCC through a long-term lease. Members of SCHCC's governing Board are nominated by board members subject to appointment by the county mayor and confirmation by the county commission. The Board does not report to any county officials and is largely independent from the county's government and political process. Its meetings are open to the public by virtue of its contract with the county, but the Med is otherwise exempt from state sunshine laws. SCHCC submits to the county an annual budget and report. While the county approves and appropriates funds for the Med's budget for indigent care, the county otherwise has no part in the facility's financing, management or operation. As a private not-for-profit corporation, the Med is not subject to public bidding and procurement procedures or (except as noted above) to sunshine laws. SCHCC does receive capital appropriations from the county but maintains independent access to other capital markets through revenue bonds and joint ventures. The Med's employees are not considered civil servants nor are they eligible for county retirement benefits. The employees are represented by the same labor unions as before the reorganization.

Reorganized to depoliticize its board, strengthen hospital management, avoid wasteful procurement restrictions, gain enhanced access to capital, and to otherwise search for more cost-effective ways to provide health services, the Med now enjoys an improved reputation in the community. Since its reorganization, moreover, the Med has maintained an array of services for the indigent population, and Shelby County provides the Med with an annual indigent care appropriation.

In 1989 the Med faced a lawsuit from a local newspaper seeking access to the facility's records. The paper argued that the Med was a public hospital subject to Tennessee's open-records laws. The court disagreed, finding that the Med is a private, nonprofit entity and is not subject to the Tennessee Public Records Act. The court found persuasive, among other things, the fact that the Med was incorporated as a private not-for-profit corporation and functions in accordance with the Tennessee General Corporation Act, that it did not claim governmental immunity from tort claims, and that the Med's employees were not considered employees of a public entity for purposes of the Shelby County Retirement Plan.[14]

Brackenridge Hospital

In October of 1995, Seton Healthcare Network assumed management and control of the city-owned Brackenridge Hospital through a 30-year lease from the city of Austin, Texas. Seton itself is owned by the Daughters of Charity National Health System (a Catholic institution that operates 46 hospitals across the U.S.). As part of the lease agreement, Seton agreed to continue Brackenridge's mission of providing indigent care and to be monitored by a five-member community board appointed by the city. In addition, Seton agreed to continue providing some of Brackenridge's "essential community services," including inpatient and outpatient pediatric care, emergency and trauma services, and maternity and women's services. Seton paid the city $10 million at closing and will pay rent of approximately $2.2 million per year for 30 years.

Prior to its reorganization, Brackenridge Hospital was a city hospital whose management reported directly to the city manager and city council. The hospital CEO was the equivalent of a city department head. The hospital had a dedicated board, but it was advisory in nature. Although the city supplied only about 12 percent of Brackenridge's revenues, city approval was required for the hospital's line-item budget, salary scales, procurement, and all capital projects. At times, these approvals became highly political, the subject of overt city council lobbying. The city had been considering a reorganization of Brackenridge for some time because of growing operating losses and fear of increased future reliance on city taxpayer funds. In addition, the hospital wished to get out from under regulations for public entities that made it difficult to attract and retain high-quality management and restricted management's effective operation of the hospital, affecting personnel, purchasing, and public disclosure.

The reorganization has been termed a success, both for the city and the hospital. Without the reorganization, the city might well have had to close the hospital because of losses. Now, city finances are improved and an inflow of capital from the Daughters of Charity National Health System has led to improvements in hospital operations and facilities, which in turn have led to an increase in market share and slight improvements for the hospital's bottom line. Brackenridge agreed by terms of its lease to hold monthly open meetings.

Truman Medical Center

The two public hospitals in Kansas City, Missouri, are operated by a nonprofit corporation, the Truman Medical Center (TMC). The corporation was created after the failure in 1961 of legislation designed to create a hospital district with its own taxing authority. As a result, TMC was one of the first public hospital bodies to restructure as a private, nonprofit entity with close ties to its local governments. The initial goals of this reorganization included: desegregating the system's facilities, maintaining the public mission, creating a medical school, streamlining purchasing procedures, and improving its personnel system. Another major impetus was the system's pressing capital needs and its desire to utilize federal guarantees for its bonds pursuant to the Federal Housing Administration's § 242 program. The reorganization is widely viewed as having resulted in a successful corporate structure.

Kansas City and Jackson County retain title to the two hospitals. These government entities maintain public accountability with respect to the operation of TMC in a number of ways. For example, the city and county contract with TMC on an annual basis (these contracts have been renewed routinely since 1962, although TMC has threatened at least once not to renew because of insufficient funding). In addition, TMC has quarterly meetings with the city manager and the county executive, and TMC provides copies to the city and county of its annual audits and quarterly financial reports and projections. The city and county help finance the operation of TMC through annual lump-sum appropriations to compensate TMC for indigent care. TMC must then provide indigent care until its funding runs out (although to our knowledge, TMC has never denied care based on the lack of public funds). If necessary, TMC may go back to the city and county to request additional support based on unanticipated costs, but this is rarely done. As a nonprofit corporation, TMC is not subject to Missouri's civil service laws nor to its sunshine laws.

John L. Doyne Hospital

In late 1995, Froedtert Memorial Lutheran Hospital, Inc. (FMLH) entered into an agreement with Milwaukee county for the purchase of the county-owned and operated John L. Doyne Hospital. This agreement came after a county-appointed management group reported that the county had stood to lose $12 million to $15 million a year in operating Doyne. The agreement was based on county board resolutions ending the county's role as a direct provider of medical services and terminating Doyne's operations. It required FMLH to provide some of the health care services the county must by law provide to medically-needy residents. Motivations for the sale, other than the county's potential losses from operating Doyne, included high executive turnover, public-sector bureaucratic rigidities, decreased tax support from the community, inability to control operating costs, and lack of managerial flexibility due to legal and regulatory restrictions governing public entities. Once the county hospital was purchased by FMLH, a non-profit corporation, all services were consolidated and the county's facility was closed as a hospital.

The medical center's reorganization or transfer had been studied and discussed for many years before the sale was effected. Reports of a Blue Ribbon Committee on the Milwaukee County Medical Complex in 1990 and 1991 recommended that a public-private partnership be created. Although no formal mayoral or executive commissions were established after that time to study the prospective transfer, the county board appointed a management group which reported in April 1995 that the county could could sustain large losses from operating Doyne. The county decided to close the hospital and begin formal negotiations with FMLH. In September 1995 a binding agreement among the parties established the sale's parameters. Although formal negotiations took only a few months, both parties had laid much of the groundwork earlier. In general, the negotiations and sale were not undertaken in a public forum. The county's board of supervisors and county executive visited Doyne to assure hospital workers that their concerns were being protected. In addition, a newsletter was created to keep labor informed about developments. In the final agreement, FMLH assumed no explicit obligations to employ Doyne staff and did not assume the county's obligation under collective bargaining agreements, employee benefit plans or other personnel programs. FMLH did, however, agree to retain qualified, interested Doyne employees pursuant to its interview and hiring process. Doyne employees hired by FMLH retained their seniority for purposes of vacation and leave time, health benefits, tuition benefits, and long-term disability insurance.

FMLH is required to provide emergency and Level–One trauma services to the indigent, medically needy and other populations of Greater Milwaukee to the extent financial support is available under the county's General Assistance Medical Program (GAMP) or other sources. In addition, for the first two years, FMLH agreed to be the exclusive non-emergent, adult acute-care GAMP provider for inpatient services. Although FMLH is currently providing these services, GAMP funds are insufficient to cover this care. In March 1998, the county began seeking a contract with a network of clinics and hospitals to provide indigent care.

St. Paul-Ramsey Medical Center

St. Paul-Ramsey Medical Center (St. Paul-Ramsey) is a county-owned hospital operated by a private, nonprofit managed-care corporation. The Medical Center underwent organizational changes in 1986 (control was transferred from the county hospital commission to a newly-created nonprofit corporation) and in 1994 transfered to an established, nonprofit managed care organization). In both cases, these changes were undertaken to improve the institution's ability to compete in the current health care environment, and with shrinking county funding, while maintaining its public mission to provide indigent care. At present, the county provides only about two percent of the hospital's operating budget.

In 1994, the hospital entered into a contract with HealthPartners, Inc., an established managed-care entity. Under this agreement, HealthPartners acquired the private, non–profit corporation that operated St. Paul-Ramsey and assumed responsibility for the management of the medical center. The two nonprofit corporations now function as one. St. Paul-Ramsey is governed by a 15-member Board of Directors appointed with minimal input from the county. Eleven members of the board are appointed by the HealthPartners board and three are appointed by the St. Paul-Ramsey medical staff. In addition, one seat on the St. Paul-Ramsey Board is reserved for a Ramsey County Commissioner in an *ex officio* capacity (with voting privileges). The medical center must provide the county with a copy of its annual financial statement and an annual report of its improvements to county property.

St. Paul-Ramsey's public mission is protected by several methods. First, the long-term lease with the county contains a provision requiring that the medical center provide services to the county's indigent. In addition, state legislation requires that St. Paul-Ramsey provide hospital and medical services for the indigent of Ramsey County, though the requirement is unquantified. This legislation also requires that the medical center continue to provide the "major or unique" services it currently provides (for example, trauma center, burn unit) for a five-year period and, thereafter, to the best of its ability.

Neither Health Partners nor the surviving nonprofit corporation that formally operates St. Paul–Ramsey is deemed a public entity for purposes of state and local law. Thus, corporate employees are not public employees, although retained employees may choose to continue participation in the public employees retirement plan. In addition, the operating entity is not a municipality for purposes of tort liability for claims occurring after its incorporation. Furthermore, the statute providing for the governance of St. Paul Ramsey authorizes closed meetings "to discuss and take action on specific matters involving contracts or marketing activity" if the disclosure of such information would harm its competitive position.

Detroit Receiving Hospital

By the time its new plant was built in 1980, the city-run Detroit General Hospital was projected to lose approximately $25 million a year in capital and operating costs. As a result of current and anticipated losses, the city sought to divest itself of the facility. Meanwhile, several area nonprofit hospitals were consolidating their operations into a new nonprofit entity, the Detroit Medical Center. Detroit General Hospital was privatized, renamed and incorporated as Detroit Receiving Hospital, one of five nonprofit subsidiaries in the new, private, nonprofit Detroit Medical Center. Detroit Medical Center paid rent of $1 million annually to the city for a long-term lease of the facilities. The new, nonprofit entity did not assume Detroit General's liabilities, and the city retained liability for debt service of $7 million a year.

Upon completion of construction of a new facility for Detroit General Hospital, it had become apparent that the could not afford to open or operate it. The city's decision to divest itself of the hospital and transfer management to the Detroit Medical Center arose from this crisis. Organized labor opposed the agreement because no successor-union provisions were included that explicitly protected workers' benefits and guaranteed the Detroit Medical Center's recognition of existing bargaining agreements. Representatives from labor challenged the agreement in court, and the mayor actually closed the facility for two weeks while the Michigan Supreme Court's decision was pending; patients were transferred to other Detroit Medical Center facilities during that period. In June of 1980, Detroit Receiving Hospital opened as a private hospital that maintained a public health mission and served Wayne State University's educational needs.

The city's ongoing role in Detroit Receiving Hospital was limited to the appointment of a minority of the subsidiary's board, its role as lessor of the hospital facilities, and the Medical Center's submission of an annual report to the city council. Of Detroit Receiving's ten member Board, the mayor nominates three members, the president of Wayne State University nominates three, the parent board nominates three from the community, and the CEO serves in an *ex officio* capacity. The parent Detroit Medical Center board makes the appointments from these nominations. The board of Detroit Receiving is responsible for day-to-day operations of the hospital, and it has traditionally been filled with professional rather than political appointments.

The statute authorizing the transfer required adherence to the hospital's public mission of accepting all patients regardless of their ability to pay. The Detroit Medical Center has allocated services among its five member-hospitals, and as suggested by its name, Detroit Receiving provides trauma and emergency services to the system. This is its sole function, and the only source of admissions is through its emergency room.

University of Louisville Hospital

Prior to 1982, public hospital care in Louisville was provided by the University of Louisville's teaching hospital. Government financial support for unreimbursed care was insufficient, and large deficits regularly occurred. The university also maintained that its teaching programs were underfunded and public and advocacy groups complained of inadequate care.

In 1982, during construction of a new public hospital, the University told the Commonwealth of Kentucky that it could not afford to open the facility. In response, the Commonwealth to leased the facility to the for-profit Humana Hospitals Corporation. Under this contract, Humana assumed all financial risks and agreed to pay 20% of its pretax profits to the University of Louisville. Care for the uninsured was required, but the corporation was fully reimbursed for these costs from a fund created by the city, county and commonwealth. If the fund was not sufficient to cover the corporation's outlays for indigent care in any given year, the liability carried over to the succeeding year and was reimbursed from the following year's government contributions to the fund.

By 1994, after a series of corporate splits and mergers, Columbia/HCA—the nation's largest health care company—had more or less succeeded to Humana's contract to operate the hospital. Columbia originally maintained that it had the legal right to continue to operate University Hospital under the relatively generous terms of the existing Humana agreement, but ultimately agreed to renegotiate the contract. In March, 1994, the university and the commonwealth signed a new contract with Columbia, under which indigent patients would continue to receive care from Columbia/HCA in return for a fixed government subsidy. Columbia/HCA would spend $7.5 million to expand the hospital's emergency room and $11.8 million to improve the hospital's Cancer Center; increase its subsidy for the university's medical education programs; and share more of the hospital's profits with the university. As an added incentive to the state, Columbia agreed to locate its headquarters in Louisville instead of Nashville, Tennessee.

Despite the agreement, Columbia/HCA announced plans to move its headquarters to Tennessee in January 1995. This was the beginning of the end of the corporation's relationship with the hospital. The governor sought bids from the private sector to manage the University of Louisville Hospital even though Columbia announced its intent to continue management. The hospital trustees voted in October 1995 to award a 15-year contract to a new nonprofit partnership between Jewish Hospital HealthCare Services and Alliant Health System. The new entity, University Medical Center (UMC) is governed by a 12–member board of which the university appoints six members; Jewish and Alliant appoint three members each. After a legal challenge from Columbia, UMC assumed management of the hospital in February 1997. Under the contract, the university keeps all profits from UMC. UMC agreed to expand the hospital's emergency room, improve its cancer center, and maintain health care education programs. The new partnership also agreed to continue to provide indigent care and to grant the University stronger control over academic programs than it had under prior management agreements with UMC's for-profit predecessors.

Conclusion

In 1999, New York Times columnist Bob Herbert eloquently described the dilemma facing America's public and teaching hospitals:

A deep financial crisis is spreading like a virus through the nation's teaching hospitals. It is undermining their honorable and historic mission, which has been to train new generations of physicians, to conduct critically important medical research and to provide treatment for, among others, the poor. . . . *Toying with the future of such a system is as dangerous as Russian roulette.*[15]

As the IOM concluded in its 1999 Report:

Failure to support these essential providers could have a devastating impact not only on the populations who depend on them for care but also on other providers that rely on the safety net to care for patients whom they are unable or unwilling to serve.

Despite the legal and competitive crises they face, to date many public teaching hospitals have managed to maintain their safety-net mission, and many have also met and embraced the challenges of competing in a rapidly evolving health care marketplace. Successful safety-net teaching hospitals are those that have been able to develop integrated delivery systems, upgrade their physical plant, recruit and retain competent clinical and operational staff, enter into effective public-private partnerships, and compete effectively for traditional Medicaid and Medicare patients, while reaching out to expand services for those with private coverage.

One of the mechanisms used to achieve these goals has been privatization or other forms of reorganization. But as the case studies in this chapter make clear, privatization is by no means a panacea; nor is privatization or restructuring easy to achieve or sustain. Substantial political skills and leadership are required even to begin the process of considering the reorganization of a major public teaching hospital, and there are also substantial pitfalls along the way. For every successful privatization described in this chapter, there have been failed efforts due to a variety of factors. Those have included the failure adequately to address the concerns of employees, medical staff, patient advocates and other key stakeholders; inability to articulate the goals and benefits of restructuring to the public and the media; and underestimating of the ability of potential competitors or political opponents to derail or undermine a privatization initiative. Even when a privatization or restructuring has been completed, some reorganized hospitals or health systems have encountered further obstacles to success. For example, constant changes in the regulatory and reimbursement environment have generated additional pressures that even restructured public hospitals have found difficult to meet. Thus, privatized or restructured public hospitals in Washington, D.C., St. Louis, Louisiana, California and elsewhere have now closed or been forced to reorganize a second time. Moreover, in some cases public hospitals have been privatized or restructured without being given all of the tools needed to implement effective reforms. In such cases, further legislative fine-tuning or renegotiation of the terms of the reorganization have proved necessary.

Despite all these caveats, privatization or restructuring has proved to be a valuable tool in improving the viability—and survivability—of safety-net hospitals and health systems in many parts of the county. Given the ever-increasing complexity of the fiscal, clinical and competitive environment for most public teaching hospitals, it is a tool that is often well worth consideration by the governmental owners and operators of such hospitals.

Notes

1. Institute of Medicine, America's Health Care Safety Net: Intact but Endangered.
2. J. Reuter, and D.J. Gaskin. The Role of Academic Health Centers and Teaching Hospitals in Providing Care for the Poor. In S.H. Altman, U.E. Reinhardt, and A.E. Shields (eds.), *The Future of the U.S. Healthcare System: Who Will Care for the Poor and Uninsured?* Chicago: Health Administration Press, 1998.
3. J.F., Sheils, and L.M.B. Alecxih, Recent Trends in Employer Health Insurance Coverage and Benefits. Unpublished study. The Lewin Group.
4. Congressional Budget Office. Responses to Uncompensated Care and Public-Program Controls on Spending: Do Hospitals "Cost Shift?" Washington, D.C.: Author, 1993.
5. R.J. Blendon, et al. Paying Medical Bills in the United States: Why Health Insurance Isn't Enough. *JAMA* 1994, 271(12), 950.
6. S.H., Altman, and S. Guterman. The Hidden U.S. Healthcare Safety Net: Will It Survive? In S.H. Altman, U.E. Reinhardt, and A.E. Shields (eds.), *The Future of the U.S. Healthcare System: Who Will Care for the Poor and Uninsured?* Chicago: Health Administration Press, 1998.
7. Teresa Dale Pupillo, The Changing Weather Forecast: Government in the Sunshine in the 1990's—An Analysis of State Sunshine Laws. 71 *Wash. U.L.Q.* 1165, 1166 (1993).
8. Charles N. Davis, et al. Sunshine Laws and Judicial Discretion: A Proposal for Reform of State Sunshine Law Enforcement Provisions. 28 *Urb. Law.* 41, 42 (1996).

9. The Economic and Social Research Institute for The Henry J. Kaiser Family Foundation. Privatization of Public Hospitals 28 (1999) ("One aspect of public governance that proved particularly troublesome for hospitals that were trying to compete for patients was state open meeting requirements.").

10. Cal. S.B. 1350 (1997), codified at Cal. Health & Safety Code § 101860 *et seq.*

11. *Haw. Rev.* Stat §§ 323F-4 and-6.

12. Health and Hospitals Public Benefit Corporation Act of 1996, D.C. Act 11–389 § 204(e).

13. New York S.B. 593 (1997) §§ 3303.11.(A) and (B).

14. *Memphis Publishing Co. v Shelby County Health Care Corp.*, 799 S.W.2d 225 (Tenn. 1990).

15. Herbert, Bob. Hospitals in Crisis. The *New York Times.* April 15, 1999.

8

SHOULD THE LAW PREFER NONPROFITS?

M. Gregg Bloche

Overtly profit-seeking firms are powerful players in the American medical marketplace. Investor-owned hospital chains, which have been around since the late 1960s, were joined in the 1980s and 1990s by a new generation of for-profit health care financing vehicles, including publicly-traded HMOs and reorganized Blue Cross plans. The rise of this vibrant, for-profit health sector has become a subject of bitter debate. Some laud investor-owned hospitals and health plans for their efficiency, access to capital, and responsiveness to changing market conditions. Profit-seeking investors, supporters contend, push providers to better accommodate patient preferences and make health plans more adaptive to consumers' (and employers') cost control needs. Others condemn the for-profit sector for putting shareholders ahead of patients, disregarding community concerns, and abandoning the neediest.[1] High-profile scandals fed the critics' concerns in the 1990s. The nation's largest for-profit hospital chain, Columbia/HCA, faced criminal charges arising from its billing of Medicare for promotional and other activities not reimbursable under federal rules.[2] The second largest chain, Tenet Healthcare, agreed in 1997 to pay $100 million to former patients who charged that the company illegally interned them against their will in psychiatric hospitals to obtain their insurance benefits.[3] Conversions of Blue Cross plans to for-profit status were tainted by revelations of large, "golden parachute" financial rewards for senior plan executives.

These and other accounts of troublesome conduct tied to investor ownership in the health sphere have inspired calls for government action to limit the for-profit sector's role. These calls have been largely reactive to specific reports of billing fraud, kickbacks, and insider enrichment. They have spurred intense debate focused on the comparative virtues and shortcomings of investor-owned and nonprofit enterprise in medicine. This debate typically conflates assessment of these virtues and shortcomings with the separate question of whether government should act to favor the nonprofit (or for-profit) sector. Systematic conceptions of government's role in shaping the mix of for-profit and nonprofit firms in the health sphere have been largely absent from the debate.

I argue in this chapter that the question of whether government should act to protect the nonprofit health sector from encroachment by for-profits cannot be answered merely by reference to the relative virtues of the for-profit and nonprofit forms. Nor can this question be answered generally, for all potential government interventions on behalf of nonprofits. Rather, the question calls for deeper, case-by-case inquiry, into whether particular state or federal preferences for the nonprofit form yield social benefits that justify their costs.

This inquiry entails more than an evaluation of whether, from a social welfare perspective, the nonprofit form is preferable to investor ownership in the health sector. It demands, in addition: (*1*) determination of whether the government intervention at issue would yield social benefits *beyond* those to be expected *absent* intervention; (*2*) assessment of whether these *additional* benefits outweigh the intervention's social cost; and (*3*) determination of whether alternative government actions (not focused on the for-profit/nonprofit distinction) might yield the same benefits at lower social cost. Public policy makers, I argue below, should assess the *costs* of government intervention pragmatically, with an eye not only toward federal and state budgets, but also toward the wider social impact of government action. As political actors, policy makers must also weigh the political costs of proposed government interventions. Within the health sphere, interest group clout and scarce legislative and regulatory agenda space often render these costs substantial. A policy initiative that is desirable, in the abstract, from a social welfare perspective may nonetheless represent an imprudent use of scarce political resources when compared to alternative legislative or regulatory measures.

This chapter concludes with the judgment that the case has not been made for a general policy of government protection for the nonprofit health sector. The putative social advantages of nonprofit over for-profit organization are too uncertain, the *additional* social benefits (if any) that such protection might yield are speculative, and the social costs are likely to be substantial. Alternative, more narrowly-tailored government actions—for example, subsidies, regulatory requirements, and direct provision of particular services—are likely in general to achieve the desired social objectives at lower cost.

Background: the legal implications of for-profit and nonprofit status

The core legal distinction between the for-profit and nonprofit forms is that only the former can distribute earnings—that is, revenues that exceed expenses—to individuals.[4] Nonprofits must retain or eventually spend their earnings.[5] For-profits can pass portions of their earnings on to persons who invest equity capital in exchange for the prospect of financial reward. From this basic difference, myriad legal and organizational consequences flow. Differences in tax status have received the most attention: nonprofits are eligible for federal and state income tax exemption, as well as state and local property tax exemption. The major financial benefit of income tax exemption is the ability to pay tax-free interest on borrowed funds. The shielding of nonprofits' earnings from federal and state income tax is of lesser financial significance.[6] These tax advantages compensate to some degree for the nonprofit firm's singular financial handicap—its inability to raise capital by selling an ownership interest to investors.[7]

This handicap renders nonprofits less able than for-profits to respond quickly to new market opportunities. Freedom from the demands of equity investors,[8] however, may offer non-profit administrators a measure of managerial flexibility, and their freedom from financial disclosure laws that apply to publicly-traded companies may sometimes yield competitive advantages. In addition, nonprofit and for-profit firms in the health sphere are treated differently in some states by licensing bodies and insurance regulators. Moreover, terms of participation in government-sponsored health insurance and biomedical research programs often favor or even require nonprofit status.

Of growing importance in recent years has been the supervisory authority of state attorneys general over the disposition of assets by public charities, including nonprofit health care providers and insurers seeking to convert to for-profit status. Prior to the 1990s, state attorneys general paid scant attention to this regulatory role.[9] But allegations of insider self-dealing and undervaluation of charitable assets during the course of ownership change have inspired more aggressive action by attorneys general in recent years. In response to proposed acquisitions, conversions, and joint ventures involving nonprofit health plans and hospitals, attorneys general in California, Michigan, New Jersey, Ohio, and other states went to court to question purchase prices and insider emoluments, demand the transfer of assets to charitable foundations, and thwart some transactions entirely.[10] State insurance commissioners, licensing bodies, and other regulatory authorities have also opposed acquisitions, conversions, and joint ventures. Legislatures in a number of states have passed laws to facilitate such challenges.

Like frictionless surfaces and perfect markets, pure government neutrality in regards to nonprofit and for-profit forms is not possible. Health care institutions, like all economic actors, operate in complex legal and regulatory environments that reinforce some behaviors—overtly, subtly, or imperceptibly—and discourage others. To the extent that nonprofits and for-profits are differently affected by these environments, government's role is not neutral. Such differences are inevitable since myriad disparities in the rights, duties, risks, and rewards of stakeholders arise from the legal distinction between investor ownership and the nonprofit form. Inexorably, these disparities translate into differential legal and regulatory effects on institutional behavior. Moreover, because the interacting effects of tax policy, corporate and contract law, and other regulatory regimes upon for-profit and nonprofit firms in the health sector are exceedingly difficult to trace, programs of government support for nonprofit (or for-profit) institutions cannot be finely tuned.

Protection for nonprofits: tallying benefits and burdens

No comprehensive theory of the roles of nonprofit and investor-owned enterprise, or of government's place in shaping these roles, has guided public policy on the for-profit/nonprofit question in the medical realm. Recent regulatory responses to proposed conversions and joint ventures have been heavily shaped by the balance of power between proponents and critics of particular transactions—and by public fears inspired by strident rhetoric on both sides. Debate over whether public policy should favor nonprofits (or for-profits) in the health sphere has centered on the comparative performance of nonprofit and investor-owned institutions from the perspective of community need. Adherents to the view that nonprofits do better than for-profits at serving community needs tend to conclude on this basis that government should act to discourage hospital and health plan conversions and joint ventures or to otherwise protect the nonprofit realm against for-profit encroachment. Proponents of the belief that investor ownership is no less effective than the nonprofit form at addressing community needs typically urge that state and federal policy eschew creating obstacles to the for-profit health sector's expansion.

This almost exclusive focus on the comparative advantages and drawbacks of nonprofits and for-profits in the medical realm misconceives the question of what, if anything, federal and state *government* should do on behalf of nonprofits. From a public policy perspective, the question to be asked regarding any proposed state or federal intervention is whether *the intervention* would yield social benefits great enough to justify its costs. This question calls for assessment of whether: (*1*) the intervention would generate social benefits *beyond* those to be expected from nonprofits *absent* intervention; (*2*) these *additional* social benefits outweigh the intervention's social cost; and (*3*) alternative public measures (not aimed at protecting nonprofits) would yield the same or greater benefits at lower social cost. The comparative performance of for-profits and nonprofits bears on this assessment only to the extent that the intervention might change the for-profit/nonprofit market mix or affect for-profit or nonprofit responsiveness to community needs.

Assessing the benefits of protection

Evaluation of the social benefits of any state or federal intervention to protect nonprofits presents multiple difficulties. It calls both for resolution of the question of to what extent, if at all, the nonprofits at issue outperform for-profits at meeting social needs, and for prediction of the intervention's impact on nonprofit and for-profit performance. Such an impact might result either from change in the for-profit/nonprofit market mix or change in for-profit or nonprofit firms' responsiveness to social needs.

The Controversy over Comparative Performance

The controversy over the comparative social benefits of investor-owned and non-profit organizations in medicine has been catalogued elsewhere, most thoroughly by Bradford Gray[11] and Jack Needleman,[12] and I will not rehash the arguments here. It suffices for my purposes to observe, as does Gray, that the question of whether for-profits or nonprofits are socially preferable can be plausibly argued either way, and that answers depend on differing conceptions of social benefit. There are many hard political and moral questions—lacking simple, right-or-wrong answers—about what ought to count as social benefits and how such benefits should be measured.

As Gray (a proponent of government preferences for nonprofits) acknowledges, conceptions of social or public benefit that focus on free care for the poor yield no clear preference for either for-profits or nonprofits. Variations between hospitals in the amounts of uncompensated care they provide as a proportion of revenues correlate closely with such factors as location[13] (e.g. blighted inner city neighborhoods versus prosperous suburbs) and academic ties—and poorly with for-profit and nonprofit status.[14] Comparisons of uncompensated care levels at hospitals before and after their conversion from nonprofit to for-profit status (or visa versa) have generally found no significant post-conversion changes.[15] In the health insurance industry, there is no variation between for-profits and nonprofits in this regard. Neither investor-owned nor nonprofit HMOs or other private insurance plans provide significant free coverage to the poor.

Comparative studies of health care quality yield no clear preference for either for-profit or nonprofit form. Recent reviews of clinical outcomes, including mortality, have not found substantial differences between investor-owned and non-profit hospitals.[16] Some studies have found differences in indices of quality between nonprofit academic medical centers and for-profit hospitals as a whole, but not between for-profit facilities and similarly situated community (i.e. non-teaching) nonprofits.[17] Comparative data on quality-of-care provided through investor-owned versus nonprofit health plans are scant. A recent study by several high-profile critics of investor ownership reported that nonprofit HMOs performed better than their for-profit counterparts on a variety of standardized quality measures.[18]

But as Needleman and others note, these performance gaps may not result from differences in ownership.[19] Other possible causes include geographical differences in health care quality[20] and disparities in the baseline health status of subscriber populations.

Changes in the organization of the health care industry since the mid-1990s have rendered causal links between health-plan ownership form and clinical quality less likely. Rather than moving toward greater integration of medical-care financing and delivery—and toward tighter managerial control of health care provision—health plans eschewed such arrangements in favor of devolution of managerial authority and financial risk to clinical providers.[21] Conventional wisdom in the early 1990s anticipated a future of competing health systems, each with its own doctors, hospitals, and other facilities. But the picture that emerged instead is one of so-called managed health plans that do little by way of management of care. Hospitals and group medical practices typically contract with multiple health plans, both investor-owned and nonprofit. The plans delegate clinical management authority to risk-bearing providers, who play the lead role as regards both cost-control and quality of care. Thus the connection between plan ownership form and clinical decisions bearing on quality is attenuated at best and may well be insignificant.

Conceptions of social benefit that incorporate a wider range of activities and concerns—for example, research and education, disease prevention, and other health promotion efforts—invite the inference that nonprofits behave in a more socially-responsive manner than for-profits. As Gray notes, nonprofit hospitals as a class devote more of their resources to research, education, and health-promoting outreach programs.[22] Supporters of government preferences for the nonprofit form in health care financing and delivery urge a broad approach to the question of social benefit,[23] arguing that focus on care for the poor fails to take full account of the nonprofit sector's advantages.

Yet whether the differences that Gray cites reflect anything intrinsic to the nonprofit and for-profit *forms*, as opposed to the histories and cultures of institutions organized as nonprofits and for-profits, is hardly clear. Nonprofit hospitals are quite heterogeneous in their production of these social benefits. A small number of elite teaching hospitals staffed by medical school faculty perform the vast majority of clinical research. The more typical nonprofit hospital, a community facility staffed by local practitioners, conducts little or no research. Likewise, although nonprofit hospitals provide disproportionately more medical training than do for-profits *as a group,* this training is concentrated in university-affiliated teaching hospitals. Almost without exception, America's major private teaching hospitals were founded along nonprofit lines, and presumably, their founders saw advantages in this choice. At many academic medical centers today, cultural commitment to the nonprofit form is strong. But this hardly constitutes proof that the nonprofit form today *induces* production of medical education or research, particularly in view of the near-absence of these activities at most nonprofit hospitals.[24] To the contrary, the interest of teaching hospital trustees and managers in for-profit options may reflect a shift in the balance of advantage, for academic medicine, from nonprofit status to investor-involvement.

A classic argument for the desirability of nonprofits, occasionally invoked by critics of investor-ownership in health care, builds on Burton Weisbrod's model of private charity as a response to the market's failure to produce a socially optimal supply of *public goods*—products and services possessing positive externalities, from which *free riders* cannot be excluded.[25] The nonprofit form's desirability, this argument holds, arises from nonprofit firms' access to government subsidies. Public subsidies for nonprofits, Weisbrod contends, leverage charitable-giving, compensating for the free rider problem's dampening effect upon donors' willingness to contribute. Weisbrod posits (*1*) that demand for many *public goods* varies among people (due to heterogeneous preferences and ability to pay); and (*2*) that persons with unusually high demand for particular public goods seek to satisfy this demand through charitable giving to private entities. The free rider problems that keep the market from producing enough of these goods also discourage charitable giving by these high-demanders, he argues. Public subsidies for nonprofits, he suggests, counterbalance this undesirable effect.

This line of argument is unpersuasive when applied to the American health care system.[26] To be sure, medical care and research are to some degree public goods in the economic sense. We derive psychic satisfaction without paying for it, i.e. we ride free, when sick people receive needed care, and to the extent that the sick put others at risk (i.e. through contagious disease or reduced productivity) medical care yields more tangible free ridership benefits. We also benefit from free access to results from research paid for by others.[27] But nonprofit health care providers and insurers are, as a rule, not charities, dependent on donors: almost all of their revenues flow from the sale of services to consumers.[28] Philanthropic support for private insurance coverage offered by nonprofit plans is virtually nil. Because these institutions benefit only minimally from charitable donations, Weisbrod's economic account of charitable giving does not apply in the medical realm, and his case for public subsidies to leverage private giving is inapposite to nonprofit hospitals and insurers.

An alternative account of the nonprofit form's social benefits in the health sphere emphasizes consumer ignorance about the quality of medical care and the consequent potential for exploitation by health care providers and insurers. This account, akin to Kenneth Arrow's classic explanation of physicians' fiduciary ethic as a market response to patients' medical ignorance,[29] concedes that nonprofit providers and insurers are commercial enterprises—that they serve mostly paying customers and receive minimal support from charitable sources. A distinctive benefit of the nonprofit form in the *commercial* realm, some propose, is its *efficiency* advantage over investor-ownership when purchasers of goods or services are unable to effectively monitor their quality.[30] When buyers are ill-informed about a firm's output, this thesis holds, for-profits are driven by their income-seeking imperative to exploit this ignorance, either by overcharging or by making unnoticed reductions in quality. Nonprofits are less inclined toward such exploitation because the absence of investors with claims on their income reduces their propensity to seek revenues that exceed expenses. When buyers are well-informed about a firm's output, and thus able to discriminate based on quality and price, income-seeking engenders production efficiencies that make for-profit organization preferable. But when purchasers lack enough information to impose market discipline on producers, welfare losses from producer-exploitation and consumer distrust can outweigh productivity gains inspired by income-seeking.

Whatever the merits of this model as a case for the nonprofit form's efficiency advantages in some economic spheres, at best it questionably characterizes today's medical marketplace. The problem of patient ignorance, which suggests an efficiency advantage for the nonprofit form in medicine, is tempered by the role of physicians as patients' purchasing agents.[31] To be sure, there is reason to doubt the efficacy of physicians in this regard. The medical profession lacks empirical data about the effectiveness of most clinical interventions, and individual physicians are subject to the managerial influences of hospitals, group practices, and HMOs. Absent a medical profession able to act in a fiduciary manner on patients' behalf, the nonprofit form's lesser propensity toward income-seeking (and thus toward exploitation of consumer ignorance) might well translate into an efficiency advantage over investor-ownership. But valuation of this putative advantage is speculative. The efficacy of most clinical interventions is uncertain, and individuals' experiences of illness and treatment are subjective and variable. Feelings of trust (or suspicion) engendered by organizational form are difficult to trace and tally.[32] The comparative costs of exploitative behavior by for-profits and nonprofits are thus not, as a practical matter, subject to assessment.

In short, the superiority of nonprofit over for-profit status in the health sector from a social welfare perspective is, at best, possible but unproven. Uncertainty and controversy abound, both about what should *count* as a social benefit and how the benefits counted should be valued. No decisive resolution of this uncertainty looms on our political horizon.

The Social Benefits of Protection

Absent such a resolution, the social benefits of government protection for the nonprofit form in the medical sphere are at least equally uncertain. Subsidies and tax and regulatory preferences that increase nonprofit sector activity levels yield social benefits only if nonprofit status per se is superior from a social welfare perspective *and* such policies raise these activity-levels from socially-suboptimal starting points to socially-preferable endpoints.[33] Not only is the superiority of the nonprofit form from a social welfare perspective a doubtful proposition; it is hardly clear that the level of medical services provided in the United States (by nonprofits or by the health economy as a whole) is socially suboptimal. To the contrary, third party payment (and consumers' consequent insulation from actual costs) has pushed demand to much higher levels than would be expected in a market populated by self-paying consumers. America's largely nonprofit hospital industry has proven itself more than able to meet this demand,[34] and a consensus of observers holds that hospitals, nonprofit and for-profit in the United States, are overbuilt, overbedded, and too technology-intensive.[35]

To be sure, inner city and other facilities that treat large proportions of uninsured patients tend to be less well-endowed than their counterparts in more prosperous locales. Overcrowding and substandard care in such hospitals suggest that pockets of socially suboptimal health care provision persist within the larger context of oversupply and overspending. But subsidies and other supports for nonprofits per se do not distinguish between such pockets and this larger context of overabundance. To the contrary, federal and state income tax exemption, perhaps the biggest financial advantage enjoyed by nonprofits, most generously rewards the *least* needy institutions.[36] If, as seems likely, nonprofit hospitals and other health care institutions are providing health care at *above*-optimal *overall* levels, from a social welfare perspective, then public subsidies and other supports that further increase these institutions' activity levels will produce social waste.[37]

Finally, we know little about the causal links between nonprofits' activity levels and the subsidies, tax preferences, and regulatory advantages available to them. Nonprofit production levels and the for-profit/nonprofit market mix may well be influenced more by institutional histories and cultures—and by shifting financial market conditions that shape the relative attractiveness of equity and debt financing[38]—than by public subsidies and tax and regulatory advantages. The idiosyncracies of institutional history and culture and the unpredictability of financial markets make it deeply problematic to predict the impact of proposed preferences on nonprofit activity levels or the for-profit/nonprofit market mix.

In short, determination of whether any government intervention on behalf of nonprofits in the medical realm will yield social benefits beyond those to be expected from these nonprofits absent intervention is fraught with multiple, large uncertainties, both as to what *should* count as a benefit and as to whether the benefits deemed worth counting will accrue.

Assessing the costs of protection

The costs of government protection for nonprofits include: (*1*) direct public spending to implement the protection at issue, (*2*) adverse effects on private interests, and (3) opportunity costs in the form of social benefits or savings, achievable through policy or program alternatives foregone in favor of protection for nonprofits.

Costs To Taxpayers and Affected Private Interests

Direct expenses to taxpayers are the least difficult to assess. Macroeconomic models can estimate the costs of subsidies and tax preferences, and budget analysts can project the costs of administering regulatory programs. Yet even these predictions are subject to large uncertainties—about future macroeconomic performance[39] and medical spending, eligibility for subsidies, and levels of regulatory compliance attainable for given expenditures on enforcement.

Adverse effects on private interests are more problematic to evaluate, especially in view of the bewilderingly complex web of economic relationships that characterizes the health sphere. Consideration of the adverse impacts of particular subsidies and tax and regulatory preferences is beyond my scope here, but I will highlight some examples of the kinds of questions that should be asked and the difficulties that inhere in seeking answers. To begin with, negative effects on the for-profit sector should be explored since the welfare of its investors and employees and their communities[40] surely matters from a social perspective. Beyond this, the possibility of adverse effects on consumers from policies that disfavor for-profits ought to be taken seriously. Are there things desirable from a consumer perspective that for-profits do better than nonprofits—for example, raising capital[41] and responding to consumer preferences[42] as to treatment options, choice among providers, hospital and health plan amenities, and health promotion programs? If so, then to what degree do these advantages offset arguable benefits of the nonprofit form?

Transition problems also require attention. How should the costs of change be figured when a new subsidy or tax or regulatory preference (or stoppage of an existing subsidy or other preference) disrupts existing webs of economic and social reliance? Some measures on behalf of nonprofits are likely to cause considerable disruption, while others are likely to result in almost none. For example, changes in Medicare reimbursement formulae that disfavor investor-owned hospitals could lead to staff reductions, facility closings, and painful ripple effects on communities that look to local for-profit hospitals as employers, purchasers, and sources of tax revenue. By contrast, barriers to hospital and health-plan conversions do not disturb preexisting patterns of reliance since they leave prior organizational arrangements intact. How should such transition costs be incorporated into the overall calculus of costs and benefits, and what should our time-horizon be when we undertake this calculus? These challenging questions, which commentators on the for-profit/nonprofit controversy too infrequently ask, lack well-defined answers.

Opportunity Costs

The problem of foregone policy and program alternatives has received even less attention. Proponents of government preferences for nonprofits typically advocate such preferences as rational responses to one or another social concern—for example, health promotion, poor people's access to care, or trustworthiness of medical care providers. Almost absent from such advocacy are efforts to compare protections for nonprofits to alternative remedies for the same concerns. To the extent that governments substitute such protective measures for other policies aimed at these concerns, *additional* social benefits and/or savings that would have resulted from these other policies represent opportunity costs.[43]

For example, assume that making hospital care available to the uninsured is a valued social objective *and* that, all else being equal, nonprofit hospitals are more inclined than for-profits to provide free and below-cost care to the needy. Government support for nonprofits per se might then be attractive as a tool for extending hospital services to the uninsured, and public debate could usefully engage the question of whether the increased access *purchased* through such support justified its cost. This debate, however, would be incomplete without consideration of whether other policy initiatives might more cost-effectively expand uninsured people's access to hospital care. Would government payments to private hospitals for indigent care, increased funding for public hospitals, vouchers for the purchase of private insurance by poor people, and/or regulation of insurance markets to suppress risk-selection by health plans achieve more "bang for the buck" than would subsidizing nonprofits per se?[44]

Alternatively, consider clinical trustworthiness as a social concern and *assume* that the nonprofit form, all else equal, is more likely to nurture it. Would it be more cost-effective for government to promote trustworthiness by favoring nonprofits per se or by limiting or proscribing particular trust-eroding practices—for instance, financial incentives for physicians to withhold care, *gag rules*, and plan *deselection* of physicians without showings of cause? The latter approach seems more precisely tailored to the problem of untrustworthiness, a problem to which nonprofit hospitals and health plans are hardly immune.

Analysis along these lines is difficult. Indeed, it is impossible when desired outcomes—and unwanted consequences—are ill-defined. The nonprofit form may well outperform investor ownership with respect to some socially desirable ends, and some government supports for the nonprofit sector may thereby yield social benefits that outweigh their costs to taxpayers and other adversely-affected interests. But, even assuming this, the prudence of such policies does not follow automatically. Other government measures, more precisely tailored to the desired ends, may more cost-effectively employ limited social resources. To the extent that preferences for nonprofits *substitute* for such measures, these preferences entail opportunity costs that may render them unwise. More precisely tailored measures may be superior for at least two of American medicine's major challenges today—providing care to the poor and preserving trustworthiness at the bedside. As for other health policy objectives—from disease prevention to cost-containment—the case for choosing government preference for nonprofits over other social measures has not been made.

Balancing benefits and costs: the case for forbearance

Generalization about the desirability of subsidies and other preferences that might be implemented by federal and state authorities to aid nonprofits is problematic.[45] Yet the large uncertainties that surround assessment of government protection for nonprofits render the case for such programs equivocal at best. To be sure, these uncertainties cut both ways: neither has it been shown that government should *not* intervene to protect nonprofits. But if, in a market economy, proponents of protectionist intervention should shoulder the burden of proof, then the uncertainties I have discussed favor forbearance.

A Risk-Averse Preference for Market-Mediated Change

To some extent, placing the burden of proof on proponents of public intervention is a matter of ideology. Preference for private ordering over public microeconomic management, softened by openness to government intervention when private ordering goes awry, is a common feature of the public philosophies that undergird western, market-oriented democracy.[46] But beyond this ideological commitment is a risk-averse preference for incremental over wholesale change. Markets bring about the former, through their ongoing field trials of institutional innovation. Legislatures, courts, and administrative agencies impose change more abruptly, typically without field-testing. As innovations spread through markets, their impact upon potentially-affected interests becomes gradually, albeit imperfectly, known.[47] By contrast, the cascading effects of government-imposed change are *empirically* unknowable (and, at best, a matter of informed speculation) until the change abruptly takes effect.[48] To the extent that we are risk-averse toward the problem of unanticipated effects, we have reason to favor market-mediated over government-imposed institutional change, all else being equal.

This argument for forbearance cuts against the investor-owned sector when well-established policies favor nonprofits. Tax preferences are a case in point. Considered in the abstract, as rationale for *proposed* policy, the case for exempting nonprofit hospitals per se from federal income taxation is weak for reasons discussed earlier.[49] But tax exemption of nonprofit hospitals is not a pending proposal; it is reigning policy with a 100-year history.[50] Abrupt elimination of the exemption's long-standing benefits would disrupt myriad stakeholders' settled expectations. Workers, clinical staff, patients, and members of surrounding communities depend upon hospitals as employers and purchasers as well as providers of medical care. The economic shock induced by sudden withdrawal of any subsidy would move outward along these webs of clinical and economic reliance. The unpredictability of this shock's scope and severity makes it difficult to say that ending the federal tax preference for nonprofit hospitals would yield public benefits (higher tax revenue) in excess of social costs. More generally, government action to force institutional change carries greater risk of unanticipated consequences than does evolutionary, market-mediated change, even when government acts to reduce its economic role, for example, by ending regulatory or other preferences for some stakeholders.[51] This argument for government forbearance when the case for action is equivocal applies equally to intervention favoring the nonprofit and for-profit sectors.

Public Policy Making and Private Influence

This argument for forbearance in the face of uncertainty would have weight even if we could count on public policy makers to seek to maximize the social benefits of medical institutions. But policy making is subject to distortions in this regard that cast further doubt on the wisdom of government intervention on behalf of nonprofits. Legislative and administrative processes are disproportionately influenced by well-organized, well-financed, politically-attentive interests. Nonprofits (and for-profits) can employ the postmodern tools of such influence—*astroturf* lobbying, artfully-targeted campaign giving, state-of-the-art polling, and communications strategies, and influential academic advocates, as well as traditional lobbying and lawyering.[52] Policy making processes open to such influence can hardly be expected to embody the deliberative, public-regarding ideals of disengaged, policy-oriented scholarship. Imbalances of power and information, neglect for the concerns of the poor, opportunistic behavior, and consequent disregard for positive and negative externalities afflict legislative and regulatory processes no less than market processes.[53] Nor are the courts immune to similar failings. Judges are vulnerable to the disproportionate influence of wealthy litigants and to the distortion that can result from the courtroom presence of parties to a dispute and the absence of others potentially affected by its outcome.[54]

Policy makers' assessments of the benefits and costs of public preferences for nonprofits are subject to the distorting influences just described. We can thus neither count on government to outperform the market at determining the relative social desirability of the nonprofit and for-profit forms in the health sector, nor treat policy makers' assessment of the costs and benefits of government action as unaffected by interest-group power. The comparative discovery capacities of government and market mechanisms concerning costs and benefits may vary for different behaviors and characteristics deemed socially desirable. For example, the trustworthiness of investor-owned and nonprofit health plans or hospitals may be best assessed via the market since trust is a matter of individual experience and impression.[55] On the other hand, clarification of what should count as a public benefit for purposes of comparing the desirability of for-profits and nonprofits might best be done through government processes, provided they are open to public involvement.[56] The point is not that government is less able than markets to *get it right*[57]—both are imperfect mechanisms—but rather that consideration of the desirability of government intervention should take into account that public policy making is not a disinterested, entirely public-regarding enterprise, able to effect, without distortion, measures that might be desirable in theory. This further supports the case for putting the burden of proof on proponents of protectionist public intervention—and for forbearance when arguments for government action are equivocal at best.

Protection for nonprofits as recognition for moral virtue

Some advocates of government protection for nonprofits eschew the balancing of social costs and benefits in favor of the claim that nonprofits possess distinctive moral virtues deserving of public recognition. This argument does not assert that the benefits of tax or other preferences outweigh the accompanying costs; rather, it portrays these preferences as symbolic reward for the nonprofit form's virtue. To proponents of this view, the social utility of these preferences is beside the point.

Whatever the moral virtues of nonprofit medical institutions, the proposition that tax subsidies or other pecuniary benefits aptly honor such virtue invites skepticism. Indeed, financial rewards may undermine appreciation of virtue through the suggestion that the things rewarded are being purchased for a price.[58] This concern inspired some early twentieth century leaders of charitable organizations to oppose tax exemption as a threat to private benevolence and a source of *mercenary motives.*[59]

Beyond this, the nonprofit health sector's claims to distinctive moral virtue, worthy of reward at taxpayers' expense, are weak. As articulated by nonprofit-sector advocates, the distinctive virtues associated with nonprofit medical care fit into four categories—community solidarity, regard for religious and social diversity, respect for personal freedom, and moral elevation of the healing role. Solidarity is said to flow from the pooled contributions of community members, from trustees and donors to candy stripers, and from provision of *charity* care and community services.[60] Regard for diversity is said to derive from the disparate religious, fraternal, and ethnic origins of nonprofit medical institutions, and respect for freedom is tied to the nonprofit sector's capacity for voluntary as opposed to state-mandated response to problems of health care access and cost. Moral elevation of the healing role is said to arise more generally from the three kinds of virtue just mentioned.

The potential import of community solidarity as a basis for public preferences for nonprofits is underscored by research documenting broad declines in Americans' civic engagement and social-connectedness since the mid-twentieth century.[61] Drop-offs in charitable giving and community volunteering are part of this larger story of civic decline.[62] To the extent that reversing this decline is desirable, either as an end in itself or as a means for pursuing other social goals,[63] public policies that build civic engagement and connectedness are desirable. But it is doubtful that government preferences for nonprofits in the health sphere can contribute substantially to civic engagement and connectedness. Nonprofit hospitals and health plans today offer only minimal possibilities for voluntary engagement and connectedness beyond their for-profit counterparts. Donations of time and money constitute a tiny fraction of the operating expenses for most nonprofit facilities. Nonprofit hospitals depend almost entirely upon paying customers to cover costs.[64] The free care they provide is financed largely by revenues from private insurers (and, ultimately, their subscribers) who pay prices that reflect the balance of market power, not the charitable intent of health plan managers or members. This involuntary levy on plan subscribers is regressive in its distribution across personal income brackets.[65] The financing of *charity* care through involuntary and regressive wealth transfers squares poorly with the ideal of social solidarity through private voluntarism. Likewise, nonprofit health plans take only paying customers and do not derive significant operating support from donors or volunteers.

The claim to virtue arising from regard for religious and social diversity is also problematic. During the eighteenth, nineteenth, and early twentieth centuries, myriad religious, ethnic, and racial groups created nonprofit hospitals and clinics responsive to their sick members' particular spiritual and cultural needs. In more recent years, however, medical facilities with disparate religious and social origins have offered converging patient-care experiences. The technology-intensive experience of contemporary hospital treatment does not differ greatly according to a facility's spiritual or social origins, and nominally sectarian nonprofits attract ethnically and religiously heterogeneous patient populations. Geography, academic affiliation, and selective contracting between health plans and providers have become more important than sectarian ties as factors in the sorting of patients among hospitals. Sectarian nonprofits employ personnel from diverse backgrounds and provide their patients with access to clergy of many faiths. Thus the practical import of nonprofits' disparate sectarian origins is much-attenuated. Regard for diversity is a function of each health care institution's hiring practices and sensitivity to patients' varying spiritual and social backgrounds. Nonprofits have no clear advantage in this respect.

The claim to distinctive virtue deriving from respect for freedom is no more persuasive. Insofar as this claim rests upon a preference for private, over government response to problems of health care access and cost, it could equally apply to investor-owned firms. Insofar as it rests on the virtues of voluntary giving, contrasted with state coercion, it is belied by coerced extraction of health-plan-subscriber wealth to pay for charity care. Moreover, the virtue of voluntarism in the health sphere is itself open to question. Provision of medical care as a matter of *charity* fits awkwardly with the proposition that health care is a matter of *right*. To the extent that we accept this proposition, reliance on charitable giving is an insufficient response to problems of health care access. The recipients of charity depend on donors' discretion; indeed the mutual psychology of discretion, dependence and gratitude is at the core of some conceptions of charity's virtue.[66] Thus, not only does charitable provision fail to insure access to care; it nurtures the sense that beneficiaries are less than entitled to the care they receive.[67]

The weakness of these claims to distinctive virtue infects the fourth, more general claim—that nonprofit status is linked to moral elevation of the healing role. The moral standing of medical-care providers matters both in itself and as a means. Caregivers, it is argued, should have high-moral standing because those to whom we reveal our intimate selves should *deserve* our trust; such standing, moreover, makes medical care more effective by nurturing bedside trust.[68] To the degree that the above claims to virtue are credible, nonprofit status conveys moral stature. Moral stature, in turn, inspires trust by signaling patients that caregivers are disinclined to exploit ignorance and powerlessness.[69]

Thus the weakness of the three just-discussed claims to virtue undermines nonprofit providers' more general claim to elevated moral standing, as a matter of both reality and appearance. Well-documented similarities in the ways that nonprofit and for-profit hospitals pay and manage staff and build relationships with physicians cast further doubt on the notion that nonprofit status signals higher moral stature.[70] To be sure, some patients may associate nonprofit status with greater trustworthiness, tied to distinctive virtue. But to the extent that these impressions of distinctive virtue are at odds with economic and organizational reality, they do not reflect moral elevation of the healing role.

In short, the nonprofit medical sector's claims to distinctive moral virtue deserving of preferential government treatment, fare poorly when subjected to more than passing scrutiny. Even if we take the reward-for-virtue argument on its own terms and treat the balance of social costs and benefits as beside the point, it is a weak basis for the general preference for nonprofits urged by proponents. This argument's disregard for the moral force of competing claims on the public fisc makes it even more problematic.

The political economy of protection for nonprofits

Were we to conclude, on cost-benefit balancing or other grounds, that government should as a rule favor the nonprofit form, the political economy of government action would give us reason for restraint. Policy makers committed to any conception of the public good must work with scarce political resources. These include agenda space, that rarest of political commodities at the legislative level, and the engagement of constituencies sufficiently powerful to counterbalance adversely affected stakeholders. Less tangibly, popular support for public responses to pressing social needs requires a measure of civic confidence in government's capacity to serve the common good. To the extent that the social benefits of state or federal action are not immediately and widely visible, and to the extent that such action draws acrimonious reaction, public confidence is put at risk, rendering government less able to respond to future needs.

Thus government cannot do all that might be wise from an Olympian, public-policy perspective. Well-meaning policy makers must exercise forbearance in fashioning initiatives, taking into account agenda constraints, the political interplay of interest groups and public engagement, and the need to sustain citizen confidence in government. The comparative social urgency of potential initiatives needs to be assessed within these constraints. Prudence requires that some worthy policy measures be foregone.

These considerations challenge advocates of government preferences for nonprofits to make the case for the priority of such preferences over other politically-costly health policy initiatives. This challenge is daunting. Public preferences for nonprofits are blunt policy instruments, poorly-matched to particular health-policy concerns. As suggested earlier, more precisely-tailored measures are often preferable—for instance, when clinical trustworthiness and poor peoples' access to care are at stake. The squandering of agenda space, activist energy, and other political resources on enactment or preservation of preferences for nonprofits leaves fewer resources available for pursuit of other, more focused measures.

Prudence thus counsels that the desirability of such preferences be assessed with a close eye to political opportunity costs. Might a campaign for restrictions on for-profit health care financing and delivery both divert public attention from the quest for coverage for the poor and complicate efforts to enlist investor-owned medical institutions as allies in this quest? Conversely, could opposition to continued tax exemption of nonprofit hospitals have a similar impact on policy-makers' ability to draw in nonprofits as allies in this quest? With respect to trustworthiness at the bedside, will emphasis on potential exploitation by for-profit hospitals and health plans divert public attention from the larger problem of conflict between the demands of cost-containment and Hippocratic loyalty to patients? This conflict today pervades American medicine: financial incentives and other pressures to limit clinical spending are central features of professional life at both nonprofits and for-profits. On the other hand, is opposition to *extension* of the charitable exemption from hospitals to nonprofit health plans prudent *today* as a way to abort a wasteful tax expenditure before expectations form and settle? When policy makers can anticipate both the prospect of wasteful spending and the emergence of potent constituencies advantaged by it, preemptive action today may yield large social benefits tomorrow.

The calculus of political opportunity cost can vary for policy makers at different levels of government, facing different political and legal constraints. State officials, for example, are limited in their ability to regulate private health plans by the federal statute that preempts state law *relating to* employer-sponsored coverage.[71] This disempowers states from acting to curb health-plan-risk selection practices—for example, strategic design of plan benefits—that increase the ranks of the uninsured. The federal government, by contrast, has sweeping authority to regulate such practices. Were it shown that nonprofit health plans are less inclined than for-profits to engage in such behavior, political focus on tax and regulatory preferences for nonprofits might make more sense for state officials (for whom comprehensive insurance market regulation is precluded by federal preemption, and for whom advocacy of federal regulation may be quixotic) than for federal policy makers.

Another problem of political economy merits brief mention. Use of a policy instrument as blunt as government support for the nonprofit form fosters lack of clarity about policy goals. This ill-definition may at times finesse conflict over policy aims. But by allowing contrary expectations to persist, it sets the stage for future disillusionment and political friction, and corrodes popular confidence in government's ability to act on behalf of public ends.

Conclusion

The overall thrust of this discussion is that forbearance is in order for policy makers contemplating opposition to the for-profit form in American medicine. The case for a general presumption *in favor* of government intervention on behalf of nonprofits has not been made. Absent a series of action-favoring answers to the questions of policy and political economy I have highlighted, government inaction regarding the for-profit/nonprofit distinction is the prudent course.

Such forbearance does not imply broader regulatory neglect. Robust policing of conversions, joint ventures, and other transactions involving the disposition of nonprofit assets is essential to suppress opportunistic behavior by insiders. Such transaction-related behaviors have included undervaluation of nonprofit assets, leading to windfalls for investors and reduced ability of successor nonprofit entities to serve charitable purposes,[72] and "golden parachute" compensation and employment arrangements for nonprofit executives and board members. Control of opportunism—and the resultant squandering of social resources—is necessary, not only to preserve the value of charitable assets,[73] but also to maintain the credibility of capital markets as means for refashioning health care financing and delivery.[74]

One might object that my call for forbearance constitutes a gamble against government intervention and in favor of deference to markets in the face of the many uncertainties noted above. To be sure, some risk is inevitable. But the availability of more precisely-tailored policy responses to the problems cited by critics of investor ownership greatly mitigates this risk. Moreover, Americans' preference for private ordering and their skepticism about government support a bias toward forbearance when the case for government action is, at best, equivocal.

A final concern deserves mention. Objections to investor ownership of medical institutions may in part reflect anxiety over the larger phenomenon of commodification of health and other social services. Medical care has become, more explicitly, a thing purchased at market price, managed through financial rewards and penalties, and even regulated via market-mimicking economic incentives. Although the commodification of medicine encompasses the entire American health economy, the rise of large, publicly-traded health care firms may be its most visible symbol. To the extent that this symbolism lies behind objections to investor-ownership, the arguments in this paper may be beside the point.

Some might dismiss this symbolic, expressive dimension as irrational, since the for-profit sector in health care is hardly the driving force behind the commercialization of medicine. Yet law often serves expressive purposes, symbolically affirming cherished values even as reality subverts them.[75] We should not dismiss such symbolism as irrational when it conveys deeply-felt moral sentiments—even if these sentiments are often disregarded in practice. The interplay between such symbolism and its contravention by our behavior reflects our ambivalence in the face of conflict between what we hold dear and what we find necessary. Our discomfort with the commodification of medicine, in concert with our attraction to the allocative efficacy of the medical marketplace, illustrates this ambivalence.

Understood in this light, objections to investor-ownership of health care institutions deserve to be taken quite seriously. From a pragmatic policy-making perspective, however, more central challenges confront us. These include the receding goal of universal access to care, cost-control, the need to reorient medicine toward health promotion while preserving the humanism that rescue-oriented care expresses, and restoration of trustworthiness at the bedside, as a way to improve medical outcomes and as a humane virtue in itself. Conflict over the role of for-profits and nonprofits in American medicine draws energy away from pursuit of these larger aims.

Acknowledgments

The author thanks Judith Feder, Lawrence Gostin, and Lynn Stout for their comments and suggestions, and Tomer Seifan and Erica Pape for their research assistance. Preparation of this chapter was supported in part by the Henry J. Kaiser Family Foundation and by a Robert Wood Johnson Foundation Investigator Award in Health Policy Research. This chapter is revised and expanded from an article published by *Health Affairs*, M. Gregg Bloche, Should Government Intervene to Protect Nonprofits?, 17(5) *Health Aff.* 7–25 (September/October 1998).

NOTES

1. Bruce. C. Vladeck, Market Realities Meet Balanced Government: Another Look at Columbia/HCA, *Health Aff.* 37–39 (March/April 1998).

2. Kurt Eichenwald, Columbia/HCA Discussions on Cost Shifting Were Secretly Taped by U.S. Informants, *The New York Times*, September 2, 1997, at D2. K. Eichenwald, U.S. Looks at Columbia/HCA Elderly Programs, *The New York Times*, August 22, 1997, at D1.

3. Kurt Eichenwald, $100 Million Settlement Seen in Tenet Suits, *The New York Times*, July 30, 1997, at D1.

4. Henry B. Hansmann, The Role of Nonprofit Enterprise, 89 *Yale L. J.* 835–901 (1980). In practice, the distinction between distribution of earnings and payment of legitimate expenses can become murky, as when nonprofit firms pay high salaries to senior executives or offer generous emoluments to staff physicians. In principle, legitimate expenses include employee salaries and benefits, payments to independent contractors, and debt interest and principle.

5. In formalistic legal terms, nonprofits' earnings, like their other assets, must be used or held in trust for charitable (broadly–defined) and/or community purposes, and must not inure to the benefit of private interests.

6. Much less important in financial terms is the deductibility of donations to qualifying nonprofits from donors' taxable incomes.

7. Henry B. Hansmann, The Rationale for Exempting Nonprofit Organizations from Corporate Income Taxation, 91 *Yale L. J.* 54–81 (1981).

8. By contrast, nonprofit managers must pay close attention to the expectations of current and potential *debt* investors—bondholders and other creditors—who can be relied upon to keep a close eye on firm financial performance, as an indicator of creditworthiness.

9. M. Gregg Bloche, Corporate Takeover of Teaching Hospitals, 65 *S. Cal. L. Rev.* 1035–1170 (1992). This regulatory authority, which empowers attorneys general to challenge the terms of conversions, sales, joint ventures, and other arrangements that enable investors to benefit from nonprofit assets, is grounded in the premise that these assets are public trusts, protected by the state on society's behalf.

10. Milt Freudenheim, New Jersey Blue Cross Takeover by For-Profit Insurer Is Canceled, *The New York Times*, June 11, 1997, at D1. Tamar Lewin with Martin Gottlieb, Health Care Dividend, *The New York Times*, April 27, 1997, at A1.

11. Bradford H. Gray, Conversion of HMOs and Hospitals: What's at Stake?, *Health Aff.* 29–47 (March/April 1997); and Bradford H. Gray, *The Profit Motive and Patient Care: The Changing Accountability of Doctors and Hospitals* (1991).

12. Jack Needleman, The Role of Nonprofits in Health Care, 26 *J. Health Polit. Policy Law* 1113 (2001).

13. Edward C. Norton and Douglas O. Staiger, How Hospital Ownership Affects Access to Care for the Uninsured, 25 *Rand J. Econ.* 171 (1994).

14. Ironically, the non-profits that benefit most from income tax exemption—those with the highest net incomes (as a percentage of revenues)—tend to provide the lowest levels of uncompensated care. General Accounting Office, *Nonprofit Hospitals: Better Standards Needed for Tax Exemption* (1990).

15. E.g. Jack Needleman, JoAnn Lamphere, & Deborah J. Chollet, Uncompensated Care & Hospital Conversions in Florida, 18(4) *Health Aff.* 125 (1999); Kamal R. Desai, Gary J. Young, & Carol Van Deusen Lukas, Hospital Conversions from For-Profit to Non-Profit Status: The Other Side of the Story, 55 *Med. Care Res. & Rev.* 298 (1998); Gary J. Young, Kamal R. Desai, & Carol Van Deusen Lukas, Does the Sale of Nonprofit Hospitals Threaten Health Care for the Poor? 16(1) *Health Aff.* 137 (1997). A more recent study, however, reported a drop-off in uncompensated care after conversion from non-profit to for-profit status. Kenneth E. Thorpe, Curtis S. Florence, & Eric E. Seiber, Hospital Con-

versions, Margins, and the Provision of Uncompensated Care, 19 (6) *Health Aff.*187 (2000).

16. E.g. Frank A. Sloan, Gabriel A. Picone, Donald H. Taylor, Jr. & Shin-Yi Chou, Hospital Ownership and Cost and Quality of Care: Is There a Dime's Worth of Difference? 20 *J. Health Econ.*1 (2001); Susan L. Ettner & Richard C. Hermann, The Role of Profit Status under Imperfect Information: Evidence from the Treatment Patterns of Elderly Medicare Beneficiaries Hospitalized for Psychiatric Diagnoses, 20 *J. Health Econ.* 23 (2001). An older study found higher mortality rates at for-profits than at non-profits. Arthur J. Hartz et. al., Hospital Characteristics & Mortality Rates, 321 *New Eng. J. Med.* 1720 (1989).

17. E.g. Zhong Yuan, Gregory S. Cooper, Douglas Einstadter, Randall D. Cebul, & Alfred A. Rimm, The Ass'n between Hospital Type and Mortality and Length of Stay: A Study of 16.9 Million Hospitalized Medicare Beneficiaries, 38 *Med. Care* 231 (2000); Mark McClellan & Douglas O. Staiger, Comparing Hospital Quality at For-Profit & Not-for-Profit Hospitals (1999) (unpublished paper on file at the National Bureau of Econ. Res., Cambridge, Mass.).

18. David U. Himmelstein, Steffie Woolhandler, Ida Hellander, & Sidney M. Wolfe, Quality of Care in Investor-Owned vs. Not-for-Profit HMOs, 282 *JAMA* 159 (1999). Another study found greater consumer satisfaction with quality for nonprofit health plans than for their investor-owned counterparts. Bruce E. Landon, et al., Health Plan Characteristics & Consumers' Assessments of Quality, 20(2) *Health Aff.* 274 (2001).

19. Needleman, supra note 12, at 1121.

20. To the extent that investor-owned health plans have a disproportionate presence in regions with lower quality of care, they can be expected to perform worse than nonprofits on quality indices for reasons unrelated to ownership form. In theory, though, the disproportionate presence of for-profit plans in some localities could *cause* regional differences in clinical quality. No reported studies address this possible causal relationship.

21. James C. Robinson, *The Corporate Practice of Medicine: Competition and Innovation in Health Care* (1999).

22. Gray, Conversion of HMOs and Hospitals, supra note 11.

23. The U.S. Treasury Department has long taken this approach in its defense of nonprofit hospitals' federal income tax exemption as a quid pro quo for activity with positive externalities. Department representatives cite biomedical research, clinical education, and community health promotion programs, as well as care for the poor. Tax-Exempt Status of Hospitals and Establishment of Charity Care Standards, Hearing before the House Comm. on Ways and Means, 102d Cong., 1st Sess. 34–37 (1991) (statement of Michael J. Graetz, Deputy Assistant Secretary for Tax Policy, U.S. Dep't of the Treasury).

24. Institutional arrangements and norms often begin as rational adaptations, conscious or otherwise, to economic circumstances, then sustain themselves through transmission from one generation to another as social habits, whether or not they remain rational as economic circumstances change. See Francis Fukuyama, *Trust: The Social Virtues & the Creation of Prosperity* 33–41 (1995).

25. Burton A. Weisbrod, *The Nonprofit Economy* (1988); Burton A. Weisbrod, *The Voluntary Nonprofit Sector: An Economic Analysis* (1977).

26. M. Gregg Bloche, Health Policy Below the Waterline: Medical Care and the Charitable Exemption, 80 *Minn. L. Rev.* 299–405 (1995).

27. Medical education's status as a public good is less certain. Potential trainees *can* be excluded, at the discretion of educational institutions, but the diffusion of medical knowledge through society may yield benefits on which people *ride free*.

28. In 1985, philanthropy covered less than 1.3% of the cost of care in American hospitals. Gerard F. Anderson et al., Providing Hospital Services: The Changing Financial Environment 47–48 (1989).

29. Kenneth Arrow, Uncertainty and the Welfare Economics of Medical Care, 53(5) *Am. Econ. Rev.* 941–73 (1963).

30. This line of argument invokes Henry Hansmann's more general thesis that nonprofits are more efficient than for-profits at both commercial and charitable activities when those who pay for the activities are not able to knowledgeably assess their quality. Hansmann, The Role of Nonprofit Enterprise, supra note 4.

31. Henry Hansmann, perhaps the leading proponent of this model, has argued that it probably does not apply to medical care for this reason. Id.

32. There have been few empirical studies of comparative patient confidence in for-profit and nonprofit health care institutions. Consumer surveys suggest that patients see nonprofit HMOs as more trustworthy (and less inclined to skimp on care) than for-profits. Gray, Conversion of HMOs and Hospitals, supra note 11. The recent explosive growth of investor-owned HMOs, relative to nonprofits, however, invites skepticism about the significance of this expressed preference for consumers' real-world health care spending decisions. Valuation of this putative preference based on consumers' market behavior is rendered exceedingly difficult in practice by confounding factors such as price and coverage differences, adverse selection, and consumer satisfaction with each health plan's choice of participating providers.

33. Henry Hansmann justifies federal income tax exemption for some nonprofits along these lines. As noted earlier, he holds that the nonprofit form is preferable when it reduces producer opportunism and consumer distrust to an extent that outweighs the productivity losses that ensue from absence of investors with equity interest. This potential advantage, he notes, comes at a cost: the inability of nonprofit firms to distribute profits to contributors of capital reduces these firms' ability to raise capital, and thus to grow. Hansmann models income tax exemption of nonprofits as market-correcting compensation for this handicap, appropriate as a way to push nonprofits' activity up from socially suboptimal levels. Henry B. Hansmann, The Rationale for Exempting Nonprofit Organizations from Corporate Income Taxation, supra note 7. The exemption, Hansmann argues, is thus economically justifiable when buyer ignorance (and the resulting potential for producer opportunism) renders nonprofit organization more efficient than investor ownership, *and* the exemption increases nonprofit activity to a socially preferable level. (For exemption to be appropriate in particular cases, its cost, in tax revenues foregone, must be less than the welfare gains it induces by stimulating nonprofit activity.) Other preferential treatment for nonprofits can be similarly defended.

34. Insurance-driven demand has drawn sufficient debt capital to make up for nonprofit hospitals' lack of access to equity capital.

35. Bloche, Health Policy Below the Waterline, supra note 26. The growing realization that health *status* is much more closely linked to education and economic opportunity than to medical spending raises new doubts about our spending on medicine, relative to investment in education, occupational training, and other activities that promote personal opportunity.

36. The largest financial benefit bestowed upon health care organizations by income tax exemption is the ability to issue tax exempt debt. The potential value of this benefit to an exempt firm is a function of the firm's financial standing as perceived by prospective lenders. Thus the organizations most in need—e.g. fiscally-troubled hospitals burdened by large numbers of indigent patients—are least able to reap this benefit. Conversely, those health care organizations best positioned to benefit are those already

producing at high, even *super*optimal levels. The case for per se income tax exemption of nonprofits as a means of *boosting* production of medical services to socially preferred levels is therefore weak, owing to both the *over*production of medical services in general and the poor match between each facility's needs, *from a social welfare perspective*, and the exemption's value to it.

37. Strictly speaking, waste might be avoided if nonprofit organization per se were superior to investor ownership from a social welfare perspective *and* the subsidy or other preference at issue *decreased* for-profit sector activity sufficiently to compensate for the increased nonprofit sector production.

38. In recent years, historically low interest rates have made nonprofit firms' ability to issue tax-exempt debt relatively less valuable, while the soaring stock market has made equity financing extraordinarily attractive. These circumstances have made investor ownership unusually attractive, in comparison with the nonprofit form, as a means of raising capital. Were we to revert to a combination of high interest rates and poor stock market performance, akin to the market circumstances prevailing during much of the 1970s, the ability to issue tax-exempt debt would become more important, and the attractiveness of the for-profit form, relative to nonprofit organization, would diminish. Decreasing marginal federal income tax rates since the Reagan Administration tax reforms have also rendered the ability to issue tax-exempt debt less valuable. Reversion to the 50% and higher federal tax rates of the 1970s and earlier would give the nonprofit form a considerable edge.

39. Interest rates (which affect the value of income tax exemption), real property values (which determine the revenue losses imposed by property tax exemption), inflation, and real economic growth are among the macroeconomic factors likely to influence the costs of tax breaks, subsidies, and other preferences for nonprofits.

40. Hospitals and health plans, both for-profit and nonprofit, tend to be major employers and buyers of goods and services within their communities; thus community prosperity is linked in myriad, unpredictable ways to public policies that affect these institutions' economic health.

41. Hansmann, The Rationale for Exempting Nonprofit Organizations from Corporate Income Taxation, supra note 7.

42. Weisbrod, The Nonprofit Economy, supra note 25.

43. Such opportunity costs would accrue to the extent that the policy alternatives foregone would constitute more cost-effective responses (than would the chosen supports for nonprofits) to these social concerns.

44. To the extent that equitable distribution of indigent care costs across society is desirable, looking to private hospitals (nonprofit or for-profit) to provide *charity* care to the needy is additionally troublesome, since this *free* care is financed largely through cross-subsidies from insured, revenue-producing patients. Because health insurance premiums constitute a diminishing portion of personal income as income rises, cross-subsidization from insureds is a regressive way to finance care for the poor, compared to use of public funds raised through a flat or progressive tax. Robert A. Carolina and M. Gregg Bloche, Paying for Undercompensated Hospital Care: The Regressive Profile of a "Hidden Tax," 2 *Health Matrix: J.L. Med.* (1992). Proponents of charity care as a means for expanding access rarely acknowledge this regressivity.

45. Not only will the uncertainties discussed earlier—about what *should* count as social costs and benefits, and about how these costs and benefits should be figured—play out differently for different interventions, the question of a proposed policy's desirability is open to varying answers depending on which existing policies are taken as givens and which are treated as changeable.

46. Bruce Ackerman, *Reconstructing American Law* (1984).
47. The problem of externalities (positive and negative consequences for interests other than the contracting parties) and the problem of transaction costs (costs of becoming informed and taking action on matters in which one is not contractually involved) are principal reason for such imperfection.
48. Federalism to some extent attenuates this disadvantage, by allowing trial of government interventions in one or a few states before decisions are made about whether to adopt them more widely. Congress occasionally accomplishes something similar by setting up small "demonstration" projects to test novel and controversial policy ideas.
49. I develop this argument in depth in Bloche, Health Policy Below the Waterline, supra note 26.
50. The federal charitable exemption today extended to nonprofit hospitals was conceived prior to the end of the 19th century, when hospitals primarily served the poor. Rosemary Stevens, In Sickness and in Wealth 17–30 (1989). Nonprofit hospitals' "promotion of health," the activity that qualified them as charities under the exemption, was thus a species of relief of the poor. Bloche, Health Policy Below the Waterline, supra note 26. The exemption's original Congressional drafters did not anticipate the 20th century transformation of the hospital into a locus for the treatment of paying patients and the consequent divergence of "promotion of health," performed by nonprofit hospitals, from relief of the poor. Unmoored from its 19th century origins, tax exemption of nonprofit hospitals nevertheless survived through the 20th century, as a creature of settled institutional expectations and reliance. Ibid. It evolved first into a near-automatic benefit conferred upon hospitals that provided even small amounts of charity care. *Rev. Rul.* 56–185, 1956 C.B. 203. By 1969, it had become a benefit conferred per se upon nonprofit hospitals. *Rev. Rul.* 69–545, 1969–2 C.B. 117.

   The Internal Revenue Service (and acquiescing appellate courts) did away with the charity care requirement without trying to discern how the exemption's original drafters might have handled the critical development they did not anticipate—the evolution of the hospital from a place for the sick poor into a center for the care of paying customers. The IRS merely asserted that the exemption's drafters had incorporated the common law of charitable trusts, which, in cases involving hospitals devoted to caring for the destitute, held that "promotion of health" was a charitable purpose. Ibid. This claim begged the question of whether the drafters, for whom hospital-based "promotion of health" was a species of relief for the poor, would have treated promotion of health for a fee as a charitable endeavor. The IRS offered no basis for inferring that the exemption's drafters would have made this leap, and the agency's illogic in this regard was compounded by inconsistency. Exemption of nonprofit hospitals that serve only paying patients fits poorly with the IRS's continuing requirement that other nonprofit health care providers render free or below-cost services to qualify for exemption. Example *Federation Pharmacy Servs. v. Commissioner*, 72 T.C. 687, 690 (1979), aff'd, 625 F.2d 804 (8th Cir. 1980) (rejecting nonprofit pharmaceutical firm's request for exemption).
51. Policy making that is risk-averse toward such consequences might therefore tolerate some preexisting government preferences (for either nonprofits or for-profits) even though the case for enacting these preferences de novo would be weak.
52. Haynes Johnson and David S. Broder, The System: The American Way of Politics at the Breaking Point (1996); Hedrick Smith, The Power Game: How Washington Works (1988). The role of state attorneys general in the controversy over regulation of nonprofit to for-profit hospital and health plan conversions illustrates this vulnerability. Under their broad, vaguely-defined authority to supervise public charities, attorneys general have enormous discretion to challenge or disapprove of such transactions. As

elected officials, often with aspirations for higher statewide office (and campaign–financing needs to match), they are correspondingly vulnerable to the influence of powerful, politically engaged stakeholders. The sum of these influences may favor either investor ownership or preservation of the nonprofit form in particular cases, but it is highly unlikely to be neutral in its impact.

53. D. Shaviro, Beyond Public Choice and Public Interest: A Study of the Legislative Process as Illustrated by Tax Legislation in the 1980s, 139 *U. Pa. L. Rev.* 64–106 (1990).

54. Frank H. Easterbrook, The Supreme Court, 1983 Term—Forward: the Court and the Economic System, 98 *Harv. L. Rev.* 4–60 (1984). In this sense, court proceedings are akin to contractual relationships in the marketplace; the parties's concerns tend to be taken into account to a greater extent than the interests of nonparties (externalities).

55. To be sure, the average health plan subscriber lacks the knowledge to make richly-informed judgments about the trustworthiness (and quality) of health plans and hospitals. But this is an information problem amenable to market-driven responses. The mass marketing of health plans and the emergence of the Internet present entrepreneurial opportunities for collectors and interpreters of information on the performance of competing plans and providers. Deborah Haas-Wilson, Arrow and the Information Market Failure in Health Care: The Changing Content and Sources of Health Care Information, 26 *J. Health Polit. Policy & Law* 1031 (2001). By contrast, legislators' and regulators' comparative judgments about the trustworthiness of investor-owned and nonprofit plans may be more subject to the influence of the plans themselves, through lobbying and other political activities.

56. Markets driven by the purchases of patients and plan subscribers are at high risk to disregard such public goods as community health promotion and medical research. To be sure, political mechanisms are vulnerable to the distorting effects of interest-group power, but they have the potential to take fuller account of externalities (including public goods), owing to (*1*) involvement of a wider range of actors (beyond health care buyers and sellers), and (2) the pull of political life toward public-regarding deliberation and behavior. Cass Sunstein, Administrative Substance, 1991 *Duke L. J.* 5–19.

57. Some commentators do suggest that the political potency of interest groups in the health sphere renders government inherently less able than the marketplace to rationally organize health care provision. Jonathan R. Macey, Health Care Reform: Perspectives from the Economic Theory of Regulation and the Economic Theory of Statutory Interpretation, *74 Cornell L. Rev.* 1434–58 (1994).

58. Margaret J. Radin, Market Inalienability, Harv. L. Rev. 1849–1937 (1987).

59. National Conference on Charities and Correction, The Division of the Work Between Public and Private Charities, in *Proceedings of the National Conference on Charities and Correction* (A. Johnson, ed., 1905).

60. J. David Seay and Bruce C. Vladeck, Mission Matters, in *In Sickness and in Health: The Mission of Voluntary Health Care Institutions*, Chap. 1 (J. David Seay and Bruce C. Vladeck eds., 1988).

61. See Robert D. Putnam, Bowling Alone: The Collapse & Revival of American Community 31–180 (2000) (exhaustively compiling empirical evidence of this decline in many spheres of civil, religious, and private life).

62. Id. at 116–33.

63. Proponents of revived civic engagement contend that it would spur economic development, strengthen democracy, yield health benefits, and improve education and child welfare. Id. at 287–349.

64. Anderson, supra note 28, at 47–48.

65. See discussion at note 44.

66. Richard Titmuss, *The Gift Relationship: From Human Blood to Social Policy*, Chap. 5 (1971).

67. To the extent that the case for a society-wide entitlement to medical care (or anything else) rests on the belief that access to it is an essential aspect of social membership, charitable provision of care devalues recipients by casting doubt on their social belonging. Michael Walzer, Spheres of Justice, Chap 2 (1983).

68. David Mechanic, Public Trust and Initiatives for New Health Care Partnerships, 76(2) *Milbank Q.* 281–99 (1988).

69. Daniel Wikler, The Virtuous Hospital: Do Nonprofit Institutions Have a Distinctive Moral Mission, in, In *Sickness and in Health: The Mission of Voluntary Health Care Institutions*, Chap. 5 (J. David Seay and Bruce C. Vladeck eds., 1988).

70. Bloche, Health Policy Below the Waterline, supra note 26.

71. Employee Retirement Income Security Act of 1974, § 514(a), as amended in 29 U.S.C.A § 1144(a); *New York State Conf. of Blue Cross and Blue Shield Plans v. Travelers Insurance Co.*, 514 U.S. 645 (1995).

72. Linda B. Miller, The Conversion Game: High Stakes, Few Rules, *Health Aff.* 112–17 (March/April 1997).

73. Nancy M. Kane, Some Guidelines for Managing Charitable Assets from Conversions, *Health Aff.* 229–37 (March/April 1997).

74. Detailed consideration of this regulatory challenge is beyond my scope here. But competitive bidding requirements, third-party review of proposed asset valuations, limits on post-transaction financial rewards for nonprofit decision makers, and monitoring of post-transaction uses of charitable assets are among the tools appropriate to the task. Patricia A. Butler, State Policy Issues in Nonprofit Conversions, 16(2) *Health Aff.* 69–84 (March/April 1997); Steven R. Hollis, Strategic and Economic Factors in the Hospital Conversion Process, *Health Aff.* 131–43 (March/April 1997); Daniel Shriber, State Experience in Regulating a Changing Health Care System, *Health Aff.* 48–68 (March/April 1997). In addition, the size and visibility of the largest investor-owned health care firms merit making them a focus for regulatory enforcement programs centering on billing practices, self-referral issues, and quality of care. The federal investigations into Columbia-HCA's business practices are a case in point. Not only have they forced Columbia's several hundred hospitals to drop a range of dubious billing and referral-inducing schemes; they have signaled the entire medical industry—nonprofit and for-profit—that failure to cease such improprieties invites aggressive enforcement action. K. Eichenwald, A Makeover May Change More than Columbia, *The New York Times*, August 8, 1997, at D1.

75. See generally Richard Pildes and Cass R. Sunstein, Reinventing the Regulatory State, *U. Chi. L. Rev.* 1–129 (*Winter 1995*); Guido Calabresi, *Ideas, Beliefs, & Attitudes in the Law: Private Law Perspective on a Public Law Problem* (1985) (discussing symbolic expression through law).

INDEX